Fur Seals: Maternal Strategies
on Land and at Sea

FUR SEALS

Maternal Strategies on Land and at Sea ≋≋≋≋≋ EDITED BY

Roger L. Gentry and Gerald L. Kooyman

PRINCETON UNIVERSITY PRESS

This book is dedicated to VICTOR B. SCHEFFER, whose pioneering research helped make land-based comparison of species the next logical step in fur seal research. It is also dedicated to JAMES O. BILLUPS, whose Time-Depth-Recorder opened the oceans to us for comparing pelagic behavior, and for integrating land and sea comparisons. Their contributions to this book illustrate the interdependence of scientific and technological advance.

Contents

List of Contributors   ix
Preface   xi
Acknowledgments   xv

Chapter 1. Introduction
R. L. Gentry and G. L. Kooyman   3

Chapter 2. Methods of Dive Analysis
R. L. Gentry and G. L. Kooyman   28

Chapter 3. Attendance Behavior of Northern Fur Seals
R. L. Gentry and J. R. Holt   41

Chapter 4. Feeding and Diving Behavior of Northern Fur Seals
R. L. Gentry, G. L. Kooyman, and M. E. Goebel   61

Chapter 5. Free-Ranging Energetics of Northern Fur Seals
D. P. Costa and R. L. Gentry   79

Chapter 6. Attendance Behavior of Antarctic Fur Seals
D. W. Doidge, T. S. McCann, and J. P. Croxall   102

Chapter 7. Diving Behavior of Antarctic Fur Seals
G. L. Kooyman, R. W. Davis, and J. P. Croxall   115

Chapter 8. Attendance Behavior of South African Fur Seals
J.H.M. David and R. W. Rand   126

Chapter 9. Diving Behavior of South African Fur Seals
G. L. Kooyman and R. L. Gentry   142

Chapter 10. Attendance and Diving Behavior of South American Fur Seals during El Niño in 1983
F. Trillmich, G. L. Kooyman, P. Majluf, and M. Sanchez-Griñan   153

Chapter 11. Attendance Behavior of Galapagos Fur Seals
F. Trillmich   168

Chapter 12. Diving Behavior of Galapagos Fur Seals
G. L. Kooyman and F. Trillmich   186

Chapter 13. Attendance Behavior of Galapagos Sea Lions
F. Trillmich   196

Chapter 14. Diving Behavior of Galapagos Sea Lions
G. L. Kooyman and F. Trillmich   209

Chapter 15. Synthesis and Conclusions
R. L. Gentry, D. P. Costa, J. P. Croxall, J.H.M. David,
R. W. Davis, G. L. Kooyman, P. Majluf, T. S. McCann, and
F. Trillmich   220

Literature Cited   265
Author Index   279
Subject Index   283

List of Contributors

DANIEL P. COSTA, Long Marine Laboratory, University of California, Santa Cruz, CA 95064, USA

JOHN P. CROXALL, British Antarctic Survey, High Cross, Madingley Road, Cambridge CB3 OET, England

JEREMY H. M. DAVID, Sea Fisheries Research Institute, PO Box 251, Cape Town 8000, South Africa

RANDALL W. DAVIS, Hubbs-Sea World Research Institute, 1700 S. Shores Road, San Diego, CA 92109, USA

D. WILLIAM DOIDGE, Dept. of Renewable Resources, MacDonald College of McGill University, 21,111 Lakeshore Road, Ste. Anne de Bellevue, Quebec HX9 1C0, Canada

ROGER L. GENTRY, NMFS, National Marine Mammal Laboratory, 7600 Sand Point Way N.E. Bldg. 4, Seattle, WA 98115, USA

MICHAEL E. GOEBEL, NMFS, National Marine Mammal Laboratory, 7600 Sand Point Way N.E. Bldg. 4, Seattle, WA 98115, USA

JOHN R. HOLT, 803 18th Ave. W., Kirkland, WA 98033, USA

GERALD L. KOOYMAN, Physiological Research Laboratory, Scripps Institution of Oceanography, La Jolla, CA 92093, USA

PATRICIA MAJLUF, Large Animal Research Group, Department of Zoology, University of Cambridge, 34A Storey's Way, Cambridge CB3 ODT, England

T. SEAMUS McCANN, British Antarctic Survey, High Cross, Madingley Road, Cambridge CB3 OET, England

ROBERT W. RAND, 1 Dudgeon Road, Rondebosch 7700, South Africa

MARINES SANCHEZ-GRIÑAN, Universidad Peruana Cayetano Heredia Depto. Ciencias Fisiologicas, Aptdo 5045, Lima 100, Peru

FRITZ TRILLMICH, Max Planck Institut für Verhaltensphysiologie, Abteilung Wickler, D-8131 Seewiesen, Federal Republic of Germany

Preface

This project began with a single behavioral observation and progressively grew with a speed and dimension that was unanticipated by any one of its participants. In 1974 one of us (RLG) noted the extreme regularity with which female northern fur seals returned to suckle their pups after having foraged at sea. Not only did they land within meters of the same site on successive returns, but the timing of their arrivals was predictable to within a day. He suggested to GLK that if a suitable recorder could be devised all the dives on a feeding trip could be measured. Until that time, unrestrained diving behavior had only been measured in Weddell seals (by GLK), which were physically captive in their ice-bound habitat. The prospect of measuring diving in fur seals that were essentially captives of their own behavioral tendencies was immediately attractive.

With a small grant from the U.S. Bureau of Land Management to RLG, GLK and J. O. Billups designed and built the first prototype Time-Depth-Recorder, which was deployed in the summer of 1975. We knew nothing of how to capture, immobilize, or harness fur seals, and our first attempts must have been amusing to the uninvolved. Our elation at the return of the first instrument carrying data could not have been greater had the animal just returned from the moon. Not only had we glimpsed the previously unknown pelagic lives of fur seals, but suddenly the behavior at sea of all eared seals lay accessible to study.

From that time onward improvements in the instrument and growth of knowledge about other species accelerated. In 1976 an improved method of recording data was devised; in 1977 a more accurate means of measuring time was developed, and the depth capability of the recorder was increased. In that year we measured diving behavior of South African fur seals and collaborated with J. P. Croxall in work on Antarctic fur seals. Meanwhile, the work on northern fur seals continued steadily. In 1980 GLK collaborated with F. Trillmich to measure diving in both the Galapagos fur seal and the sea lion, and more measurements were made on the Antarctic fur seal. In 1983 the South American fur seal was added to the list of species studied.

Attendance behavior—that is, the patterns with which females al-

ternate between feeding at sea and suckling their pups on shore—
was being measured independently of the diving measurements on
each species. The initial reasons for making these measurements
varied among researchers. Nevertheless, the attendance records
combined with diving data gave a quantitative measure, unlike any
previous measurements, of all behavior devoted to rearing the
young.

GLK envisioned the present monograph while in the Galapagos
Islands in 1980. His intention was to provide the first systematic
comparison of activity patterns on land, and especially at sea, for
any group of marine mammals. One goal of this comparison was to
determine whether differences in diving capabilities might reflect
physiological limitations. Moreover, because the six species lived in
very different marine environments, there was some expectation
that their diving, foraging, and pup-rearing patterns might be related to aspects of their ecology.

In June 1983 seven of the authors met in San Diego to compare
their component chapters and to write the summary chapter. This
collaborative effort had a truly synergistic result: broad patterns
emerged from the comparison that were not apparent in the data
from a single species. Furthermore, it became clear that the lifetime
reproductive outputs of females were very different among species,
and that these could be related to the breeding environments. Not
one of us anticipated all the results of the comparison, nor could any
one of us have written the final chapter in its present form.

It is our hope that the excitement of this work, as well as the ca-
maraderie of colleagues working together with a single purpose,
will be transmitted through this book. Our intent is to make this volume interesting and informative to the student and nonspecialist in
vertebrate biology. We also wish to call attention to the eared seals as
subjects worthy of increased scientific attention. They live in re-
mote, spectacular places, usually as part of rich and diverse com-
munities. They are easily approached and breed in predictable locations, usually in dense groups. Their attendance patterns are the
key to studying their previously inaccessible pelagic lives. We believe
that the Time-Depth-Recorder is only the first of many instruments
with which new aspects of their pelagic behavior, physiology, and
ecology will eventually be measured.

These studies mark a substantial breakthrough in both our general approach to studying marine mammals and in our knowledge
of their pelagic lives. The comparative method has produced results
and new questions that are far greater in scope than any study of a

single species could have identified. The use of instrumentation on free-ranging marine mammals has just begun, and prospects are exciting for extending the techniques to other species of seals. Nevertheless, even for fur seals, this volume constitutes only a preliminary review of some aspects of maternal strategies. There is great potential for future research, and we hope this synthesis of current progress will stimulate it.

May 15, 1985   Roger L. Gentry and Gerald L. Kooyman

Acknowledgments

The Time-Depth-Recorder was designed and built by James O. Billups (Meer Instruments, Del Mar, Calif.) under a grant from the U.S. Bureau of Land Management (now Minerals Management Service) to R. L. Gentry, and under a grant from the U.S. Marine Mammal Commission to G. L. Kooyman. The 3-dimensional plots used in the diving chapters were produced by M. E. Goebel, who also provided data analysis for several of the chapters. We gratefully acknowledge the National Oceanic and Atmospheric Administration, National Marine Fisheries Service, Seattle, Washington, for its support in preparing this manuscript. Two directors of the NMFS National Marine Mammal Laboratory, Michael Tillman and Howard Braham, supported the senior editor, R. L. Gentry, during all phases of the project and provided personnel and facilities for manuscript preparation. The manuscript was typed by R. L. Gentry, S. Perry, B. Lander, and M. Wood. Many of the illustrations were provided by B. Kuhne of NMFS, and Susan Gale edited the copy before it went to the publisher. Various parts of the manuscript were critically reviewed by D. Lavigne, W. Roberts, P. Shaughnessy, and C. Short. C. W. Fowler discussed life history strategies with us. Judith May and Alice Calaprice were our helpful editors at Princeton University Press. We are deeply indebted to James Estes for consulting with us during the preparation of Chapter 15, and to him and to Craig Packer for a thorough, critical review of the completed manuscript. Finally, we acknowledge the importance of the 1982-83 El Niño to our thinking. If this example of environmental fluctuation had not occurred during our studies, its long-term effect on fur seal maternal strategies may not have been recognized.

Reference to trade names in this book does not necessarily imply our endorsement.

The authors of the various chapters would like to acknowledge the following for their help:

Chapter 2: J. O. Billups, Red Howard, G. V. Sarno, and D. L. Urquhart assisted in designing and testing the TDR, and provided a computer program for data analysis. Support for the TDR design and record analysis was provided by NOAA contracts 03-5-208-310, 01-78-19-02-01924, 80-ABC-00094, and Marine Mammal Commission contract 17176AC019 to G. L. Kooyman.

Chapter 3: J. Calambokidis, S. Carter, S. Clayton, D. Christel, E. D'Arms, R. Felt, E. Jameyson, J. Johnson, D. Lestenkof, M. Lester, S. Macy, R. McGee, A. Merculief, P. Merculief, S. Merculief, S. Merculief, T. Meyer, M. Ryan, and C. Short helped collect the data; V. Malavansky and G. McGlashan captured and marked animals held in captivity; John Francis helped design and execute field experiments and assisted in data analysis; additional data analysis was performed by M. E. Goebel. Anne York and Robert Lander gave advice on statistics and criticized earlier drafts of the paper along with Burney LeBoeuf, Edward H. Miller, Charles Repenning, and Alton Roppel. James Estes offered encouragement and advice throughout this work. The research was supported by the National Marine Fisheries Service's program of research on the northern fur seal. The senior author, R. L. Gentry, was hosted by the Center for Coastal Marine Studies, University of California, Santa Cruz, during the initial writing of this chapter.

Chapter 4: D. Costa, J. Francis, C. Heath, P. Thorson, and R. Spaulding helped capture instrumented females; A. York gave advice on statistics; and C. Bouchet and S. Mizroch gave advice on the use of computer programs for analysis. The study was supported by the National Marine Mammal Laboratory of the National Marine Fisheries Service, NOAA.

Chapter 5: This study was supported by the National Marine Fisheries Service's National Marine Mammal Laboratory (NOAA Contract No. 81-ABC-00164), National Institutes of Health postdoctoral fellowship F32 AM 06093, and National Science Foundation grant DPP-8311799 to D. P. Costa. Philip Thorson, Steven Feldkamp, and Michael Goebel gave invaluable assistance in the field. Jim Herpolsheimer and Lesley Higgins assisted in sample analysis. Ken Nagy critically read a previous draft of this chapter. Thanks are extended to the Pribilof Islands Program, and the northern fur seal task of the National Marine Mammal Laboratory, Seattle, for logistic and field support.

Chapter 6: Bob Bell, Paul Copestake, Lyndon Kearsley, Paul Martin, Bruce Pearson, Andrew Stewart, and Gerry Thomas gave field assistance on this project, which was initiated by Mike Payne; Dr. Chris Ricketts gave advice on data analysis; and Mike Hammill gave helpful criticism of the manuscript.

Chapter 7: J. O. Billups, M. A. Castellini, I. Hunter, S. Hunter, and T. S. McCann provided assistance and T. S. McCann commented on the manuscript. This work was supported by NSF grant DPP 78-22999.

Chapter 8: The authors thank P. B. Best for critical reading of the manuscript.

Chapter 9: Peter B. Best and the Sea Fisheries Research Institute, Cape Town, South Africa, hosted us during this research, gave permission to study at the Kleinsee site, and provided logistic support; the De Beers Consolidated Mining Company allowed us access to the study site; and Mike Meyer gave valuable field assistance. The project was supported by grant no. MM6ACO19 from the U.S. Marine Mammal Commission to G. L. Kooyman, and by the National Marine Mammal Laboratory of the National Marine Fisheries Service, NOAA, Seattle.

Chapter 10: This work was supported in part by the Max-Planck-Institut für Verhaltensphysiologie, the National Geographic Society, the New York Zoological Society, and the Percy Sladen Memorial Fund. The Peruvian governmental organizations Pesca-Peru and Hierro-Peru kindly provided facilities and accommodation in San Juan. Commander Gustavo Salcedo allowed us to fly the blood samples to Lima, and Mrs. Lucha Magan de Contreras provided laboratory facilities in the Hierro-Peru hospital in San Juan. The Universidad Peruana Cayetano Heredia provided laboratory facilities in Lima.

Chapter 11: Parque Nacional Galapagos and the Charles Darwin Research Station gave me permission to work at Fernandina Island and supported me during the field work; W. Arnold, H. and B. Biebach, C. Kasche, D. Limberger, M. Taborsky, and K. Trillmich provided much help in the field work; J. Lamprecht, C. Rechten, W. Wickler, R. Gentry, and G. L. Kooyman gave constructive criticism of various drafts of the manuscript. This study was supported by the Max-Planck-Gesellschaft. I am in great debt to W. Wickler for his continuous support of this study. This is contribution no. 329 of the Charles Darwin Foundation.

Chapter 12: Parque Nacional Galapagos and the Charles Darwin Research Station gave us permission to work on fur seals in the Galapagos and provided continuous support during the field work; W. Arnold gave great assistance in the collection of the data. This study was supported by the Max-Planck-Gesellschaft and the National Geographic Society. It is contribution no. 377 of the Charles Darwin Foundation.

Chapter 13: Parque Nacional Galapagos and the Charles Darwin Research Station gave me permission to work on sea lions in the Galapagos and I am grateful for their continuous support during the field work; J. Cilio, D. Nakashima, and K. Trillmich assisted in the collection of the data; I am grateful to G. L. Kooyman for his hospitality while I was writing this manuscript; G. L. Kooyman, R. Davis, S. Feldkamp, C. Heath, and J. Francis gave constructive criticism of the manuscript. I am in great debt to W. Wickler for his continuous support of this study. This study was financed by the Max-Planck-Gesellschaft and is contribution no. 375 of the Charles Darwin Foundation.

Chapter 14: Parque Nacional Galapagos and the Charles Darwin Research Station gave us permission to work on sea lions in the Galapagos and provided continuous support during the field work; W. Arnold gave great assistance in the collection of the data. The study was supported by the Max-Planck-Gesellschaft and the National Geographic Society. It is contribution no. 376 of the Charles Darwin Foundation.

Fur Seals: Maternal Strategies
on Land and at Sea

1 Introduction ≅ *R. L. Gentry and*

G. L. Kooyman

INTRODUCTION

Marine mammal science has always been thwarted by the difficulty of collecting data on free-ranging animals at sea. This problem has hindered research on cetaceans (whales and porpoises) somewhat more than on pinnipeds (seals, sea lions, and walruses) because, except in rare circumstances, all data on cetacean biology must be collected at sea. Since pinnipeds mate and rear young on land where measurements are more easily made, some aspects of their behavior and biology are relatively well known. However, just as the pelagic lives of cetaceans remain obscure, those aspects of pinniped biology that occur at sea, such as feeding ecology, diving physiology, predator avoidance, and causes of mortality, remain little known. It is essential to collect data at sea if we are ever to obtain for marine mammals the breadth of information that is now available for some terrestrial groups.

The problem of gathering data on pelagic animals has been partially solved with the advent of new technology. A special instrument, attached to marine mammals, has been developed that continuously records time and pressure. Pressure can be translated into depth, so the instrument is called a Time-Depth-Recorder, or TDR. Up to 2 weeks, this instrument records the time of day, depth, and duration of all dives; the amount of time spent at any given depth; and the interval and kind of activity (resting, swimming, and grooming) between dives. These data allow us to make many new inferences about the behavior, physiology, and ecology of marine mammals at sea. The TDR also enables us to study the pelagic behavior of fur seals, which already have known histories on land, and to compare different species closely. The ability to obtain this information and to make such comparisons constitutes a major breakthrough for marine mammal research.

The authors of this book have applied this new technology to the study of eared seals (family Otariidae), a group whose land-based activities are, by marine mammal standards, under extensive study. In this book we integrate the on-land and at-sea behavior for each of six species. This integration in itself is a unique step forward for marine mammal studies because such integration was not possible for even one species until the TDR was developed. We also make detailed comparisons among the species studied. These comparisons allow us to see broad patterns in the life histories of fur seals and enable us to discuss some of the factors that shape these patterns.

Background Information on Eared Seals

The different species of fur seals are remarkable for their similarity in size, morphology, social behavior, and ecological role (as top carnivores). Their mating systems are also very similar. All otariids are polygynous, gregarious, and sexually dimorphic in body size (Bartholomew, 1970). Adult males range from two to four times larger than adult females, depending on the species. Males mate multiple times over a 2- to 3-year period, usually between the ages of 9 and 14 years, whereas females may bear one young per year from ages 3 to 20 years. Females wean their young at ages varying from 4 months to 3 years. This long neonatal dependency demands that the female alternate between feeding at sea and suckling onshore, and it creates longlasting social groupings on land, some of which never disband.

Otariid life histories are far more homogeneous than those of "true" seals (family Phocidae). Most phocids lack sexual dimorphism in size, but some are extremely dimorphic and others have reversed dimorphism (i.e., females are larger). Most phocids have adult sex ratios of approximately 1:1 and are solitary; others are highly polygynous and gregarious (Stirling, 1975, 1983). Finally, the phocids have a greater range in adult body size and occupy more diverse habitats than otariids. Phocids are similar to otariids in that females may bear a single young each year. However, phocid females fast throughout suckling and wean at 1 to 8 weeks. After weaning, social groupings, if they form at all, break down.

Fur seal life-history patterns are shaped by two major environmental factors: seasonality and the degree of environmental uncertainty. The seasonal factor is relatively straightforward. Otariids breed from approximately lat. 60° N to 60° S. Two species, the northern fur seal *Callorhinus ursinus* and the Antarctic fur seal *Arctocephalus gazella*, breed at the ends of this range where waters are cold and productive but highly seasonal. They occupy these sites only in summer and autumn and migrate in winter. Most other otariids live in temperate latitudes where seasons are less extreme. Temperate fur seals usually depend on upwelling systems or on productive ocean currents that provide food throughout the year.

Two species, the Galapagos fur seal *A. galapagoensis*, and the Galapagos sea lion *Zalophus californianus wollebaeki*, live at the equator, where seasonal changes are perceptible but not profound. These species, and the Peruvian populations of the South American fur seal *A. australis*, depend on upwelling plumes around islands or on a thin band of coastal upwelling. These small areas of upwelling are surrounded by vast areas of warm, equatorial water.

Environmental uncertainty also varies in the area inhabited by fur seals and may have a more profound effect on life-history patterns than does seasonal change (Orians, 1969; Colwell, 1974; Wilbur et al., 1974). One major source of uncertainty is a meteorological and oceanographic phenomenon termed an "El Niño/Southern Oscillation" (hereafter abbreviated EN) that affects the entire equatorial Pacific Ocean (Cane, 1983). Its oceanographic effects in Peru, Ecuador, and Chile include intermittent suppression of upwelling and productivity around islands and along mainland coasts. When productivity is suppressed the fish on which otariids depend die, migrate, or descend to unreachable depths (Barber and Chavez, 1983). Under such conditions female otariids cannot find sufficient food and their young die (Limberger et al., 1983; Barber and Chavez, 1983). In severe ENs several cohorts of young may die along with some adults. EN events are known to have occurred since at least the 1700s and recur on average once every 4 years, although the interval varies from 2 to 10 years (Cane, 1983). Furthermore, no two ENs are alike in severity, timing, spatial distribution, or biological consequences (Barber and Chavez, 1983). Therefore, the timing and severity of food shortages for fur seals are unpredictable, though they are likely to occur within a female seal's reproductive lifetime (ca. 15 years).

Sea surface temperatures can be used as an index of the environmental uncertainty that exists for otariids. Figure 1.1 shows the mean annual sea surface temperatures for the Bering Sea and Chicama Beach, Peru. These locations represent the most extreme environments (subpolar and tropical) inhabited by otariids, and are at rookeries or close to them. The overall mean temperatures differed greatly, but variance around the means was similar. The sites differed most in the rapidity of change around the overall mean. In the Bering Sea the mean annual temperatures changed relatively little between successive years, describing a long sine wave having a period of 13 to 14 years. However, the Peruvian temperatures changed very quickly from one extreme to the other in an unpredictable pattern (EN years coincide with peaks in the graph). Com-

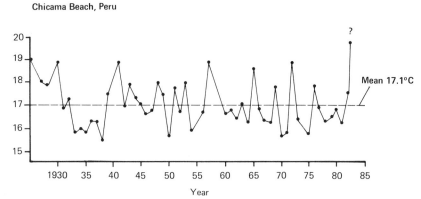

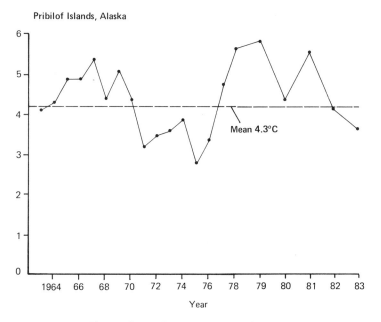

Fig. 1.1. Sea surface temperatures for Chicama Beach, Peru
(data from Pesca Peru, unpubl.; figure reprinted from
IMARPE, unpubl.), and the Bering Sea (figure modified from
Niebauer, 1981a).

puter modeling would be required to quantify the differences in these graphs.

The environmental uncertainty imposed by ENs on otariids may not be restricted to the equator, but may be graded according to latitude and severity of the event. Warm water from the equator flows poleward along land masses via the California and Peru countercurrents. In the severe EN of 1982-83, female feeding patterns and pup mortality among northern fur seals breeding at lat. 34° N were markedly different than in previous years (Antonelis and DeLong, 1985). No measurable effects were demonstrated on northern fur seals breeding in the Bering Sea (lat. 57° N), but measurable effects on water temperature and fish distribution were reported at lat. 50° N. The direction of current flow makes a similar effect south of the equator also likely. Furthermore, a phenomenon analogous to the EN has been reported for the equatorial Atlantic (Merle, 1980; Hisard, 1980; Shanon, 1983) and may affect fur seals of the temperate south Atlantic Ocean.

To summarize, fur seals face a gradient of seasonal change from very large in the subpolar areas to very slight in the tropics. They face a reverse gradient (or at least seals at the ends of the range face reversed extremes) in the predictability of their food supply while rearing young. Seals at one extreme (subpolar) begin a sharply defined breeding season with the high likelihood that sufficient food will be available for a brief period. Seals at the other end begin a longer, more equable season, but face the possibility that catastrophic food declines may occur before the young are independent. These opposing alternatives are shown graphically in Figure 1.2, which is a modification of Figure 7 in Stearns (1976). We show only the subpolar and tropical extremes because information is lacking on the extent of environmental uncertainty for temperate fur seals; presumably they would be intermediate between these extremes in both seasonality and environmental uncertainty.

The Central Issue

The purpose of this book is to show what suites of adaptive responses females have developed for producing the maximum number of young in their lifetime, given the different ways their environments fluctuate. To address this issue we compared a wide range of maternal behavior, using approximately forty variables, for each of the six species we studied. Attendance behavior—the pattern in which females deliver nourishment to their growing young—was observed from shore. Attendance included such measures as the

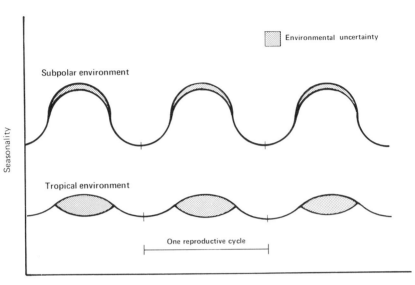

Fig. 1.2. Differences in seasonality and environmental uncertainty faced by fur seals at the extremes of their range. Subpolar seals face extreme seasonal variation (wave amplitude) but little environmental uncertainty (amplitude of shaded area). Despite these differences all species have a yearly breeding season (wave lengths are the same). The figure is modified from Fig. 7 of Stearns, 1977.

number and duration of visits to shore from birth to weaning, the number and duration of trips to sea, changes in trip duration as a function of the pup's age, and suckling frequency while ashore. We view these parameters as components of the maternal strategy on land. Some direct results of female attendance were also measured, such as growth rates of suckling pups and the weight of the pup at weaning.

Using TDRs we measured pelagic behavior among foraging mothers. The measures included the transit times between shore and feeding areas, depth and duration of feeding dives, relationship between depth of dive and time of day, repetition rate of dives within bouts, number of feeding bouts per day, and the occurrence of rest periods at the surface. We regard these parameters as components of maternal strategies at sea because they are central to maternal efforts to rear young. Finally, we measured the interval from birth to weaning, the timing of births relative to weaning the previous young, and the partitioning of suckling where competing, dependent young exist.

Although the measures we made are extensive, they do not include all the components that are usually considered in life-history theory (such as juvenile and adult mortality schedules, age at first reproduction, and reproductive life span; Wilbur et al., 1974; Stearns, 1977). We refer to our subset as maternal strategies. We define these strategies as combinations of short- and long-term options by which females produce the largest number of weaned offspring in their reproductive lifetime. Short-term options are those associated with rearing a single young to weaning and include attendance and pelagic behavior. Long-term options affect the frequency with which females attempt to rear and wean young. The terms "option" and "strategy" refer to adaptive responses shaped by natural selection over time; they do not imply that animals have cognitive awareness of their actions, or that systems are teleological.

Our results will show two different maternal strategies. Seals breeding at high latitudes, where seasonal change is extreme and the environment is highly predictable from year to year, have brief, nonvariable periods of neonatal dependency; these females always wean their young at the same age (ca. 4 months) and size (ca. 40% of adult female mass) each year. Seals breeding at low latitudes, where seasonal changes are small and environmental uncertainty is large, have longer, highly variable periods of neonatal dependency; these females wean their young at 40% of adult female mass but suckle them for 18 to 36 months to attain this size. Thus, females adjust the weaning age according to the vicissitudes of the environment. We will show that attendance behavior, diving behavior, and the energy content of the mother's milk all covary with the age at weaning. We will contend that environmental uncertainty is more important than seasonal change in shaping these suites of characters. These results are not consistent with the r- and K-selection theory of life-history strategy, which holds that predictable environments should lead to longer neonatal dependency. Instead, our results are in general agreement with the bet-hedging alternative in which juvenile mortality is variable (see Table 4 in Stearns, 1976).

These broad patterns of maternal strategies among fur seals are apparent only from detailed comparisons among all species. Therefore, we will delay discussion of comparative maternal strategies until Chapter 15, leaving Chapters 3 through 14 to set forth unique aspects of the overall comparison.

This work is the first detailed investigation of diving behavior in any group of marine mammals. Other diving studies have been conducted, but they were brief or involved only a few dives (Evans, 1971; Lockyer, 1977; Ichihara and Yoshida, 1972). Only Kooyman's ongoing studies of diving in Weddell seals exceed this work in scope (Kooyman, 1968, 1975, 1981). This is also the first systematic attempt to compare the behavior of closely related marine mammals, although the need for such comparisons was recognized earlier (Gentry, 1975).

EVOLUTIONARY HISTORY OF OTARIIDS

The ancestors of modern otariids, the Enaliarctids, evolved approximately 22 million years ago in the early Miocene. With little diversification or change, the Enaliarctids gave rise to the earliest true otariids beginning about 12 million years ago (Mitchell and Tedford, 1973; Repenning and Tedford, 1977; Repenning et al., 1979). The otariid stock began to diversify around 6 million years ago when the lineage leading to modern northern fur seals arose. Aside from the divergence 3 million years ago of a form leading to modern sea lions, the basic otariid stock continued to evolve in the direction of modern *Arctocephalus* (Repenning et al., 1979).

Because the earliest fossils are found in the north Pacific Ocean, the otariids are believed to have evolved there. About 5 million years ago the first fur seals crossed into the southern hemisphere concomitant with the closure of the Central American Seaway and the cooling of the central Pacific, which occurred when the warm Atlantic equatorial current was diverted northward as the Gulf Stream (Repenning et al., 1979). Sea lions appear to have crossed the equator about 3 million years ago.

Despite the otariids' origins in the north Pacific, their diversification has been greater in the southern hemisphere, where five *Arctocephalus* species and three genera of sea lions live. Two kinds of fur seals (one *Arctocephalus* species plus *Callorhinus*) live in the northern hemisphere, as do two genera of sea lions. A subspecies of one of the northern hemisphere sea lions (*Zalophus*) and one fur seal species also breed at the equator (Repenning et al., 1971, 1979).

DISTRIBUTION AND ABUNDANCE

All fur seal populations were exploited for furs soon after their discovery. The distributions and population sizes of today's herds are therefore derived from disrupted populations. This section briefly traces the history of each species we studied. The approximate distributions of breeding sites for these six species are shown in Figure 1.3.

The Northern Fur Seal, *Callorhinus ursinus* (Linnaeus, 1758)

This is the most ancient and distinct of all fur seals; its generic name means "beautiful nose." The adult male's maximum mass is about 185 to 275 kg, and that of the adult female is about 30 to 50 kg (Fig. 1.4). It is a generalized feeder, taking over sixty-three species of prey (Kajimura, 1983). The worldwide population was estimated to be 1,765,000 in 1976 (Lander and Kajimura, 1982). About 865,000 now breed the Pribilof Islands in the Bering Sea, and 265,000 breed on the Commander Islands. Thus most of the population breeds between lat. 54° and 58° N (Fig. 1.5). Smaller populations breed on Robben Island in the Sea of Okhotsk, on the Kuril Islands, at San Miguel Island off California, and at Bogoslof Island (Lander and Kajimura, 1982). The population on all Soviet islands is presently estimated from 325,000 to 350,000.

The species was discovered on the Commander Islands in 1741 by G. W. Steller, and the Pribilof population was discovered in 1786 by Gerasim Pribilof. Sealing activities nearly exterminated the Pribilof herd twice before 1834, when the Russian stewards, under the first fur seal management program, prohibited the killing of females. The herd had recovered by 1867, when the Pribilof herd came under U.S. jurisdiction. Immediately thereafter, huge numbers of females were again taken for three years. With the onset of pelagic sealing in about 1889, seals were killed with few restrictions. The Pribilof herd declined to about 200,000 animals by 1910, and western Pacific populations were dangerously low.

In 1911 the United States, Great Britain (for Canada), Japan, and Imperial Russia agreed upon a sealing convention that prohibited pelagic takes and provided for sharing the land-based collections. This agreement resulted in a rapid herd expansion of about 8% per year. In 1941 the treaty was abrogated but was reinstated in 1957, at which time the Pribilof herd numbered about 1.5 million. New colonies formed in the Kuril Islands in 1950, at San Miguel Island in 1967, and on Bogoslof Island in 1980. Since 1974 the Pribilof population has declined from some unknown cause at an annual rate of 5% to 8% (North Pacific Fur Seal Commission, 1982).

The northern fur seal is one of three fur seal species still being harvested for pelts. The United States take ended in 1985. The So-

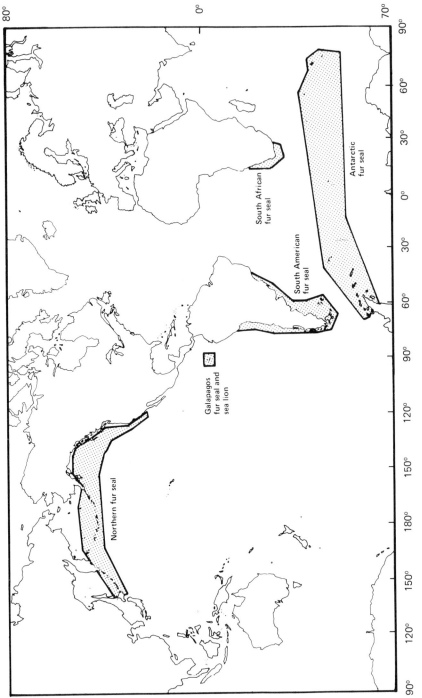

Fig. 1.3. World map showing the approximate range of each species studied in this volume.

Fig. 1.4. Adult male (top) and female (bottom) northern fur seals.

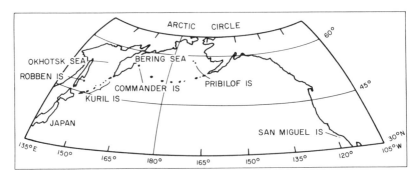

Fig. 1.5. Distribution of breeding sites for northern fur seals.

viet Union takes about 9,000 pelts annually. Only males 2 to 5 years old are killed.

Antarctic Fur Seal, *Arctocephalus gazella* (Peters, 1875)

The generic name for all fur seals other than *Callorhinus* means "bear head." The first specimen of the Antarctic fur seal returned from Kerguelen Island aboard the German vessel *S.M.S. Gazelle,* hence the species name *gazella* (King, 1964). The maximum mass of adult males is 150 to 200 kg, and their mean mass is ca. 130 kg (Fig. 1.6 top). The mass of mature females is 20 to 50 kg (Payne, 1979b; Fig. 1.6, bottom).

Breeding populations of Antarctic fur seals all occur south of the Antarctic convergence and north of lat. 65° S in the Atlantic and Indian Ocean sectors of the southern ocean (Erickson and Hofman, 1974; Fig. 1.7). The winter dispersal patterns of this species are unknown, but breeding areas are not occupied by females during the winter.

The Antarctic fur seal has experienced the most spectacular recovery from exploitation and near extinction of any fur seal. The breeding colonies were discovered in the late 1700s, and by 1821 this species was commercially exterminated. Only two years were required for the species to be eliminated from the South Shetland Islands, where at least 250,000 skins were taken by fifty sealing vessels. Through the rest of the 1800s sporadic takes occurred as odd pockets of fur seals were discovered and collected. By the late 1800s the species appeared to be extinct.

Rediscovery occurred in 1915 when a single juvenile male was found on South Georgia Island. Five were found there in 1919, and

Fig. 1.6. Adult male (top) and female (bottom) Antarctic fur seals. The male shown is in the unusual white color phase.

Fig. 1.7. Distribution of breeding sites for Antarctic and South African fur seals.

in 1933 a serious search of the island revealed a breeding group of thirty-eight animals at Bird Island near South Georgia. By 1956 Bonner (1968) estimated that 8,000 to 12,000 fur seals inhabited South Georgia and the smaller islands near it. Payne (1977) estimated that between 1963 and 1973 the South Georgia population grew at the phenomenal rate of 16.8% per year.

The present population is difficult to estimate because the census of some islands is poor, and the population is still expanding rapidly. By 1983 the South Georgia population was estimated to be about 1.1 million, with an estimated 20,000 animals in the remainder of the range (Doidge and Croxall, 1985). The Antarctic fur seal is unusual among fur seals in that the diet, at least in summer, consists largely of krill (Croxall and Pilcher, 1984; Doidge and Croxall, 1985). Some fish are also taken (North et al., 1983), but they are probably more important in winter.

South African Fur Seal, *A. pusillus* (Schreber, 1776)

Ironically, the species name of the South African fur seal means "little," even though it is the largest of the fur seals (Fig. 1.8). Apparently the first description was based on a picture of a young pup (King, 1964). The mass of adult males at maximum breeding size is about 300 kg, but a mass of 363 kg has been reported. The female's mass is about 40 to 80 kg, with a maximum of about 100 to 120 kg (Rand, 1956; Shaughnessy, 1982; Fig. 1.8, bottom). Morphologically and behaviorally, this species shares many features in common with sea lions (Repenning et al., 1971).

The species breeds on the South African and Namibian coasts, and the subspecies *A. pusillus doriferus* breeds on the southeastern Australian and Tasmanian coasts (Fig. 1.7). Shaughnessy (1982) estimated the South African and Namibian populations in 1971 at about 850,000, of which 211,000 were pups of the year. The 1982 population was about 1.1 million (Butterworth et al., in press). The Australian population numbers approximately 20,000 (Warneke, 1979). This species does not appear to migrate but instead remains in the vicinity of its breeding islands year-round. Individuals are seen routinely 130 km offshore, and feed mostly on fish such as maasbankers, pilchards, and anchovies, as well as on crustaceans and cephalopods (Rand, 1959).

Sealing has occurred in South Africa since 1610 (Best and Shaughnessy, 1979). At least twenty of the original island populations were exterminated (Shaughnessy, 1982), and conservation measures were not exercised by the government until 1893, when the population was probably at a low level. The main breeding colonies are now on the mainland, but it is known they did not exist during a survey in 1828 (Best and Shaughnessy, 1979). Rand (1972) and Best and Shaughnessy (1979) attribute this shift to increasing disturbance of the original breeding sites, a decline in large land carnivores, and protection of coastlines in existing breeding colonies by diamond-mining interests.

The population of South African fur seals is presently increasing at about 3.9% per year (Butterworth et al., in press). Six new colonies have formed since 1940. The 1971 population was estimated to be at 73% of the previous, unexploited population (Shaughnessy and Butterworth, 1981) and to exceed the level of 1828 (Best and

Fig. 1.8. Adult male (top) and female (bottom) South African fur seals.

Shaughnessy, 1979). This increase occurred in the face of very heavy fishing for pilchards and anchovies. Until 1982 the mean harvest consisted of about 75,000 young of the year and 1,200 adult males harvested from ten seal colonies in South Africa and Namibia.

South American Fur Seal, *A. australis* (Zimmerman, 1783)

This species is widely distributed in South America from Tierra del Fuego in the south to the latitude of São Paulo, Brazil, and southern Peru in the north (Vaz-Ferreira, 1982; Bonner, 1981). The mass of adult males is about 150 to 200 kg, and for females about 30 to 60 kg (Fig. 1.9). The species name means "southern."

The history of exploitation started early for this species. Harvesting in Uruguay began shortly after that country was discovered by Juan Diaz de Solis in 1515. Excellent records of harvests show a sustained take of about 16,000 pelts per year from 1873 until the turn of the century (Vaz-Ferreira, 1982). The take declined to 3,400 yearly from 1943 to 1947, so the government prohibited the killing of females. The Uruguayan herd subsequently increased, bringing annual kills from 1979 until 1982 to 12,000. This species is now harvested only in Uruguay, which has the largest population in the species' range (Fig. 1.10).

Commercial sealers took 13,000 skins from the Falkland Islands in 1784 (Strange, 1973). Apparently only the discovery of the larger colonies of Antarctic fur seals at South Georgia Island saved the Falkland population from total extermination.

The total world population of South American fur seals cannot be estimated closely because of the wide distribution and lack of simultaneous censuses from all areas. If the censuses reported by Vaz-Ferreira (1982) had all been made in the same year, the world population would have been about 325,000.

The species does not appear to migrate. Although some animals disperse in winter, most females maintain contact with breeding sites year-round (Vaz-Ferreira, 1982). Their diet is poorly understood but consists of fish, cephalopods, and crustaceans (Vaz-Ferreira, 1982). Animals breeding in the Pacific populations probably depend on the major upwelling band along the coasts of Chile and Peru.

Galapagos Fur Seal, *A. galapagoensis* (Heller, 1904)

This is the smallest of the fur seals with a maximum mass for adult males of about 70 kg, and for females about 30 to 35 kg (Fig. 1.11).

Fig. 1.9. Adult male (above) and female (at right) South American fur seals.

Breeding populations are found only on islands of the Galapagos
archipelago, with the largest colonies on Isabela and Fernandina islands (Fig. 1.12). Animals use these colonies year-round, and there
appears to be no annual dispersion or migration. An unusual feature of reproduction in this species is that young are usually suckled
for 2 years. The species undoubtedly feeds in association with upwelling plumes around these islands because these plumes are far
more productive than the surrounding tropical waters. Little is

known about the diet, but it includes squid and small schooling fish.

The breeding islands were discovered by sealers in 1535, and sporadic sealing continued thereafter. The last of the large takes, consisting of 5,000 skins, was in 1823. By 1900 the species was believed to be extinct (Clark, 1979). Despite several surveys of the islands in the early 1900s, no large concentrations were reported again until the 1960s. The herd appears to have increased steadily in the past 30 to 40 years; the population before the 1982-83 EN event was es-

Fig. 1.10. Approximate breeding range of South American fur seals.

timated to be 40,000 (Trillmich, pers. commun.). Although the full impact of the 1982-83 EN on the herd has not been determined, all pups of the year and some adults died (Limberger et al., 1983).

Galapagos Sea Lion, *Zalophus californianus wollebaeki* (Sivertsen, 1953)

These animals are widely distributed throughout the Galapagos archipelago (Fig. 1.12), but breed on different beaches and substrate than the Galapagos fur seal (Trillmich, 1979). Sivertsen (1953) estimates the mass of adult males as 200 kg, and Kooyman and Trillmich (Chapter 14) list the mass of adult females as 50 to 100 kg (Fig. 1.13). These sizes are considerably smaller than California sea lions, *Z.c. californianus*, of the same sex. The taxonomic status of this species was in question until Sivertsen clearly distinguished it from *Otaria*. He assigned the specific name after Alf Wollebaek, who collected the type specimen in 1925 (Sivertsen, 1953). Scheffer (1958) and King (1954) reassigned the Galapagos sea lion to subspecific status.

No commercial exploitation of these animals has been recorded,

Fig. 1.11. Adult male (top) and female (bottom) Galapagos fur seals.

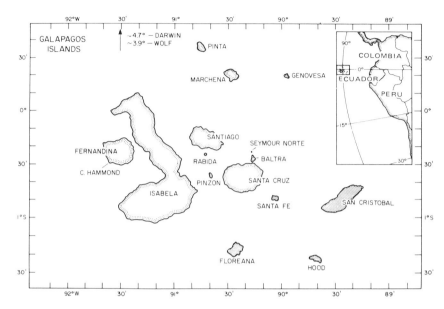

Fig. 1.12. Distribution of breeding sites for Galapagos fur seals and Galapagos sea lions.

although occasionally animals were taken for skins. The present distribution is probably very similar to the original, but present numbers may be below historical levels. A disease of unknown etiology swept through the herd in the 1970s and may have killed 50% of the animals. Furthermore, periodic ENs, such as the 1982-83 event, affect survival of newborns (Limberger et al., 1983). The population before the 1982-83 EN was estimated to be 40,000 (Trillmich, 1979), but its present size is not known.

Although brief accounts of behavior and biology have been published for this species (Eibl-Eibesfeldt, 1955; Orr, 1967), the most comprehensive treatment is given in Chapters 13 and 14 of this book. The most significant feature of their mating system is the long duration of the pupping season and the prolonged neonatal dependency. The species does not migrate, but some local dispersion may occur. Nothing is known of their diet. Like the Galapagos fur seal, these sea lions probably feed in association with local upwelling.

Fig. 1.13. Adult Galapagos sea lion male (top) and female (bottom).

TABLE 1.1 Comparisons of otariid species studied in this work.

	Northern	Antarctic	South African	South American	Galapagos Fur Seal	Galapagos Sea Lion
Adult mass (kg)						
Male	185–275	150–200	300–363	150–200	70	200
Female	30–50	20–50	40–80	30–60	30–35	50–100
Diet*	1, 2	4, 1	1, 2, 3	1, 2, 3	1, 2	1, 3
Population size	1,215,000	1,120,000	1,100,000	325,000	40,000	40,000
Population trend	Decreasing @ 5–8%	Increasing @ 16.8%	Increasing @ 3.9%	Unknown	Generally increasing	Unknown
Environment	Mostly subpolar	Subpolar	Temperate	Temperate-tropical	Tropical	Tropical
Being exploited	Yes	No	Yes	Yes	No	No
Migratory	Yes	Yes	No	No	No	No

* 1 = fish; 2 = cephalopods; 3 = crustaceans other than krill; 4 = krill. Numbers given in order of importance of that item to the known diet.

OVERVIEW

The species we studied are compared in Table 1.1 according to data given in these brief species sketches. Our data show that the subpolar species migrate, and that population sizes are larger for the subpolar and temperate species than for the tropical species. The size range among these females represents the extremes among all fur seals.

Even though our comparisons emphasize fur seals, we studied one species of sea lion to detect possible competition with the Galapagos fur seal. However, because sea lions are different from fur seals in many regards, our conclusions are meant to characterize mainly the latter. The comparison also emphasizes maternal strategies at the extreme ends of the subpolar-equatorial range of fur seals. The temperate fur seals are represented here only by the South African species. The South American fur seal is also a temperate species, but we studied it in southern Peru, where it is subjected to an equatorial environment. The fur seals that we did not study (the subantarctic, New Zealand, Juan Fernandez, and Guadalupe fur seals, and the Australian subspecies of A. pusillus) are all temperate in distribution. In addition to latitudinal differences, our comparison includes seals that are feeding generalists and one that is a specialist; those that feed in upwelling systems; and those that feed on widespread spring blooms in subpolar waters.

The chapters of this book are organized primarily according to the similarities we found among the species, and secondarily according to latitude. The two subpolar species were the most similar, and therefore are presented first. The chapters on attendance and dive behavior are presented separately for each species to facilitate cross-species comparisons of similar data types. The diving chapters are more homogeneous in content and emphasis than the attendance chapters because the data were collected by the same means (the TDR), and the same questions were being asked in each case. Studies of attendance behavior predated both the TDR and the idea of a comparative work and focused on problems relevant to each species. We have retained these differences in order to present as much new information as possible for each species.

Chapter 5 departs from the main theme of comparison that unifies this book. It shows that, in addition to attendance and pelagic behavior, maternal strategies can be compared by measuring, with isotopic tracers, the amount of energy flow from the mother to the young. Specifically, it shows how energy flow was measured in female northern fur seals and their pups using ^{18}O, tritiated water, or both. Comparable measures were not made on the other species because the technique is new to marine mammal research. Energetic measurements are now being made on the Antarctic and Galapagos fur seals.

2 Methods of Dive Analysis

≅ *R. L. Gentry and G. L. Kooyman*

INTRODUCTION

Chapter 1 stated that the maternal strategies of fur seals would be compared largely through data on attendance and dive behavior. Attendance data were obtained with conventional behavioral research methods, already described in an extensive literature (e.g., Altmann, 1974; Fagen and Young, 1979). However, the methods used to measure dive behavior require introduction because the technology evolved along with this research project. The existing literature contains only a brief description of the instrument (Kooyman et al., 1983a) and one kind of result obtainable with it (Kooyman et al., 1976). In this chapter we discuss the design requirements of the Time-Depth-Recorder (TDR), capture and restraint methods devised for instrument attachment, methods of data analysis, possible effects of the instrument on the measurements obtained, and tractability of the species that were instrumented.

REQUIREMENTS

When this project began, no suitable instrument existed for measuring diving. Therefore, we designed an instrument that was small enough for a 30 kg animal to carry, inexpensive to build, and reliable. Furthermore, it could record continuously, function without an extensive support system, and collect large amounts of data in a short period of time. Many of these design features were based on the size and attendance behavior of northern fur seals (Table 3.1; Fig. 3.6), the first species we instrumented. Because northern fur seals were known to forage 100 km or more from the Pribilof Islands (Kajimura, 1983), we rejected telemetry as a means of collecting data. Not only did these foraging distances exceed radio transmission distances, but the expense of chartering a vessel for tracking at sea was too great. In addition, ships could follow only one instrumented animal at a time, resulting in limited data collection per season.

A mechanical TDR met all the requirements. It also offered the advantage of being easy to repair and adjust by people in the field who had little previous experience with the instruments or lacked technical skill. Because northern fur seal females return to land with great regularity, we believed that instrument recovery was assured; the animals did prove to be exceptionally precise in site fidelity compared to other species. Had this project begun on another species, we might not have assumed recovery and might have designed the instrument differently.

THE TIME-DEPTH-RECORDER

The only precedent for design of a TDR was an earlier model devised for Weddell seals (Kooyman, 1965). The previous instrument, based on a simple 60-minute kitchen timer mechanism, rotated a smoked glass disc past a recording needle that was attached to a pressure transducer. This transducer, a C-shaped bourdon tube, straightened as pressure increased and inscribed an arc proportional to depth. Time was estimated by laying a time grid over a photograph of the time-depth arc. The limitations of this instrument for fur seals were its weight (1.5 kg) and its short running time.

Two features of the Weddell seal recorder—the bourdon tube and the stylus method of inscribing data—were retained for the first fur seal recorder, produced in 1975. To record for two weeks, the instrument was designed like a strip chart recorder with time on the abscissa. Time was not recorded but was estimated from the rate at which a long strip of pressure-sensitive paper passed under the pressure stylus. This rate increased as the uptake spool filled with paper, so time was estimated from a geometric constant.

The paper spools were driven (through gears) by a constant speed motor powered by two AA lithium batteries (Fig. 2.1). The motor could be run at 3 or 6 volts by wiring it either in series or in parallel with the batteries. A helical bourdon tube was substituted for the previous C-shaped tube. The motor, gear train, paper spools, and bourdon tube were mounted on a rigid aluminum chassis sealed by O-rings inside a cylindrical aluminum housing measuring 20 x 5.3 cm (inside) diameter. Bourdon tubes of varying maximum depths could be installed into one instrument; a tube with a maximum of 300 psi (ca. 206 m) was selected for fur seals. The thickness of the pressure-sensitive paper limited the amount that could be wound onto a spool. Therefore, the actual recording time was about 1 week, whereas the motor ran 16 days. A further limitation was hysteresis caused by the friction of the stylus on the paper.

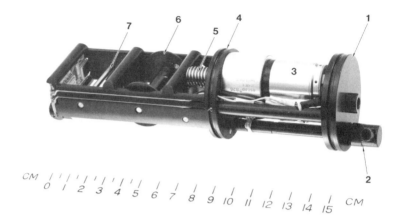

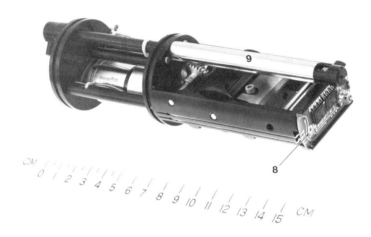

Fig. 2.1. Two views of the Time-Depth-Recorder (TDR) used to measure diving in otariids. (1) External bulkhead with O-ring forms a watertight seal with TDR housing. (2) Pressure transducer port. (3) DC electric motor. (4) O-ring creates light seal to protect film. (5) Worm gear drives gear train that turns takeup spool. (6) Takeup spool. (7) Axle of film supply spool. (8) Timing circuit. (9) Transducer housing. Figures reprinted from Kooyman et al., 1983a.

Some of the instrument's limitations were overcome in 1976 by substituting 32 mm wide, ultra-thin (0.05 mm) high contrast photographic film for the pressure-sensitive paper, and by substituting a light-emitting diode (LED) for the stylus. This friction-free system reduced hysteresis, and the thinner film allowed a greater film length to be wound onto a spool, thereby increasing the recording life of the recorder to 2 weeks. As in the first instrument, time was estimated by a constant. The first published dive records for fur seals (Kooyman et al., 1976) and the records for South African fur seals (Chapter 9) were obtained with such recorders.

A final change in 1978 brought the instrument to its present state of development, although improvements continue (Kooyman et al., 1983a). The previous estimated time base assumed a constant motor speed. But trials with the Weddell seal showed that, in fact, the motor ran slower at lower temperatures. A method was needed to record time independently of the fluctuating effects of environmental temperature. A timing circuit, composed of a crystal oscillator and CMOS (low power requirement) down counters, solved this problem by placing timing marks on the film at 12-minute intervals with a second LED (Fig. 2.1).

Two limitations of the present design are important to this volume. First, resolution on the time base is 30 seconds when the instrument runs at 3 volts (running time 16 days). That is, the instrument cannot resolve two events occurring <30 seconds apart. Fur seals dive so quickly that some dive times cannot be resolved on the film, nor can they be accurately converted to digital form for computer analysis. Errors result, especially in calculating the duration of fast dives and the intervals between them. When the instrument is run at 6 volts, the time base resolution increases to 8 seconds. But since the instrument runs only 7 days at that speed, an entire trip to sea may not be recorded. The phocid seals instrumented to date (e.g., Weddell seals; Kooyman, unpubl. data) dive at slower rates, and resolution on the time base is not a problem.

A second limitation is that deviation of the LED arm is not proportional to depth until 10 m has been exceeded. Instead, the LED arm oscillates slightly, creating a wide baseline that we term "chatter" (Fig. 2.2). Chatter obscures all dives of less than 10 m and misrepresents overall diving effort if fur seals feed on surface prey. However, chatter is not a total liability. It ceases when the animal is motionless and the baseline then becomes a thin line (Fig. 2.2). That is, the LED arm acts like an accelerometer, recording the difference between activity and inactivity at sea, as well as entry into and exit

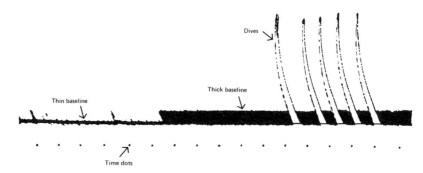

Fig. 2.2. Photocopy of film trace obtained from a TDR on a northern fur seal showing (1) timing dots every 12 min; (2) a thin baseline indicating the animal was inactive at the surface; (3) a thick baseline termed "chatter" indicating activity at the surface; (4) dives.

from the sea. Thus the thickness of the baseline can be analyzed to show activity budget.

Small radio beacons transmitting in the 150–160 MHz range were attached to the TDR to help locate returned animals where terrain was rough or where animals moved great distances on successive visits (South American and Antarctic fur seals). The beacons were located with a Telonics or AVM brand radio direction finder and handheld antenna. The telemetry unit added only 25–50 g to the 500 g weight of the TDR.

CAPTURE AND RESTRAINT

Most females were captured with a hoop net measuring 0.75 m in diameter, with a fine mesh nylon bag ca. 1.5 m deep on a flexible plastic hoop attached to a rigid handle (Fuhrman Diversified). Net captures differed depending on the behavioral characteristics of the species. With the South African fur seal, researchers crawled to within 10–20 m and then sprinted to net the animal before it entered the sea, often clearing nearby areas of other fur seals in the process. The Antarctic and Galapagos fur seals were much less wary of human approach and no stalking was necessary. Captured animals were carried in the net to a quiet work area. Northern fur seals were captured with a noose attached to a 5-meter-long pole and were carried in a box to a quiet work site (Gentry and Holt, 1982). After northern fur seal males abandoned their territories, females

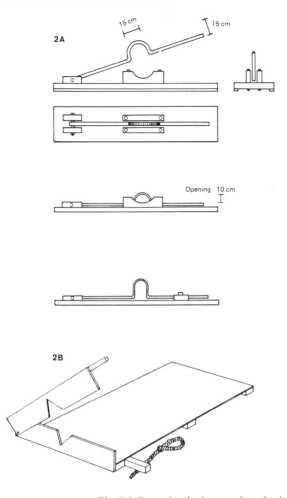

Fig. 2.3. Restraint devices used to physically immobilize otariids for attachment of TDR and harness. (A) Four views of a "plank" type restraint. (B) The preferred restraint device. Figure reprinted from Gentry and Holt, 1982.

became more wary and were taken with a hoop net by the stalk-and-sprint method.

Netting was not sufficient with some species. Because of their wariness, the South American fur seal and Galapagos sea lion were captured by drugs delivered from a blowpipe or blowgun. A light dose was given, usually 2–4 mg kg^{-1} ketamine mixed with 0.3–0.4

mg kg^{-1} xylosine, which reduced coordination without causing loss of consciousness. Most animals were able to swim within 30 minutes of being immobilized by drugs.

Females were removed from the hoop net using a 2-meter-long pole with a rope noose attached to the end, and were physically restrained while the TDR was attached (Fig. 2.3). Two types of restraint were used. One type pressed the animal's neck down onto a heavy wooden plank, 30 cm wide and 120 cm long (Fig. 2.3A). The other type locked the female's neck in a diamond-shaped opening (Fig. 2.3B). The latter type was preferable because the animal was prevented from rising, and could be tied and left unattended or carried around while restrained. A hole in the center of this second device allowed milk samples to be collected from restrained females (Chapter 5).

INSTRUMENT ATTACHMENT AND ENCUMBRANCE EFFECT

The TDR was held between the seal's scapulae by a harness with either one or two dorsal straps, to which the instrument was attached with hose clamps (Fig. 2.4). The harness was made of the brightly colored, tubular nylon webbing (2.5 cm wide when flat) used by mountaineers and was held together by steel rivets, which slowly rusted in seawater. Because of this rusting it is doubtful that harnesses would last more than one month at sea if the animal failed to return to land. The sizes and proportions of harnesses varied among species.

The nylon harness material was easy to cut with a knife. When instrumented females returned to shore they were recaptured with a hoop net, and the harnesses were cut off. With the Galapagos sea lion, harnesses were retrieved with a long hooked knife without recapturing the animal.

The instrument and harness affected the seal's swimming ability, and, by extension, probably altered its dive performance. The duration of feeding trips was longer for instrumented than for uninstrumented females, at least for species such as the northern fur seal that undertook long trips to sea. The harness design with two back straps (Fig. 2.4, bottom) eliminated most of this effect.

We estimated the effects of the instrument and harness by measuring (a) the drag they created on captive sea lions, and (b) the total energy expenditure of instrumented and uninstrumented, free-ranging fur seals. Drag was measured by towing an immature female California sea lion behind a cart being driven around a ring-

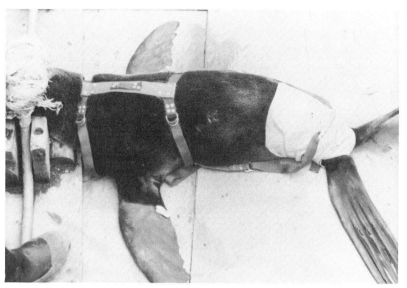

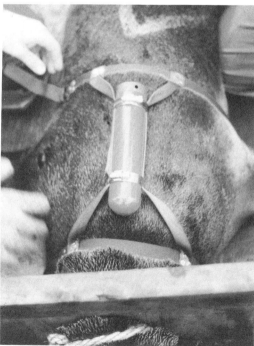

Fig. 2.4. Harnesses used to attach TDRs to otariids. Top: Harness with a single back strap to which the instrument is attached. Bottom: Type with two back straps that prevent the instrument from falling sideways.

shaped sea-water tank at Scripps Institution of Oceanography. This procedure is described elsewhere (Williams and Kooyman, 1985). In brief, the sea lion was trained to bite a rubber mouth piece held ca. 1.0 m below the surface of the water by a streamlined hollow pipe (a standoff). A nylon cord holding the mouth piece passed over pulleys, through the hollow standoff, and up to a load cell linked to a strip chart recorder atop the cart. A tachometer on the cart wheel indicated velocity in m sec^{-1} attained by the motor driven cart. The unswimming subject was pulled by its teeth at various speeds up to 3.5m sec^{-1} with and without the harness and TDR. Although total drag increased continually with speed (Fig. 2.5),* the proportion contributed by the harness leveled off at approximately 70% of total drag at speeds greater than 3 m sec^{-1} (Fig. 2.6).

We also estimated the effects of the instrument and harness by making energetic measurements. Metabolic rate was measured using doubly-labeled water methods for five females on ten feeding trips (one each with and without an instrument). For each animal metabolic rate was higher while wearing the harness (Table 5.7); interindividual variation was substantial. The TDR and harness caused an average 19% increase in mean metabolic rate of females while at sea (Chapter 5).

From the drag and energetic measurements it is not clear how the instrument affects foraging animals. The energetic measurements show only that average energy expenditure in total pelagic activities is greater. The drag measurements suggest, more specifically, that any activity requiring high rates of speed would be especially affected. For example, if chase involves high speeds (no data on this subject exist), then the success of prey capture may be reduced and the number of dives may be increased in compensation. This would decrease the estimated foraging efficiency (Chapter 15). It is also possible that dive depths and durations are reduced by carrying the TDR, which would mean that our estimates of total dive effort are minimal values only. To fully evaluate the effect of the instrument on diving, either swim speed should be measured directly or the diving patterns should be measured by an instrument that causes less drag, such as the Depth Histogram Recorder (Kooyman et al., 1983a).

*Figure 2.5 is based on unpublished data from S. Feldkamp. Further information on this source and on other unpublished sources of information mentioned throughout the book is available from the Editors.

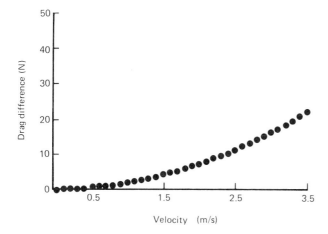

Fig. 2.5. Differences in drag measured on a harnessed and an unharnessed sea lion being towed underwater at various velocities (S. Feldkamp, unpubl. data, Scripps Institution of Oceanography, La Jolla, CA).

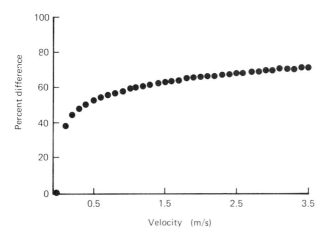

Fig. 2.6. Porportion of drag increase (TDR-SL) SL^{-1} due to the presence of a TDR harness as a sea lion is towed underwater at various velocities (S. Feldkamp, unpubl. data, Scripps Institution of Oceanography, La Jolla, CA).

DATA ANALYSIS

While retrieved instruments were still running, they were attached to a calibrated pressure gauge and a pressure curve was plotted on the record. Immediately thereafter the film was removed from the instrument and processed with appropriate developing chemicals.

The film record was enlarged seven times by copy-flow xerography. The enlarged image was converted to digital form by following the dive trace with the electronic cursor of a digitizing pad interfaced with a computer (originally an IBM 1800, but more recently by an Apple II). The digitized record, including the dive trace, time dots, and pressure calibration marks, was stored on magnetic tape or disk. A computer program plotted the digitized dive trace on a compressed time base using a variety of scales, such as 0.5 cm hr^{-1} and 2.5 cm 100 m^{-1} depths (Fig. 2.7). The program calculated the time of day, duration of each dive, and interval to the next dive from the time dots, and calculated depth for each dive using the pressure calibration. Finally, it summarized all dives into a series of frequency distributions for depth, duration of dive, hour of day, and combinations of these three, and gave ranges and median values for depth and duration.

Plots for most species, such as those shown in Figure 2.7, suggested that dives occurred in natural clusters, which we termed dive bouts. To derive an operational definition for dive-bout length, a log survivor curve of interdive (surface) intervals was plotted for several individuals of each species. The log survivor function was derived by first calculating the number of surface intervals with a duration greater than time t, then plotting the log of these values against t. The curves for fur seal records had two break or inflection points (Fig. 2.8), each representing a change in probability. The longest interdive intervals (to the right of the second inflection point) consistently had a much lower probability of ending than did shorter intervals. For that reason we defined dive-bout length as the time t at the second inflection point. This point differed considerably among species, but was consistent among individuals of a given species. Biologically, the first inflection point appeared to coincide with a change in recovery times from dives of different durations within a bout. The second inflection point correlated well with the apparent breaks between dive bouts on the records.

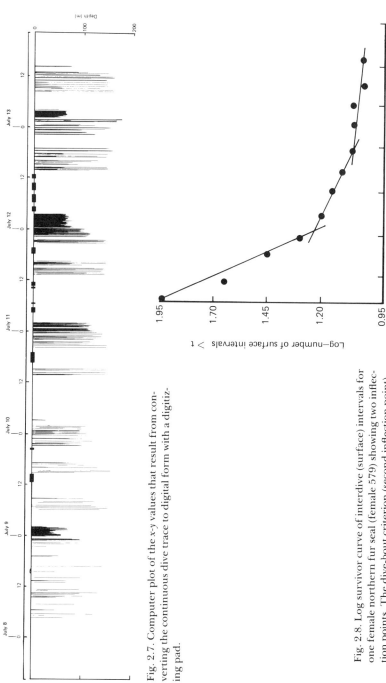

Fig. 2.7. Computer plot of the x-y values that result from converting the continuous dive trace to digital form with a digitizing pad.

Fig. 2.8. Log survivor curve of interdive (surface) intervals for one female northern fur seal (female 579) showing two inflection points. The dive-bout criterion (second inflection point) was 40 minutes, i.e., a "bout" contained no surface intervals exceeding 40 minutes.

TRACTABILITY OF SPECIES

The six species were not equal in ease of capture and handling. Clearly the most difficult species, at least at the time of season and study site used, was the South American fur seal, which fled to the water at the sight of distant humans. The second most difficult was the South African fur seal. These animals did not flee from distant humans (>100 m), but did flee from nearby humans. An entire beach could be cleared from one capture attempt. Furthermore, these animals rolled and twisted so strongly upon capture that three people were required to immobilize them. The Galapagos fur seal and sea lion also move at first sight of humans, but within a week they could be habituated so that researchers could sit beside them and remove harnesses without capture. The northern fur seal did not flee from humans during the pupping period, June and July, but did flee later. The Antarctic fur seal was as easy to capture as the Galapagos fur seal, but females wandered so far into rough terrain that radio telemetry was needed to relocate them. In all species individual females learned to avoid humans after having been captured once or twice, but this effect did not generalize to uncaptured animals.

3 Attendance Behavior of Northern Fur Seals ≅ *R. L. Gentry*

and J. R. Holt

INTRODUCTION

When we first began this study in 1974 our purpose was to monitor female attendance behavior as a fur seal herd changed in size and age/sex composition. We knew that these changes were imminent because the commercial harvest of fur seal pelts had been terminated at our study site (St. George Island, Alaska) in 1973 specifically to create such changes. Terminating the harvest was part of a research program to investigate the effects of the northern fur seal management program on herd composition, behavior, and size (Anonymous, 1973). Female attendance was only one of many parameters that were to be compared simultaneously between a harvested (St. Paul Island, Alaska) and an unharvested population.

Our second purpose was to investigate the potential impact of commercial fisheries on the growth of a fur seal herd. Females from the Pribilof Islands feed on and at the edge of a broad continental shelf. Extensive data exist on their pelagic distribution and food habits in the eastern Bering Sea (Kajimura, 1983). The diet in summer consists largely of walleye pollock, *Theragra chalcogramma*, the target species of one of the world's largest fisheries (Pruter, 1973). The pollock fishery began in the 1950s and peaked in the 1970s at about 2 million metric tons per year. Chapman (1961) suggested that the fishery might affect the growth of the fur seal herd, and that the effect might be measurable through the pattern of female attendance on shore.

Most northern fur seals occur in the north Pacific Ocean in winter and the Bering Sea in summer; females and young males regularly migrate between these two areas. Their migratory pathways are relatively well known because of extensive pelagic sealing at the turn of the century (Townsend, 1899; Zeusler, 1936; Kenyon and Wilke, 1953). Their distribution suggests adaptation to cool environments; about 90% of the population breeds at the Commander and Pribilof Islands, lat. 54°–57° N (Lander, 1979), where sea and air temperatures rarely exceed 5°C. The species spends November to June on

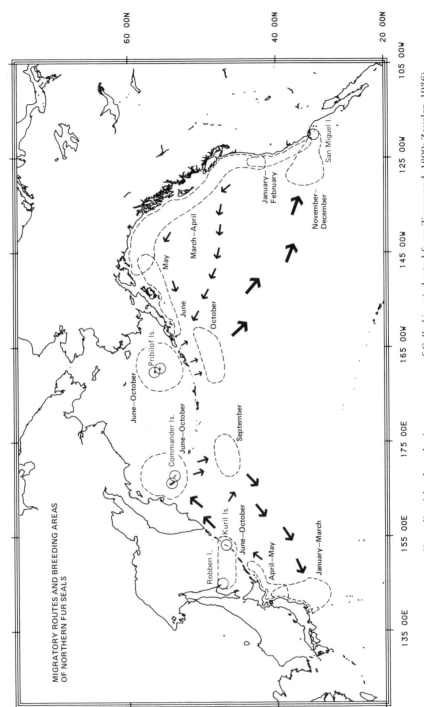

MIGRATORY ROUTES AND BREEDING AREAS
OF NORTHERN FUR SEALS

Pribilof Is.
June—October

Commander Is.
June—October

Robben I.
Kuril Is.
June—October

San Miguel I.

January—
February

November—
December

March—April

May

June

October

September

April—May

January—March

Fig. 3.1. Locations of breeding islands and migratory routes of *Callorhinus* (adapted from Townsend, 1899; Zeusler, 1936).

the high seas, and is then usually found 20–200 km from shore (Fig. 3.1).

METHODS

We collected attendance data at two study sites on St. George Island (East Reef and Zapadni), and at one site (Kitovi) on St. Paul Island, 65 km away (Fig. 3.2). East Reef (hereafter called East) is a long, narrow beach covered with large boulders. Zapadni is a flat but sloping hillside with few rocks, located about 200 m from the sea. Kitovi is a broad beach covered with large boulders on top of bedrock. Data were collected at East from 1974 to 1977, at Zapadni from 1975 to 1977, and at Kitovi in 1976 and 1977. East and Zapadni represented different types of terrain, whereas Kitovi was selected because comparative data were collected there in 1951 (Bartholomew and Hoel, 1953) and 1963 (Peterson, 1968). At each site, observations were made from blinds (hides) only a few meters from the animals. A grid with intersections every 10 m was painted on the rocks at each site to facilitate locating marked animals on daily distribution maps.

Observation efforts differed among years. At Kitovi in 1976 and 1977 and at East in 1976 observations began in July and extended through the entire suckling season until weaning in November. In other years and at other locations, observations extended only through the first ten weeks of the breeding season. Scans were made for marked females on alternate hours, 8 to 16 hours each day through July and August. The frequency of scanning decreased after August so that by November usually no more than one observation of known females was made per day. No night observations were made.

Females were permanently marked with plastic identification tags applied to their front flippers, and by number/letter combinations bleached or clipped into the pelage. Some were branded with a hot iron. Offspring of these females were marked whenever possible.

The data from one study site for one year are referred to as a data base; ten such data bases are presented in this paper, including Kitovi in 1951 (a recalculation of Table 2, Bartholomew and Hoel, 1953) and 1963 (reanalysis of original data collected and reported by Peterson, 1968). Females that were seen onshore once in a day were scored as spending the entire day onshore, and females that were not sighted were scored as spending a day at sea. Trips to sea that exceeded 15 consecutive days were treated as a failure of the

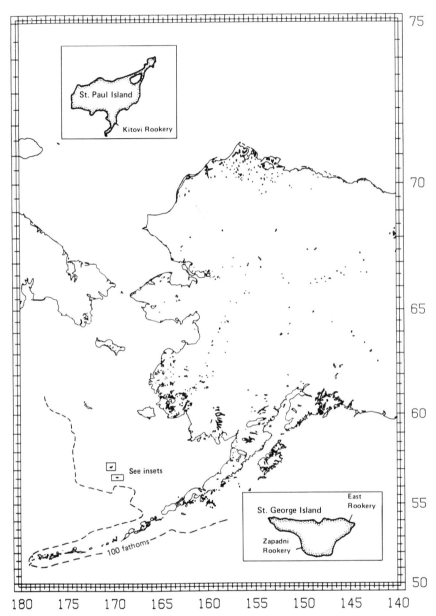

Fig. 3.2. Map of Pribilof Islands showing study sites used in this work.

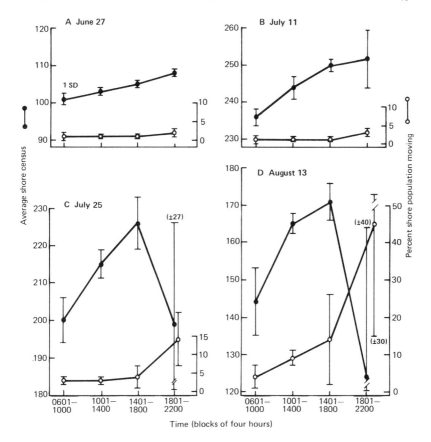

Fig 3.3. Average number of females on shore and proportion
of the shore population seen moving on 4 days in 1975.

observers to see a female during one visit, and were deleted from
most analyses to bring our methods into agreement with Peterson's.
All statistical hypotheses were tested at the 0.05 level.

Arrival/departure rates were quantified during 8 days at East in
1975. On 2 days each in the early, middle, and late parts of the pupping season, and on 2 days after pupping had ceased, we tallied all
arrivals and departures on the study grid from 0600 to 2200 hours.
Daily censuses were made near noon at each site.

An experiment to determine the effect of suckling and of pregnancy on female attendance patterns was conducted at East in 1976
and 1977. The two variables were paired in a four-cell experimental

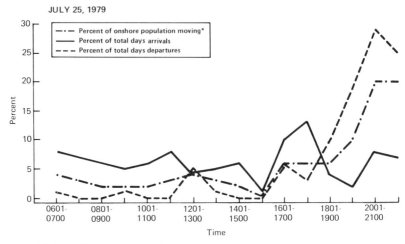

JULY 25, 1979

—·— Percent of onshore population moving*
—— Percent of total days arrivals
--- Percent of total days departures

* Arrivals and departures per number onshore

Fig. 3.4. Hourly arrival and departure rates of females on one typical day at East Rookery, St. George Island.

design. The classes of females were designated S/P, suckling, pregnant; S/NP, suckling, nonpregnant; NS/P, nonsuckling, pregnant; and NS/NP, nonsuckling, nonpregnant. S/P females were those presented in Tables 3.1 and 3.2 for East for 1975 and 1976. Females intended to be S/NP were held captive from parturition to day 10 postpartum and were then released and studied the remainder of that year. None of these animals returned with a pup the following year (hence were NP in the study year). Of females intended to be NS/P some were the mothers of stillborn pups, and others were S/NP females observed in the year after their initial captive period. Of females intended to be NS/NP, some were the mothers of stillborn pups and were held captive for 10 days postpartum. Others were S/NP the year before and were held captive for a second 10-day period in the season following their initial captivity.

RESULTS

Seasonal and Daily Pattern of Attendance

Females attended the breeding islands from late June through mid-November, or approximately 125 days, which was the duration of neonate dependence. Weaning was abrupt; no young were suck-

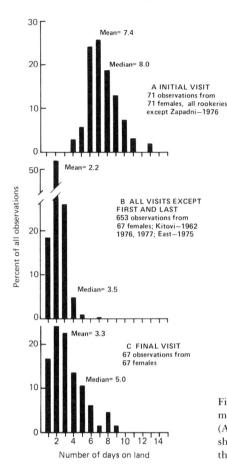

Fig. 3.5. Frequency distributions, means, and medians for the duration of (A) the first visit to shore, (B) all visits to shore except the first and last, and (C) the last visit to shore.

led beyond the first year of life. In a separate study, 77% of pups weaned themselves by disappearing from the island before their mothers did, and 33% disappeared simultaneously with or after the mother did (Macy, 1982). Females and young have never been observed together on the open sea, and are not known to move between rookeries during the period of dependency.

Daily movements changed throughout the pupping season. In early and mid-pupping season (late June to early July), the population increased steadily throughout the day due to the arrivals of new females (Fig. 3.3A, B.) After most births had occurred (late July onward) and when daily movement patterns were not obscured by new arrivals, the population peaked in afternoon hours and declined

TABLE 3.1. Visits to land by northern fur seal females; comparisons among different breeding sites and years.

1.	2.	3. Arrival to parturition	4. Parturition to copulation	5. Copulation to first departure	6. Total first visit	7. Number of subsequent visits	8. Duration subsequent visits	9. Duration of last visit	10. Length pup-rearing season	11. Days available to pup
Area	Year	x̄ SD N	x̄ SD N	x̄ SD N	x̄ SD N	x̄ SD N	x̄ SD N	x̄ SD N	x̄ SD N	x̄ SD N
Kitovi	1951[a]	2.6	6	1	9		1.5(0.7)27			
Kitovi	1962[b]	0.6(0.8)12	5.4(0.9)5	2.2(0.8)5	7.9(1.4)15	8.0(1.5)15	2.3(1.2)120	2.9(1.9)15	111(18)15	26(5)15
Kitovi	1976	0.7(0.7)10	— — 2	— — 2	8.0(1.7)11	9.6(1.2)12	2.6(1.3)105	3.9(2.0)11	122(12)11	31(5)11
Kitovi	1977	— — 2	— — 1	— — 1	— — 2	12.2(2.4)25	2.3(1.0)314	3.6(2.2)25	125(16)25	35(6)25
East	1974	1.2(0.9)10	5.7(1.1)7	2.1(1.1)7	8.2(1.7)10	—	2.1(0.9)128	—	—	—
East	1975	1.4(1.0)11	— — 2	— — 2	8.5(1.9)10	12.2(3.3)16	2.0(1.1)244	2.8(1.6)16	112(22)14	35(5)14
East	1976	0.8(0.8)5	— — 1	— — 1	8.7(2.2)4	—	2.1(1.2)60	—	—	—
East	1977	1.1(1.0)14	6.0(1.3)7	1.0(1.2)8	8.8(2.3)16	—	2.1(0.9)67	—	—	—
Zapadni	1976	—	—	—	—	—	1.8(0.9)356	—	—	—
Zapadni	1977	0.7(0.5)6	5.3(0.6)3	0.75(1.0)4	7.7(1.6)10	—	2.3(0.8)77	—	—	—
ANOVA	1-way	p = 0.26		= 0.94		>0.99		= 0.65	= 0.96	>0.99

ANOVA 2-way[c]

		Arrival to parturition		Total first visit	Duration subsequent visits
Main effects		p = 0.78		= 0.26	>0.99
Rookery		p = 0.37		= 0.74	>0.99
Year		p = 0.33		= 0.04	>0.99
2-way interactions		—[d]			>0.99

Note: All units are days.

[a] Reanalysis of data from Bartholomew and Hoel, 1953.
[b] Reanalysis of raw data cited by Peterson, 1968.
[c] Each column was compared by 2-way analysis of variance (ANOVA), or by 1-way ANOVA if insufficient data existed. Tukey's Q-test was done if significant differences were found.
[d] Suppressed.

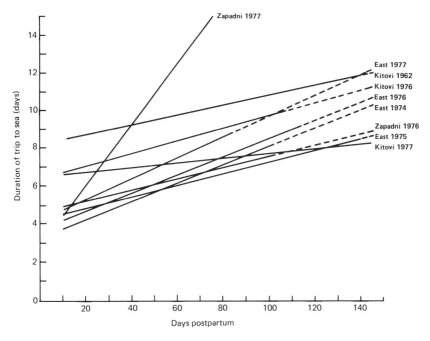

Fig. 3.6. Group regression lines for the duration of trips to sea as a function of days postpartum for all data bases. Solid lines show period over which data were collected.

markedly overnight (Fig. 3.3C, D). Clearly, females departed on feeding excursions in the evening, but this does not suggest when feeding occurred because feeding excursions lasted several days. Females arrived on shore in relatively low numbers throughout daylight hours (Fig. 3.4).

Time on Shore

At the start of the pupping season, females arrived, gave birth, and copulated on the first visit to shore, which lasted 7 to 8 days for most females (Table 3.1; Fig. 3.5A). No information is available on feeding just prior to parturition. The intervals between biological events within the first visit did not differ among sites or years (Table 3.1, columns 3, 4, 5). Estrus usually occurred on day 5 or 6 postpartum, only a few hours to one day before departure on the first feeding trip.

After the first trip to sea, females made a number of brief visits to shore for suckling. Kitovi females usually (2 out of 3 years) made

TABLE 3.2. Trips to sea by northern fur seal females; comparisons among different breeding sites and years.

1.	2.	3.	4.	5.	6.	7.	8.	9.	10.	11.
				All trips excluding first trip			All trips including first			
Area	Year	N	Duration first trip (SD)[a]	N (no. trips)	Mean duration (SD)	Slope (95% conf. interval)	N (no. trips)	Mean trips per season	Mean duration (SD)	Slope (95% conf. interval)
Kitovi	1951	11	7.0(1.1)	11(18)	8.1(1.7)	—	11(29)[b]	—	7.7(1.5)	.16(.06)
Kitovi	1962	15	7.8(3.8)	15(97)	10.1(2.5)	.02(.02)	15(112)	7.5	9.8(2.8)	.03(.01)
Kitovi	1976	11	5.0(2.2)	11(95)	8.9(2.0)	.02(.01)	11(106)	9.1	8.5(2.4)	.03(.01)
Kitovi	1977	26	5.7(2.1)	26(288)	7.2(2.1)	.01(.003)	26(314)	12.0	7.1(2.1)	.01(.01)
East	1974	11	3.7(2.1)	11(120)	5.9(2.3)	.05(.01)	11(131)	—	5.7(2.4)	.05(.01)
East	1975	16	3.8(1.6)	16(169)	5.9(1.8)	.03(.01)	16(185)	10.8	5.8(1.8)	.03(.01)
East	1976	6	3.8(2.8)	6(60)	6.7(2.3)	.04(.02)	6(66)[b]	—	6.4(2.5)	.05(.02)
East	1977	15	5.0(2.2)	15(48)	5.9(1.4)	.04(.04)	15(63)[b]	—	5.7(1.7)	.05(.04)
Zapadni	1976	31	3.4(1.4)	31(311)	6.4(2.9)	.02(.01)	31(342)	—	6.1(2.9)	.03(.01)
Zapadni	1977	20	4.6(2.6)	20(95)	6.4(3.2)	.14(.07)	20(115)[b]	—	6.1(3.2)	.16(.05)
ANOVA 2-way										
Main effects			$p > 0.99$		>0.99				>0.99	
Rookery			$p = 0.97$		>0.99				>0.99	
Year			$p = 0.998$		>0.99				>0.99	
2-way interactions			$p = 0.14$		>0.99				>0.99	

[a] N same as column 3; all units are days.

[b] Data collection ended in August with not more than four trips to sea for a given female.

fewer visits throughout the season than females at East (Table 3.1, column 7), but these visits usually lasted longer than for females at East or Zapadni (Table 3.1, column 8). These subsequent visits were always shorter than the initial shore visit; 94.5% of all subsequent visits lasted only 1 to 3 days (Fig. 3.5B).

The data indicated that the duration of shore visits did not change progressively throughout the season. However, the last visit to shore before weaning was significantly longer than any other except the initial visit to shore (Fig. 3.5C; Table 3.1, columns 6, 8, 9, compared for Kitovi 1962 and 1976 by 2-way analysis of variance [ANOVA], $p > 0.99$ for type of visit, $p = 0.98$ for year; East 1975 by 1-way ANOVA, $p > 0.99$; Tukey's Q-test shows differences in type of visit).

The pup-rearing season lasted an average of 111 to 125 days, about 12 days longer at Kitovi than at East (Table 3.1, column 10), although not in all years. Females were usually on shore suckling only 31 to 35 days of the year (Table 3.1, column 11). This constituted an average of 27% of the pup-rearing season.

Females did not move great distances between suckling sites throughout the season. The mean distance between the parturition site and all subsequent suckling sites in 1974 was only 11 m at East ($N = 179$ sites for 12 females, SD = 8.4) and 21 m at Zapadni ($N = 288$ sites for 213 females, SD = 24.7). Frequent searches failed to show that any females moved from the study site to adjacent rookeries.

Time at Sea

We noted in the field that the duration of trips to sea became longer over time. Therefore, we expressed all female records as "on day x postpartum the female returns from a feeding trip of y days duration," and compared all data bases by regression analysis. The seasonal increase existed in all data bases (Table 3.2, column 11; Fig. 3.6) and averaged 1.2 days for every 30 days postpartum, or 5 days for a pup-rearing season of 120 days. Only one data base (Kitovi-1977) had a different slope (its 95% confidence interval did not overlap with the others). We cannot explain this result. The first trip to sea after parturition was shorter than the regression line predicted (compare Table 3.2, columns 7 and 11).

The pattern of seasonal increase probably did not result from depletion of local food resources, which would have forced females to forage farther from the island over time. If food depletion had occurred, females giving birth in the latter half of the pupping season

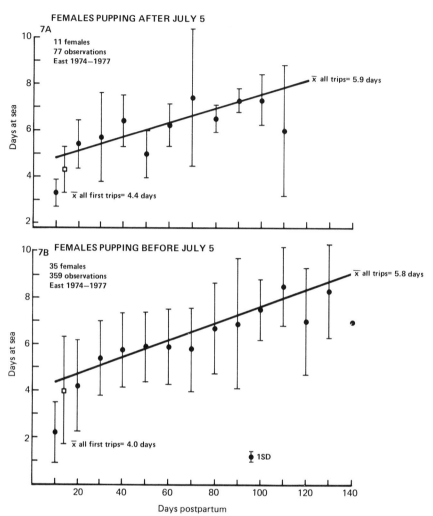

Fig. 3.7. Group regression line for the duration of trips to sea
for (A) females bearing young later than July 5, and (B) those
bearing young before July 5.

would have faced local shortages caused by foraging efforts of ear-lier-arriving females, and longer initial trips to sea would be ex-pected. The first trip to sea was not significantly different for 35 fe-males that gave birth from June 20 to July 5 (the median pupping date) compared to 11 females that pupped from July 5 to July 25 (t-test p = 0.35). Furthermore, the regressions of seasonal increase did not differ significantly, although the y-intercept for the late-bearing group was greater by one-half day (Fig. 3.7).

The mean time spent at sea per trip differed by rookery. Kitovi females had longer first and subsequent trips than females at East or Zapadni (Table 3.2, columns 4, 6, 10; Fig. 3.6). This difference was not attributable to individual seal variability, which was substan-tial in all data bases. A pooled estimate of individual seal variability and a test of homogeneity of variances (Cochran's test, p < 0.95) showed a wide range of variance but no trends by site or year.

The duration of trips to sea has not changed progressively since 1951. The 1962 and present data were restricted in numbers of fe-males and trips to sea comparable to Table 2 of Bartholomew and Hoel (1953) and were compared by 1-way ANOVA. The results showed that feeding trips were longer in 1962 than in 1951 or re-cent years, and that 1951 and recent years were not significantly dif-ferent from each other. This result suggests a difference in data-col-lection methods more than a directional change in feeding patterns over time.

Effects of Reproductive Status on Attendance Behavior

The attendance patterns considered so far were for females that were lactating and simultaneously pregnant (carrying an unim-planted blastocyst). Pregnant animals comprised on average 79% of the entire female population (York, 1979). Were attendance pat-terns of pregnant, suckling females different from those of non-suckling or nonpregnant ones? Because these animals were uncom-mon onshore, we produced numbers of them for study through short periods of captivity (see Methods) and compared their attend-ance patterns against those of normal females just described.

The durations of visits to shore differed among the four experi-mental groups (Fig. 3.8). Suckling females (S/P and S/NP) were not significantly different from each other, but both had significantly shorter visits to shore than either of the nonsuckling groups (2-way ANOVA, p > 0.99). Nonsuckling females (NS/P and NS/NP) made proportionately more visits to shore in excess of 3 days than did suckling females (Fig. 3.8). Pregnancy was not an important deter-

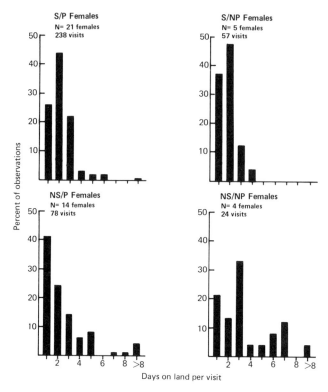

Fig. 3.8. The frequency of observing visits to shore of various duration for females of different reproductive status. S/P = suckling, pregnant. S/NP = suckling, not pregnant. NS/P = not suckling, pregnant. NS/NP = not suckling, not pregnant.

minant of shore-visit duration. Nonsuckling females made five to six visits to shore, respectively, compared to twelve to fourteen visits for S/NP and S/P females; this difference was statistically significant (2-way ANOVA, p > 0.99).

Suckling females made eleven to twelve trips to sea throughout the season, whereas nonsuckling females made only five to six, a significant difference (2-way ANOVA, p > 0.99). Furthermore, the days at sea were distributed very differently for suckling versus nonsuckling females (Fig. 3.9). Nonsuckling females interspersed long and short trips to the extent that arrivals and departures were not predictable. Pregnancy seemed to have no effect on the duration of trips to sea. The frequency distributions of S/NP and S/P females were similar, as were those of NS/P and NS/NP females.

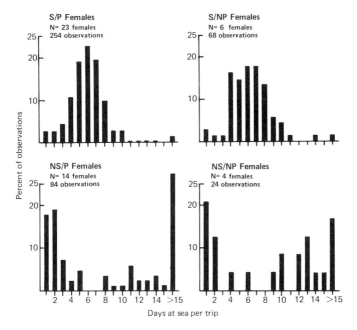

Fig. 3.9. The frequency of observing trips to sea of various duration for females of different reproductive status.

Flexibility in Shore Visits

The most unvarying aspect of attendance behavior was the duration of shore visits by S/P females (Table 3.1; Fig. 3.5). We performed two experiments to determine the extent to which this usually stable interval was variable, and to identify the determinants of shore-visit duration. Four marked pups were taken from the rookery on the day their marked mothers were expected to return from foraging trips. When the mothers arrived, the pups were held for additional intervals (12–72 hours on ten different withholdings) before being allowed to reunite with the mothers. After reunion, mothers remained onshore for an interval that was not different from control visits on which the same pup was not held captive (about 2.2 days). This control value was subtracted from the total hours spent onshore during each visit, and the remainders were regressed on the hours the pup was withheld. The slope of this regression was close to 1 (Fig. 3.10), indicating that for each hour that reunion was delayed the female spent an extra hour onshore. The total time mothers spent onshore, including pre- and postreunion

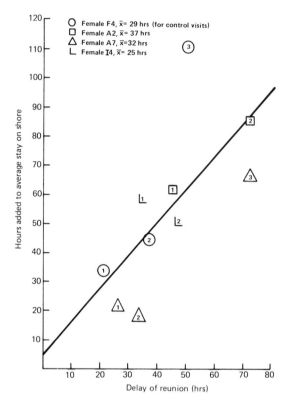

Fig. 3.10. Hours added to the average shore visit by withholding the pup from reunion with the mother for various periods. Numbers indicate different experiments for each female.

intervals, was often three to four times longer than the control visits. Therefore, the typical visit to shore was not determined by the female's inability to remain ashore longer, but was determined during contact with the pup.

We performed a second experiment to determine whether pup demand for milk may alter the duration of female shore visits. Four different pups were captured just before their mothers were expected to return from feeding and were held until the mothers appeared. Each pup was then fed a quantity of fresh milk by stomach tube (collected by tube from "donor" pups actively suckling at a different rookery) and was immediately allowed to reunite with its

TABLE 3.3. Effects on duration of shore visits of artificially feeding pups milk prior to reunion with mothers.

Female No.	Duration of control visits (hrs)		No. visits	Amount of milk fed (ml)	Feeding interval[a] (hrs)	Prereunion interval (hrs)	Duration of experimental visit (hrs)
	x̄	SD					
1	44	3.5	3	800	12	1.50	74
2	36	10	4	1,000	25[b]	0.25	47
3	39	13	4	800	1	1.50	64
4	40	2	2	900	1	0.50	79

[a] The number of hours prior to release when milk was given at least once.
[b] Subject was fed last 14 hours prior to release. All others were fed within minutes of release.

mother. The duration of shore visits for mothers of fed pups exceeded control values plus 1 SD on visits when the same pups were not fed. In three trials this duration exceeded or approximated the control mean plus 2 SD (Table 3.3). The brief prereunion intervals could not have caused these unusually long periods on shore. Therefore, decreasing the pup's demand for food lengthened the usually uniform (2.2 days) duration of shore visits for mothers.

DISCUSSION

In comparing northern fur seals on different sites, or in comparing different fur seal species, we must consider that consistency in expression of a trait may not equate with inflexibility. For example, undisturbed northern fur seals were very consistent in the duration of visits to shore. The same will be shown for other species in this work (specifically, Tables 6.4 and 8.4; Figs. 11.8 and 13.5). Also, the Steller sea lion and New Zealand fur seal, A. forsteri, are highly consistent (Gentry, 1970; Stirling, 1971). But under experimental conditions, shore visits of northern fur seals were very flexible, depending on prereunion interval and pup demand for milk. This suggests that even the major differences among seal species probably reflect responses to local environments more than genetically fixed traits.

Responses to local environments can be seen clearly in those aspects of northern fur seal attendance behavior that were consistent at a given site, but that differed consistently between sites. For example, St. Paul and St. George islands were different distances from the edge of the continental shelf where feeding occurs. Kitovi females, starting 65 km farther from the shelf, made fewer trips to sea through the season, stayed at sea longer on the first and all subsequent trips, and appeared to compensate for this absence by having a slightly longer suckling season than females at St. George Island. Nevertheless, pup growth rates at St. George Island exceed those of same-sex pups at St. Paul Island (Gentry et al., unpubl. ms.).

The regularity and predictability of the attendance patterns are also determined by reproductive status, specifically lactation. Suckling females have a longer season at the island, spend a greater proportion of this season onshore, have a greater number of both visits to shore and trips to sea, and spend more days onshore per season than do nonsuckling females. Nonsuckling females have either longer or shorter trips to sea than suckling females, and their movements are not predictable. Most females (79%) in the population suckle every year, which explains the regularity of land/sea movements of the female population as a whole. Pregnancy is not an important determinant of movements. Therefore, suckling appears to be the main factor that brings the females of this otherwise pelagic species to shore on a regular basis.

Trips to sea became longer throughout the season in all data bases. It seems unlikely that, for northern fur seals, this increase results from a depletion of local food resources. Females that give birth late in the pupping season have short first trips to sea indistinguishable from those of earlier-bearing females. Also, one early female (539, Table 4.1) dived repeatedly to 175 m on her first postpartum feeding trip, a depth that was clearly at or beyond the continental shelf break. The abundance of walleye pollock there is so great, forming shoals 20–50 km long and having densities of 9 metric tons per hectare (Smith, 1981), that fur seal foraging may have no measurable effect on local prey abundance.

The seasonal increase is also not likely to result from the stress of lactation on the long first visit to shore. Chapter 5 will show that females regain normal body weight and produce milk of normal composition within the first two to three feeding trips after parturition.

The most likely explanation for the increased duration of trips to sea is that females are responding to increased nutritional needs of the young. Chapter 5 will show that females transfer increasing amounts of milk over time, which is apparently a measure of increased need.

These data do not support Chapman's (1961) suggestion that the impact of the pollock fishery might be measurable in the duration of female feeding excursions. A comparison of present with past data shows no increase in the duration of feeding trips during the past 26 years, the interval when the pollock fishery increased from zero to 2 million metric tons annually. The slight differences in the attendance data appear to result from different sampling methods. This conclusion does not imply that fur seals have not been affected by the fishery, only that the duration of feeding trips is an inadequate measure. The marine ecosystem of the Bering Sea is very complex; walleye pollock comprise only one part of the seal-carrying capacity. Fur seals may have responded to the pollock fishery by foraging in different areas, feeding at different depths, taking fish of different size or species, or diving more frequently—none of which need increase the total duration of the trip to sea. We therefore believe that for feeding generalists, such as the northern fur seal, the duration of foraging trips is not a good indicator of fish abundance except when catastrophic declines occur, such as in the 1983 EN conditions. Chapman's suggestion that foraging effort will increase as a result of competition with the fishery will be tested by instrumenting future females with TDR's as the fishery continues to change.

SUMMARY

Attendance behavior of the northern fur seal was studied at East Reef and Zapadni rookeries (St. George Island) for 4 and 2 years, respectively, and at Kitovi rookery (St. Paul Island) for 2 years. The breeding season extends through June and July. No females attend the breeding sites in winter (November through April) because of migration to southern waters. Males remain in the Bering Sea in winter. Weaning is abrupt and total, and is initiated by the offspring. No females suckle yearlings or remain with young beyond 125 days of age. Prepartum feeding patterns are unknown because females arrive on land only 1 day before parturition. The interval from parturition to copulation is 6 days, and females make no trips to sea in this interval. Between parturition and weaning, females make twelve to fourteen visits to land, each lasting approximately 2.2 days. Females are on land 31 to 35 days (27%) of the pup-rearing season. The percentage of time pups spend suckling on each visit was not measured. When females go to sea they depart in the evening, although arrivals and departures occur throughout the day. Absences last on average 6.9 days and progressively increase in duration at the rate of 1.2 days for every 30 days postpartum. No consistent change in the duration of feeding absences has occurred over the past 26 years. Nonsuckling females make longer visits to shore, but spend less total time on land than do suckling females, and they move to sea and back in an unpredictable pattern. Pregnancy is not an important determinant of attendance patterns. The length of a female's visit to shore is determined by contact with the pup, not by the total time she is ashore. Pup demand for milk is an important determinant of shore-visit duration. Females at St. Paul Island are 65 km farther from the edge of the continental shelf where pollock are concentrated and they make longer feeding trips, fewer trips to sea per season, and have a longer pup-rearing season than females at St. George Island.

4 Feeding and Diving Behavior of Northern Fur Seals ≅ *R. L. Gentry,*

G. L. Kooyman, and M. E. Goebel

INTRODUCTION

When we began research on northern fur seal diving in 1975, our goals were modest compared to the global view presented in Chapter 1. Initially, we hoped only to characterize the depth, duration, number, and temporal occurrence of dives made by foraging mothers (Kooyman et al., 1976). Since diving had not previously been measured in any free-ranging otariids, even these modest goals seemed optimistic. But when initial success showed that these goals were easily attained, we shifted from simply describing diving behavior to studying interrelationships among the variables that make up the foraging pattern. For example, some of our newly defined goals were to identify variations in the diving patterns of different individuals, examine the relationship between depth and duration of dives, study the effect of dive depth on recovery times, and measure the frequency of dives to various depths as a function of time of day. In addition, the present work focuses on a different unit of measure. Our previous work emphasized the measurement of single dives because our interest was in showing physiological capabilities. Our present work stresses dive bouts because ecologically these are the units by which seals interact with their prey populations.

Before the present data were collected, a modification was made in the instrument attachment system. In 1975 and later, instrumented females spent up to three times longer at sea than uninstrumented females. We surmised that instrumented females were delayed because the TDR was attached to a single harness strap that could flutter. Therefore, we suspended the instrument between two opposing straps (Fig. 2.4) and the duration of trips to sea became almost normal.

All diving measurements were made at East Reef rookery (hereafter called East; Fig. 3.2), a beach on the north side of St. George Island, facing away from the continental slope where much feeding occurs. The long (150 m), narrow (20 m) configuration of the beach contributes to high site fidelity of breeding females (Chapter 3).

Summer weather consists of continual heavy overcast, moderate winds, and air temperatures of 4°–5°C. The female population on-shore peaks from 1200 to 1700 hours each day, and is low from dusk until dawn. The moon is rarely visible throughout the year due to overcast. Tidal excursion is less than 2 m.

Dive measurements reported here were made in July of 1980 and 1982. Previous dive measurements had been made at East in September and October 1975 (Kooyman et al., 1976). Because the previous results were obtained with a different model TDR (Chapter 2), they are not included here.

METHODS

We usually captured females with a noose fixed to the end of a 5-meter long pole while working at low tide from the seaward edge of the rookery. This approach caused fewer flight responses than any other and blocked the escape of animals at recapture. The presence in July of adult males on territories also reduced flight responses. Only tagged females of known reproductive and attendance history were instrumented. These animals unerringly returned to within 2–3 m of the same site on successive visits to shore, and their arrival dates could be anticipated to within ± 1 day. The daily presence of an observer at the rookery made it possible to capture any desired female on any given visit to land, and facilitated recapture soon after instruments returned. Females made wary by multiple captures moved laterally along the beach up to 100 m, and were taken with hoop nets as they fled to the water.

All animals to be instrumented were carried away from the rookery in a box before being immobilized on a restraint board (Fig. 2.3). Harnesses were removed from returned females without carrying them from the rookery. Most females showed little response to the harness and TDR, and calmly returned to suckle their pups before going to sea.

Dive-bout duration was defined by plotting the log survivor curve for interdive intervals, described in Chapter 2. For three females the first inflection point was at 15 or 20 minutes, and the second was at 40 minutes. Therefore, bouts were defined as diving sequences having no interdive intervals greater than 40 minutes and consisting of five or more dives (a stipulation that was necessary for calculating dives per hour). Transit times were measured from departure to the onset of the first dive bout, and from the end of the last bout to return onto shore.

TABLE 4.1. Summary of northern fur seal dive records.

Female no.	Total dives	Hours at sea	Depth (m)		Dive duration (min.)	
			Aver.	*Max.*	*Aver.*	*Max.*
539	292	141	99	184	2.8	5.7
1133	296	239	60	207	1.8	5.5
1208	302	231	48	139	1.8	6.1
1789	362	192	32	86	2.4	5.8
542	325	192	62	172	2.4	5.7
579[a]	176	135	126	193	4.0	7.6
540[b]	122	130	150	196	3.1	6.4
Average	268	180	68	168	2.2	6.1
SD ±	86	45	53	42	1.4	0.7

[a] Baseline was slightly off film, so dives less than 50 psi not represented.

[b] Baseline faint, so shallow dives, if any, may not have been recorded.

We conducted a special analysis of rest periods occurring on trips to sea. Periods of rest, which we infer to be sleep, were indicated by a flat baseline with none of the "chatter" typical of diving and active swimming (Chapter 2). Rest periods showed on the baseline of six TDR records. Five records had adequate detail for analysis of three separate behavioral categories: (a) resting at the surface; (b) active at the surface without diving; and (c) active at the surface while diving. The consecutive minutes spent in each category were tallied for each record. Time in each category was read to the nearest 12 minutes, the interval between time dots on the baseline. This method of measuring dive times was more accurate than the estimate derived from the dive-bout criterion, and explains the differences in some of the tables and figures.

RESULTS

In July of 1980 and 1982 seventeen TDR deployments were made, during which three instruments were lost, seven partial or blank records were obtained from instruments that malfunctioned, and seven complete records were acquired.

The duration of trips ranged from 5.5 to almost 10 days, with an average for seven females of 7.5 days (Table 4.1). This average is 2% to 12% greater than the average duration of trips to sea of uninstrumented females from East rookery (5.9 to 6.7 days; Table 3.2). The difference may result from drag caused by the instrument and harness. The record baseline showed that females did not land in unob-

TABLE 4.2. Activity patterns during trips to sea for northern fur seals.

Female no.	Dives per hour	Rest time (%)	Transit times (h)	
			Outbound	Inbound
539	2.1	14.0	6.1	7.0
1204	—[a]	25.0	—[a]	—[a]
1133	1.2	—[b]	7.3	15.0
1208	1.3	15.0	26.7	6.6
1789	1.9	20.0	6.0	7.8
542	1.7	6.0	25.1	12.1
579	1.3	—[c]	11.5	6.6
540	0.9	10.0	22.5	15.9
Average	1.5	15.0	15.0	10.2
SD ±	0.4	6.8	9.4	4.1

[a] Baseline adequate for analysis of rest, but record too faint to analyze for depth.

[b] Baseline too free of "chatter" to analyze for rest patterns.

[c] Baseline off film; sleep patterns and dives <50 psi not discernible.

served locations during this interval. Individual variability in the records was marked as indicated by an almost five-fold difference in mean dive depth among females. Dives were simple spikes with no time spent at maximum depth. Most seals apparently fed at or beyond the continental shelf break because five of the seven records (Table 4.1) showed dives exceeding the 140 m maximum shelf depth between the island and the shelf break (which occurs at 170 m).

The low frequency of dives on a trip (average 1.5 dives per hour spent at sea; Table 4.2) was attributable in part to long rest periods, long periods of activity at the surface without diving, and long transit times in both directions. Rest at the surface sometimes accounted for a quarter of all time spent at sea. Transit times for seven females (Table 4.2) were relatively long, averaging 15.0 hours outbound and 10.2 hours inbound. When transit times were measured to the first or last single dive, rather than to the first or last dive bout, the averages were 6.2 and 7.2 hours, respectively. The dive-bout criterion of 40 minutes and five dives per bout excluded from bouts 3%–14% of the dives on a record. The average record consisted of sixteen bouts (Table 4.3).

The dives excluded from defined bouts by the dive-bout criterion had special characteristics that distinguished them from other diving. Not only were they spaced farther apart, but also 27% of the

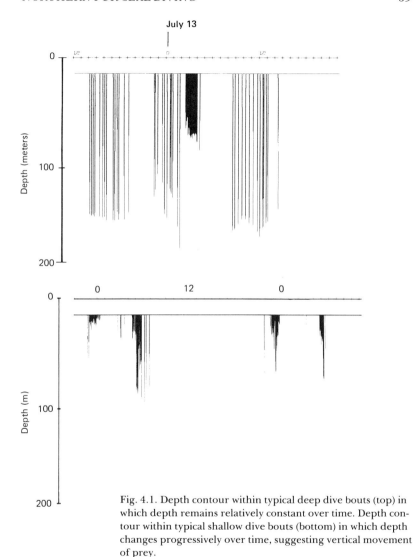

Fig. 4.1. Depth contour within typical deep dive bouts (top) in which depth remains relatively constant over time. Depth contour within typical shallow dive bouts (bottom) in which depth changes progressively over time, suggesting vertical movement of prey.

excluded dives occurred within the first twenty-five dives of the trip. Some excluded dives occurred at the transition from shallow to deep diving, and others occurred after the last definable dive bout. Most excluded dives (67%) occurred during daylight hours (0500–2100), and the mean depth of excluded dives exceeded the mean of overall dives by 11–30 m (for three females).

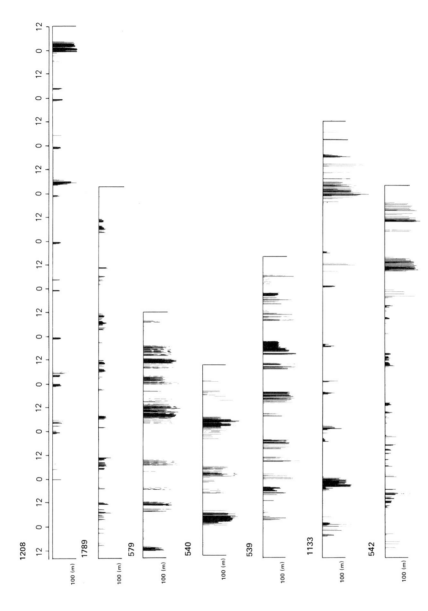

Fig. 4.2. Dive records for seven females showing the tendency for shallow dive bouts to occur at night, for deep bouts to occur at any hour of day.

TABLE 4.3. Dive bout average characteristics for northern fur seals.

Female no.	Dive bouts	Dives excluded (%)	Dives per bout		Bout duration (h)		Dives/h in bouts		Time of bout under water (%)	
			Mean	Range	Mean	Range	Mean	Range	Mean	Range
539	17	3	16.6	5–65	2.6	1.4	5.8	4.2	29	11
542	18	14	15.6	5–44	1.9	1.7	9.9	4.5	16	11
1133	12	11	23.6	7–62	2.8	2.5	11.5	5.4	21	6
1208	14	7	20.1	11–41	1.6	1.4	16.4	8.4	39	11
1789	18	12	17.6	5–52	2.2	1.5	8.6	4.7	33	12
Average	15.8	9.4	18.2		2.2		10.1		28	
SD ±	2.7	4.4		5–65		1.7		6.4		13

Notes: Includes all bouts that fit the dual criterion of including no interdive intervals >40 min, and including at least five dives. Note that bout duration does not equate with percentage of time spent diving in Fig. 4.13, which was tallied differently.

Both dives per bout and bout duration were highly variable. Bouts averaged 18.2 dives each, and bout durations averaged 2.2 hours (Table 4.3).

The depth of dives within a bout followed two distinct temporal patterns. In some bouts the depth remained relatively constant over time (Fig. 4.1A). In other bouts the depth consistently changed over time, suggesting that the prey were moving vertically (Fig. 4.1B). The mean depth of the latter bouts was always 75 m or less (hereafter called *shallow* bouts), whereas the mean depth of the former type was always greater than 125 m (hereafter *deep* bouts).

The tendency for shallow bouts to occur in the nighttime and for deep bouts to occur throughout both day and night was clear from examination of complete records (Fig. 4.2). More specifically shallow bouts with changing depth contours were bimodal on a daily basis (i.e., had peaks at dusk and dawn; female 1789, Fig. 4.2). Resting periods usually occurred during daylight hours.

Depth of dives was not random, but instead clustered around two main intervals, at approximately 50–60 m and approximately 175 m (Fig. 4.3). Shallow and deep dives tended to occur at different times of day, and, if performed by the same individual, they often occurred on different days.

The majority of dives occurred at night (Fig. 4.4), with two distinct peaks. The onset of diving coincided with local dusk (about 2200 hours in July), and diving ended about one hour after local dawn (about 0500 hours in July).

Northern Fur Seal

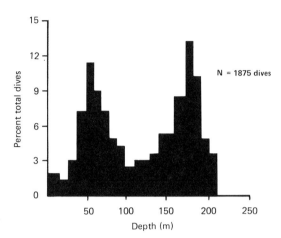

Fig. 4.3. Frequency distribution for dives by 10 m depth increments. Bars are labeled with the deepest dive (20 = 11–20 m). This figure combines data for seven females.

Northern Fur Seal

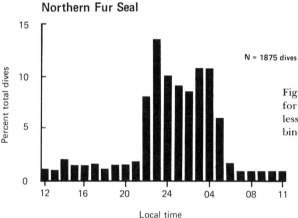

Fig. 4.4. Frequency distribution for dives by hour of day regardless of depth. The figure combines records for seven females.

The most frequently attained depth interval showed trends with the time of day, but considerable hourly variation occurred. Taking all records together, shallow depths predominated at night and deeper depths predominated in the daytime (Fig. 4.5). However, such grouping obscures the preferences of individual females for deep or shallow diving. Individuals making mostly shallow dives predominated the records, and for these animals the above generalizations are true. The generalization does not apply to the two females that dived deeply at all hours. Therefore, Figure 4.5 reflects

Northern Fur Seal

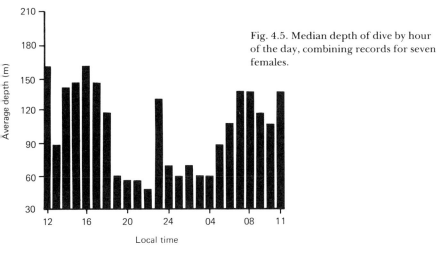

Fig. 4.5. Median depth of dive by hour of the day, combining records for seven females.

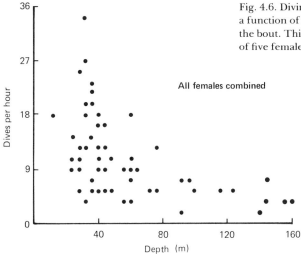

Fig. 4.6. Diving rate in dives per hour as a function of the mean depth of dives in the bout. This figure combines records of five females.

an average tendency for the whole sample that accurately portrays some individuals but misrepresents a few.

The rate of dives per hour within bouts varied with the mean depth of the bout. Generally, the deeper the diving, the slower the diving rate (Fig. 4.6). Virtually all the variability in dive rates occurred at mean depths of 75 m or less. The shape of this distribution

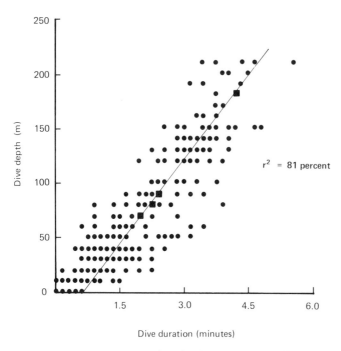

Fig. 4.7. Linear regression of dive depth on the duration of the
same dives. This figure plots all dives for female no. 1133.

was determined mainly by the interdive intervals within groups because the relationship between depth and duration of a given dive
was linear with little variability ($r^2 = 0.81$; Fig. 4.7). The data in Figure 4.6 were not plotted as recovery time from individual dives because poor resolution in the time base created errors in reading dive
duration (Chapter 2). Calculation of dives per hour averaged these
errors over the duration of the entire bout and was therefore more
accurate.

The amount of time spent underwater per bout differed according to the depth of the bout. Deep bouts with their long interdive
intervals averaged 26% submerged time (SD = 9.5, N = 3 females,
14 bouts to depths of 125–200 m), whereas shallow bouts with
shorter surface intervals averaged 37% submerged time (SD =
16.7, N = 4 females, 16 bouts to depths of 10–40 m). This difference was significant (ANOVA, p = 0.96). Shallow dive bouts were
highly variable in the percentage of time submerged because the interdive intervals, which largely determined bout duration, were

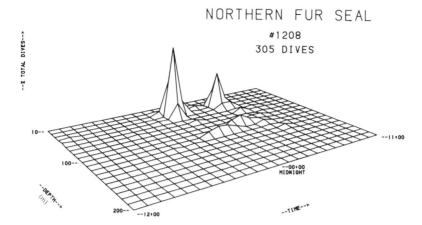

Fig. 4.8. Three-dimensional representation of all dives performed by one shallow diving female during an entire trip, grouping dives by hour of day regardless of date.

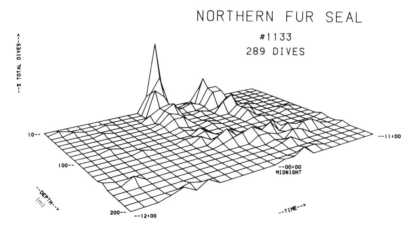

Fig. 4.9. Three-dimensional representation of all dives performed by one mixed (shallow and deep) diver on one trip, grouping dives by hour of day regardless of date.

Fig. 4.10. Three-dimensional representation of all dives performed by one deep diver on one trip, grouping dives by hour of day regardless of date.

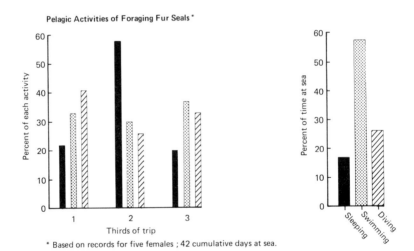

Fig. 4.11. Activity budget of females at sea by thirds of the trip and overall. The figure combines data from six females. Time spent diving was calculated to the nearest 12 minutes, not by the dive-bout criterion.

most variable in bouts of <75 m (Fig. 4.6). The average proportion of time spent submerged for all seventy-nine bouts was 28%.

All dive records fit one of three basic patterns. Two records (females 1789 and 1208) had all shallow dives, and these occurred in a distinctly bimodal pattern with peaks just after dusk and just before dawn (Fig. 4.8). The depth contours within bouts changed with time, suggesting that the prey were moving vertically during feeding.

Three females (nos. 539, 542, and 1133) showed a mixture of shallow diving at night and deep diving at all hours of the day and night (Fig. 4.9). Their shallow dives, too, were bimodal with peaks near dusk and dawn; the depth contours within shallow dive bouts changed consistently with time. For an individual, deep dive bouts did not usually occur on the same day as shallow bouts, but usually took place on the first and/or last day of the trip. Deep bouts were not bimodal in distribution and did not change depth consistently with time.

Two females (nos. 540 and 579) showed only deep diving (>100 m; Fig. 4.10). Their bouts were not bimodal in distribution, but occurred throughout the day and night, and their depth contours within bouts did not change consistently over time as in shallow diving. These females usually had many fewer dives per trip than did shallow or mixed (shallow and deep) divers.

The activity budget during feeding trips, inferred from the nature of the baseline, showed that 57% of all time at sea was spent active at the surface but without diving, while diving and resting accounted for 26% and 17%, respectively (Fig. 4.11). However, activity cycles did not remain constant throughout the trip. Resting behavior was significantly more frequent in the middle third of the trip than in other thirds (ANOVA, p = 0.99). The times spent in the other two categories did not differ significantly in each third when considering all records together (ANOVA, p = 0.85, p = 0.27, respectively), although diving was significantly less frequent in the second third for some individuals, especially the mixed divers.

Resting behavior (inactive) at the surface was not uniformly distributed throughout the day; 80% of all minutes spent resting occurred within 12 daylight hours (0800–2000 hours; Fig. 4.12). Resting behavior, active without diving, and diving occurred in periods of different duration. Periods of uninterrupted resting rarely exceeded 6 hours, and 72% of the periods lasted 4 hours or less (Fig. 4.13). Periods of uninterrupted diving did not exceed 13 hours, and

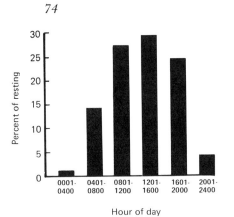

Fig. 4.12. The occurrence of resting at sea by hour of the day. The figure combines data from six females.

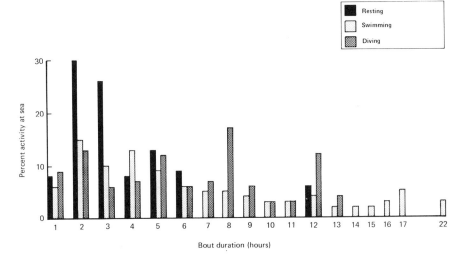

Fig. 4.13. The durations of uninterrupted rest, swimming, and diving periods at sea. Diving time was read to the nearest 12 minutes, and therefore values do not correspond to Table 4.3, which was based on the dive-bout criterion.

77% of the periods lasted 8 hours or less. Active periods without diving were longer than the other categories. One period lasted 21 consecutive hours, but 76% of them lasted 10 hours or less.

DISCUSSION

Northern fur seals show more individual variation in diving than other species discussed in this volume except, perhaps, the South

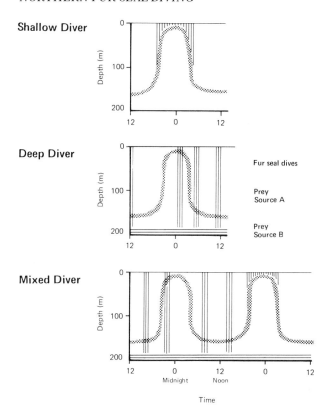

Fig. 4.14. Diagrammatic representation of three dive patterns observed in northern fur seals. (A) Shallow pattern. Individuals feed mostly at dawn and dusk, when the deep scattering layer is closest to the surface; depth of dive changes over time. (B) Deep pattern. Animals bypass prey associated with the deep scattering layer and feed at the same depth throughout day and night; dive depths do not suggest that prey move vertically. (C) Mixed (shallow and deep) pattern. Individuals alternate between A and B on different days.

African fur seal. We do not know the extent to which individuals specialize in one of the three diving patterns identified. Some evidence indicates that diving patterns change according to season. For example, diving was significantly deeper in the July 1980 and July 1982 data than in the September 1976 data (Chi-square contingency table, $p < 0.99$). This difference may reflect the tendency of juvenile walleye pollock to inhabit shallower depths in September than earlier in the year (Lynde, 1984).

In contrast to most other marine mammals, the northern fur seal diet is relatively well known from examination of stomachs collected from dead animals at sea. About sixty-three species of fish and cephalopods are taken in all parts of the range, but only eight species (five fish, three squid) constitute the principal prey species in the Bering Sea. The frequency of these prey items in stomachs changes by location within the Bering Sea, and by month in the same area (Kajimura, 1983).

The three diving patterns may reflect the vertical movements of the prey species being taken. Shallow divers, which are active at dawn and dusk and which have changing depth contours over time, may be feeding as the deep scattering layer moves relative to the surface at night. Fur seal prey species that fit this description are juvenile walleye pollock and Atka mackerel. Deep divers, which dive throughout the 24-hour period and have no consistent change in depth within bouts, may be taking species that have no vertical movement. Mixed shallow and deep divers may alternate between these two types of prey. The three patterns are shown diagrammatically in Figure 4.14.

Shallow and mixed divers show a consistent crepuscular diving pattern. The interval between peaks of dive activity matches gut clearance time (R. L. DeLong, pers. commun., 1983), and therefore it may reflect a period of satiation during the night. It may also reflect the fact that some fish are more susceptible to predation at dawn and dusk when available light wavelengths in the water column rapidly shift out of their range of peak spectral sensitivity (e.g., the Twilight Hypothesis; Munz and McFarland, 1973; McFarland and Munz, 1975; Hobson et al., 1981).

Although the favored depths for diving were 50–60 m and 175 m, seals may not have an equal impact on food resources at both depths. Seals are unable to dive to 175 m as often per hour as they can dive to 60 m or less, probably because of disproportionate recovery times from deeper dives (Fig. 4.6). Perhaps because of recovery times, few seals (2 of 7 records) chose the deep-diving pattern, and thus the total number of feeding dives to greater depths is much smaller than to shallow depths. Based on frequency of dives, the northern fur seal's major impact on fish stocks may occur in the top 75 m. However, more research on prey-capture success, as well as size, age, and reproductive status of prey at the two depths are needed to test this conjecture.

Repenning's (1976) hypothesis that feeding patterns ultimately direct breeding patterns was supported in an unexpected way by our research. The records showed that most animals had peaks of diving near dawn and dusk, and that they rested during daylight hours (0800–2000 hours). Unpublished data (and discussions with G. A. Antonelis) indicate that mating aggregations on shore have peaks of general activity and of copulations at dawn and dusk, and that individuals rest during much of the daylight hours. It is possible that the pelagic activity cycle of northern fur seals is ultimately determined by the hourly availability of prey, and that this cycle is simply maintained for the brief periods that the animals are on shore each year.

Activity patterns at sea may also be determined by thermoregulatory needs. Figure 4.13 shows that 72% of pelagic rest periods lasted 4 hours or less, much shorter than periods of diving or of nondiving activity at the surface, which we interpret as swimming. Rest periods were often interrupted by brief (12–48 min) periods of activity. We suggest that these short interruptions were grooming bouts that were necessitated by cold sea water infiltrating the pelage and reducing the skin temperature. Rest periods may also be brief due to a reduction in the heat that is produced when food is assimilated (Specific Dynamic Action), which may raise resting metabolic rates for 1 to 3 hours after eating (Costa and Kooyman, 1984).

We suggest that the dives excluded from bouts by the dive-bout criterion may have represented exploration. Their nongrouped nature and their occurrence either at the onset of feeding or at a transition between shallow and deep feeding suggest that these were attempts to locate food patches. This hypothesis could be tested by including in the TDR a device to record actual prey capture.

SUMMARY

Diving in the northern fur seal was studied at East Reef rookery, St. George Island, during July 1980 and 1982. Seven records, one each for seven individuals, were obtained. Trips to sea were longer when females carried TDRs than when they did not ($\bar{x} = 7.5$ versus 6.9 days). The outbound transit times averaged 15 hours and return times averaged 10.2 hours. The number of dives made on trips to sea varied from 122 to 362. Shallow-diving seals fed just after dusk and just before dawn in a distinctly bimodal pattern. Deep-diving seals fed at all hours of the day with no obvious temporal pattern. About 69% of all dives occurred at night. Some individuals had all shallow bouts, others had all deep bouts, and some had both types.

The dive-bout criterion was 40 minutes. Females averaged 15.8 dive bouts per trip, and each bout lasted on average 2.2 hours. The dive rate within bouts was 10.1 dives per hour. On average 28% of each bout was spent below the surface, but this portion was significantly different (greater) in shallow than in deep bouts. Depth changed continuously with time during dives; seals did not linger at any given depth. Dives lasted on average 2.6 minutes, with a maximum of 5 to 7 minutes. The mean depth of all dives was 68 m, and the maximum depth was 207 m. The most frequently attained depths were 50–60 m and 175 m. The correlation between depth and duration of a dive was high ($r^2 = 81\%$). The surface interval between deep dives was longer and less variable than between shallow dives. The activity budget on foraging trips was 17% resting, 26% diving, and 57% swimming or active at the surface. About 80% of all resting occurred during the day, and rest was most frequent during the middle third of a trip to sea. Rest bouts were shorter (4 hours or less) than bouts of either swimming or diving.

5 Free-Ranging Energetics of Northern Fur Seals ≅ *D. P. Costa*

and *R. L. Gentry*

INTRODUCTION

The two preceding chapters showed the behavior associated with prey capture and subsequent delivery of nourishment to young northern fur seals. From the viewpoint of energetics, this behavior represents two categories in the overall allocation of maternal energy resources: foraging and travel costs. Other categories are the energy expended while avoiding predators, energy loss to parasites and diseases, milk production, and maintenance metabolism. The pattern of energy allocation among these categories has undoubtedly evolved in response to environmental pressures balanced against physiological limitations. Because environmental pressures differ among fur seal species, the allocation of maternal energy resources, or energy budget, also varies and is therefore central to the concept of maternal strategies.

The investigation of female energy budgets complements the behavioral measures made in Chapters 3 and 4. For example, studies of energetics can show differences in the energy costs of different foraging strategies. Nagy et al. (1984) showed that widely foraging lizards expended more energy but had higher rates of prey capture and greater growth rates than lizards using a sit-and-wait strategy. A similar analysis could perhaps show whether the deep-diving fur seals in Chapter 4 expend energy on a trip to sea equal to that of shallow divers making three times as many dives. Interspecific comparisons could show differences in the amount of energy devoted to foraging in an energy-rich compared to an energy-poor environment, the extent to which the richness of a food resource is offset by the distance to foraging grounds, or whether the cost of milk production varies with body size. These differences are best studied by combining diving and attendance studies with direct measures of energy budget.

In this chapter we systematically quantify the onshore and offshore components of the energy budget for females and pups during the first half (two months) of the reproductive cycle. We focused specifically on the energetics of lactation because, as in other mammals, this is the most costly phase of reproduction and is, therefore, most susceptible to failure (Millar, 1977). One such failure, emaciation syndrome, which is starvation coupled with disease and injury, is the largest single cause of death among northern fur seal pups of less than four months of age (Keyes, 1965). Clearly, some aspect of the northern fur seal's energy-flow system, either in the mother's ability to produce milk or the pup's ability to fast between suckling periods, appears to fail.

The techniques described in this chapter have been used to measure rates of food and energy intake in lizards, birds, and mammals (including humans), and to quantify milk intake and maternal energy investment in northern elephant seals (Ortiz et al., 1984; Costa et al., in press). Maternal energetics and milk production have been studied in the grey and harp seals using different techniques (Fedak and Anderson, 1982; Stewart and Lavigne, 1984). The present study is the first to measure both onshore and offshore components of maternal energetics in a marine mammal. Similar studies are currently being completed on the Antarctic and Galapagos fur seals by several contributors to this monograph.

METHODS

To quantify the components of the energy budget, we divided it into segments and measured each one using isotopic tracer methods. We measured food intake while at sea and energy utilization of lactating females, maintenance metabolism of lactating and nonlactating females on the rookery, the rate of milk and energy intake by pups, fasting metabolic rate of pups, and the changes in milk composition with time. Animals were captured and restrained using the techniques described in Chapter 2. We completed field measurements during the summer months (July–August) of 1981 and 1982 at East Reef rookery, St. George Island, Alaska.

Milk Composition

Changes in milk composition through time were measured in samples taken from twenty-seven females of known parturition date. Milk collection was facilitated by the IV or IM injection of 40 U.S.P. units of oxytocin. Milk samples were analyzed for fat, water, and ash content. Water content of milk was measured by drying duplicate 1 g aliquots at 80°C overnight. The fat content of dried milk samples was calculated as the weight change after fat extraction with six rinses of di-ethyl ether. Ash weight of milk samples was determined by drying 1 g aliquots of milk overnight in 30 ml covered ceramic crucibles and then ashing for 5 hours in a muffle furnance at 600°C. The protein content of milk samples was taken to be the weight of fat-, water-, and ash-free milk samples. This assumption is valid since carbohydrate, the only other component of milk, is insignificant in fur seal milk (Ashworth et al., 1966). The caloric content of milk was calculated from standard caloric values of the protein and fat components (fat = 39.8 kJ g^{-1}, protein = 23.9 kJ g^{-1}; Kleiber, 1975).

Milk Ingestion

The rate of milk ingestion by pups was estimated from total body water influx. Water influx includes both preformed water and metabolic water. Since milk is the only source of preformed water available to suckling pups, the amount of milk ingested is the difference between total water influx and metabolic water production divided by the fractional water content of fur seal milk. Total water turnover and metabolic water production are equivalent in fasting, non-drinking pups. Therefore, measures of total water turnover in fasting pups were used to solve this equation for an estimate of milk ingestion rate in the same pups while suckling.

Water turnover in fasting pups was measured by following the decline in plasma-specific activity of tritiated water (HTO) through time. A small quantity of water containing tritium (a radioactive isotope of hydrogen) was injected into an animal; after 3 hours of isotopic equilibration, a blood sample was drawn. The initial dilution of HTO in this sample reveals the initial total body water (Foy and Schneiden, 1960). The dilution rate in subsequent samples is proportional to the rate of the metabolic processes that add water to the system. Ideally, serial samples are taken over time to assure that water flux is constant. This, or a similar procedure, has been used to measure milk intake in dairy cattle, caribou, reindeer calves, elephant seal pups, and dingo dogs (Macfarlane et al., 1969; Yates et al., 1971; McEwan and Whitehead, 1971; Holleman et al., 1975; Green and Newgrain, 1979; Ortiz et al., 1984). Errors in the measure of water influx were analyzed by Nagy and Costa (1980).

Two experimental groups were used to measure milk ingestion in suckling pups: one group for the 7-day perinatal period (Chapter 3), and the other for the interval from 10 days to 2 months. The first group consisted of females and newborn pups captured on the rookery and held for 8 days in a holding facility (Chapter 3). The pups were injected with HTO and blood samples were taken after 3 hours and on days 3, 5, and 6. On day 6 they were reinjected, and final total body water was calculated from a sample taken 3 hours later. All blood samples were drawn from the interdigital vein of the rear flipper; all injections were made intraperitoneally. The mothers were periodically weighed, and milk samples were collected for content analysis as described above.

The second group comprised thirteen pups (eight males, five females), in which fasting metabolic rate (total water turnover) was measured when their mothers were absent on feeding trips. Such pups were captured 24 to 36 hours after the mother's departure, prevented from suckling from other females, and injected with HTO. Periodic blood samples were taken, the last of which was usually just before the mother's expected return to shore (or after she was sighted). A final total body water was calculated for most, but not all, pups by a final HTO injection and subsequent sample. The rate of milk ingestion (total water influx) was measured by injecting these pups with HTO before release to their mothers, then recapturing them and taking blood samples immediately after the mother's next departure, usually 2 days later. For each pup a regression equation was derived for the relationship of total body water to mass. This equation was used to estimate final total body water in cases where no final measurement was made but mass was known.

As a validation of the HTO technique for measuring milk intake, seven pups were injected and were then fed known quantities of milk by stomach tube while their mothers were at sea. The milk was collected from "donor" pups actively suckling at a different rookery. A maximum of 360 ml of milk was taken from each donor via stomach tube. Milk was collected at least twice a day and was kept refrigerated until warmed immediately prior to feeding, always within 24 hours of collection.

Lactation and Parturition Costs

The cost of lactation was determined by comparing total metabolism in six lactating females during the 7-day perinatal fast against that of two mothers of stillborn pups and two barren females fasting for a comparable interval. Because water influx in fasting, non-drinking animals is derived totally from metabolic processes, the rate of water influx, measured by dilution rate of HTO, gives an indirect measure of total metabolism. An overestimate of water influx occurs during respiration when unlabeled water vapor is inhaled and exchanged for labeled water. Since this error is a function of metabolic rate, it is constant and cancels out in the milk intake estimates but may cause a 10% to 15% overestimate in metabolism (Costa et al., in press). Water influx was converted into values representing fat and energy utilization (Nagy, 1975; Ortiz et al., 1978). Total water influx and efflux were calculated using Lifson and McClintock's (1966) equation for animals with exponentially changing body mass as described by Nagy and Costa (1980).

Pregnant females for the lactating group were captured at East Reef rookery, weighed, and held undisturbed in separate pens until they gave birth. Within a day of parturition the females, separated from their pups, were injected with 0.5 mCi (millicurie) of HTO. A blood sample for initial body water was taken after 3 hours of equilibration, with subsequent samples on days 3, 5, and 6. On day 6 they were reinjected, and final blood samples were taken to calculate final body water. Females were weighed and milk samples were collected whenever blood samples were taken. The female and pup remained together except when such samples were being collected. Total metabolism was measured in the four nonlactating females using the same sampling regime.

In addition to lactation costs, the energy budget of females included the costs of parturition—specifically, the energetic content of the fetus, amnion, and amniotic fluids. The fetus and other tissues were weighed, but their energetic contents were not measured.

Foraging Energetics

Food consumption at sea was estimated from a combination of HTO turnover (Shoemaker et al., 1976) and metabolism as measured by the doubly labeled water method (Nagy, 1980). HTO turnover alone measures water influx of free-ranging animals (Nagy and Costa, 1980), and the difference between HTO and ^{18}O labeled water measures CO_2 production, a direct index of energy metabolism (Lifson and McClintock, 1966; Nagy, 1980). An RQ of 0.81 was assumed in calculating energy consumption from CO_2 production, and 0.0286 ml H_2O kJ^{-1} was used as metabolic water production (Brody, 1945). The ^{18}O samples were analyzed using the low level enrichment method, which, as a sensitive measure, allows smaller doses of labeled substance to be used on large animals. The total energy obtained at sea was calculated from the equation by Shoemaker et al. (1976), which combines water influx measurements with standard values for the energetic content of various prey items and with the ratio of metabolizable energy to energy available in the food. Actual prey captured by these animals was unknown, so a hypothetical diet was constructed from the results of Kajimura (1983).

Standard prey composition and metabolic efficiency values used were as follows: water content—pollock 76% (3.545 g H_2O g^{-1} d.w.$^{-1}$), capelin 78% (3.545 g H_2O g^{-1} d.w.), squid 84% (5.25 g H_2O g^{-1} d.w.); caloric density—pollock 24.6 kJ g^{-1} d.w., capelin 25.0 kJ g^{-1} d.w.; squid 22.8 kJ g^{-1} d.w.; metabolizable efficiency—pollock 94%, capelin 93%, squid 85.3% (Miller, 1978).

The amounts of food ingested and energy consumed while at sea were calculated for five females during their first postpartum trip in 1981; a repeat measurement was made one month later for one of these females. The same measurements were made for six females in 1982. Five of the latter females were injected with HTO and sent to sea one time wearing a TDR. The same five were injected another time (one month earlier or later) and sent out without a TDR as a control. Comparison of experimental and control trips to sea showed the metabolic cost of carrying the TDR. Complete metabolic measurements were obtained for four of the five females, and water flux was measured for all five.

All females were injected with 1 mCi (3ml) of HTO and 3 ml 95% ^{18}O water; blood samples drawn 3 hours later gave initial total body water. After being weighed, the females were released on the rookery, and they left for sea from within a few hours to a day of release. Daily surveys were made until the females were resighted, whereupon they were recaptured and reweighed, and repeat blood samples were drawn. Final total body water determinations were made for ten of the twelve females by reinjecting them with HTO and taking subsequent blood samples.

Accurate calculation of food intake and water influx measurements require that preformed water comes only from food, not from ingested sea water. To determine whether significant amounts of water were ingested when animals fed at sea, three juvenile males were captured from the hauling grounds and were trained to eat commercially obtained herring (*Clupea* sp.) while swimming in seawater holding pens. When captives had maintained weight on the herring diet for at least 48 hours they were injected with HTO, and serial blood sampling was begun. At least four times daily thereafter, injected animals (one per sea-water tank) were fed weighed quantities of fish. Aliquots of the food from each feeding were frozen for later analysis of water and caloric content. These simultaneous food consumption and water flux determinations were made for up to nine days.

Sample Analysis

The H_2O content in samples of herring (50–200 g aliquots), seal blubber (10–50 g aliquots), and seal milk (1 g aliquots) were measured by comparing freeze-dried weight against wet weights. The caloric content of herring and of seal blubber was measured by combustion in a nonadiabatic bomb calorimeter (Lieth, 1975) using duplicate determinations on 1-gram pellets prepared from dried samples ground in a ball mill. Tritium-specific activity was determined by scintillation spectrometry in triplicate 100 ml aliquots of pure water distilled from the serum samples (Ortiz et al., 1978) in 10 ml of Betaphase cocktail (Westchem). The specific activity of ^{18}O water was determined by mass ratio spectrometry (Global Geochemistry, Canoga Park, Calif.) of pure water distilled from plasma samples. Delta ^{18}O values were converted to atom percent using 2005.2 for the absolute $^{18}O/^{16}O$ ratio for Standard Mean Ocean Water (Gonfiantini, 1978).

RESULTS

Milk Composition

The mean composition for all fifty-eight fur seal milk samples was fat = 41.5% (± 7.0 SD), water = 44.4% (± 6.9 SD), protein = 14.2% (± 2.2 SD), and ash = 0.50% (± 0.10 SD), with a caloric content of 19.9 kJ g^{-1}. However, fat and water content of milk changed inversely during the suckling cycle. Fat content was greatest and water content was least immediately after birth or after arrival from a feeding trip. As suckling proceeded in either the perinatal period or in 2-day visits, the fat content steadily decreased while the water content increased until maximum values were reached at the termination of the suckling bout (Table 5.1; see Fig. 5.1 for fat only). The fat content was significantly correlated with the time elapsed since parturition (Fig. 5.2). Fat content was least (Pearson product moment correlation r = 0.572, N = 22, p > 0.99) and water content was greatest (Pearson product moment correlation r = -0.516, N = 22, p > 0.95) after the first feeding trip. Thereafter, fat content gradually increased while water content decreased to postpartum values within 40 days after parturition (Fig. 5.2). Protein content of milk increased significantly in the perinatal period (two-sample t-

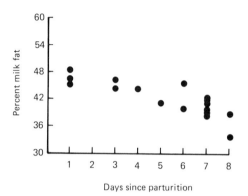

Fig. 5.1. The relative proportion of fat in the milk of northern fur seals is plotted as a function of time since parturition to show that fat content decreased during the perinatal period.

TABLE 5.1. Change in the relative proportion of fat, protein, and water in northern fur seal milk as correlated with stages in the suckling cycle.

Milk components[a] (%)		Feeding period		Perinatal period[b]	
		Arrival	Departure	Parturition	Departure
Fat		44.0[c]	37.5[c]	46.3[d]	39.6[d]
	SE	1.4	2.1	0.9	1.1
Protein		14.3	14.3	11.7	15.5[d]
	SE	0.2	0.5	0.6	0.6
Water		41.7[d]	48.4[d]	42.0	45.0
	SE	1.4	2.1	0.4	1.4
	N	22	17	7	12

[a] Milk composition while feeding refers to milk samples collected on arrival from foraging trips to sea and just prior to the anticipated departure 2 days later.
[b] Milk composition during the perinatal period refers to samples collected during the initial 7-day postpartum period immediately after birth and prior to the female's first trip to sea.
[c] Means found to be significantly different using two-sample t-test, $p > 0.95$.
[d] Means found to be significantly different using two-sample t-test, $p > 0.99$.

test; $v = 17$, $t = 4.453$, $p > 0.99$). Thereafter, it did not change significantly with time elapsed since parturition, nor did it change between arrival and departure on 2-day suckling intervals (Table 5.1; Fig. 5.2).

Milk Intake

Milk intake during the entire 7-day perinatal period was 500 ml d^{-1} (a total of 3,500 ml) for four female and two male pups (Table

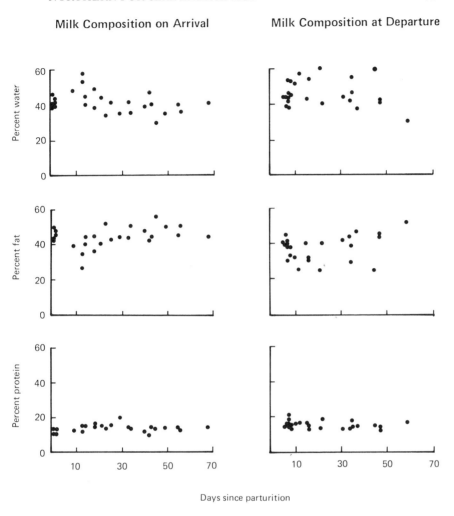

Fig. 5.2. Water, fat, and protein content of northern fur seal milk during 2-day visits to shore are plotted as a function of days since parturition.

TABLE 5.2. Milk ingestion of northern fur seal pups during the perinatal period.

Pup no.	Sex of pup	Average mass (kg)	Total water influx per day	Metabolic water production per day	Milk water flux per day[a]	ml d^{-1}	ml 7d^{-1}
				Water flux[a]			Milk input[b]
				. . . . ml kg^{-1}d^{-1}			
1134	Male	7.14	61.6	20.5	41.1	673	4710
592	Male	7.01	47.8	22.3	25.5	402	2810
580	Female	5.55	49.2	20.5	28.7	366	2560
1138	Female	5.54	69.0	20.5	48.5	616	4310
1140	Female	5.29	43.2	20.5	22.7	276	1930
1137	Female	6.23	67.1	20.5	46.6	666	4660
Average		6.13	56.3	20.8	35.5	500	3500
SE		0.33	4.5		4.6	70	490

[a] Milk water flux was calculated from the difference between metabolic water production measured on fasting pups and the total water influx measured on these suckling pups.

[b] Total milk intake was calculated by dividing the milk water influx by the milk water content.

TABLE 5.3. Milk ingestion rates of female and male northern fur seal pups from 10 days to 2 months of age.

Sex	Age (days)	Mass (kg)	Mean samples per pup	Milk intake (ml bout^{-1a})	Fasting water flux[b] (ml kg^{-1}d^{-1})
	Pup				
Female (N = 5)					
Mean	42.0	7.37[c]	2.4	2650[c]	24.50[d]
SE	3.0	0.17		260	2.01
Male (N = 8)					
Mean	39.0	8.99[c]	3.8	4270[c]	18.50[d]
SE	2.5	0.47		400	0.90

[a] Milk intake was calculated as the difference between metabolic water production of fasting pups and total water influx of suckling pups divided by the milk water content.

[b] Fasting water flux measurements were made between suckling bouts while the mother was at sea.

[c] Means found to be significantly different using two-sample t-test, p > 0.95.

[d] Means found to be significantly different using two-sample t-test, p > 0.99.

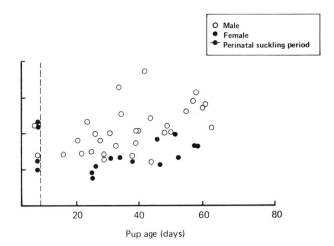

Fig. 5.3. The total amount of milk (in ml) consumed by pups during 2-day suckling periods is expressed as a function of pup age and sex. Values for male pups are denoted by clear circles, females as solid circles. The data points to the left of the dotted vertical line are quantities of milk consumed during the entire 7-day perinatal period.

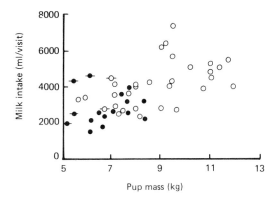

Fig. 5.4. Total volume of milk consumed by male and female pups during the 7-day perinatal period and subsequent 2-day suckling bouts is expressed as a function of pup body mass.

5.2). During the subsequent 2-day suckling bouts, eight male pups consumed significantly more milk than five female pups (4,270 versus 2,650 ml/bout; two-sample t-test; $v = 10$, $t = 2.921$, $p > 0.98$; Table 5.3). Furthermore, male pups had a significantly lower fasting water influx than female pups (18.5 versus 24.5 ml kg^{-1} d^{-1} two-sample t-test; $v = 11$, $t = -4.471$, $p > 0.99$; Table 5.3). The quantity of milk consumed was positively correlated with the age of male pups ($r = 0.553$, $v = 28$, $p > 0.99$ linear correlation), the mass of male pups ($r = 0.539$, $v = 28$, $p > 0.99$ linear correlation), and the mass of female pups ($r = 0.5879$, $v = 10$, $p > 0.95$ linear correlation; Figs. 5.3, 5.4). Milk ingestion estimated from HTO flux was within -4% to 7% of the actual milk intake measured in the validation tests. This range varied as a function of the rate used for metabolic water production.

Metabolism during Lactation

Lactation did not increase the female's metabolism. Lactating females had metabolic rates similar to nonlactating females (4.67 versus 4.77 W kg^{-1}, respectively; Table 5.4). However, one nonlactating animal had an unusually high metabolic rate that increased the mean for nonlactating individuals from 4.10 (± 0.04 W kg^{-1}) to 4.77 (± 0.72 W kg^{-1}).

Energetic Costs of Parturition

The mass of pregnant females averaged 51.1 kg; those that gave birth to male pups were slightly larger than those with females. This difference persisted after parturition (Table 5.5). Mean placental mass was 0.55 kg, and the average pup's birth weight was 5.57 kg (Table 5.5). The 3.28 kg difference between pregnant mass and the sum of nonpregnant mass, placenta, and pup mass was assumed to be amniotic and other fluids. Male pups were significantly heavier than females at birth (two-sample t-test; $v = 17$, $t = 4.471$, $p > 0.99$) and at the end of the perinatal period ($v = 11$, $t = 3.963$, $p > 0.99$; Table 5.5). During this period females with male pups appeared to lose mass faster than those with female pups, and they may have come ashore with more absolute weight than mothers of female pups. However, when growth was expressed on a weight-specific basis this difference was not as great (Table 5.5, column 7). During the perinatal period, male pups gained 14.3% of the mass lost by their mothers and female pups gained 12.8% (Table 5.5, last column).

FORAGING ENERGETICS

The mean water influx at sea, combining both years (1981 and 1982), was 184 ml $kg^{-1} d^{-1}$; influx was significantly greater (t-test; $t = 2.014, v = 9, p > 0.95$) in 1982 than in 1981 (Table 5.6). These values were combined with other assumptions and constants (see Methods) to calculate the amount and energetic value of food that may have been consumed during trips to sea. The estimated wet mass of food consumed varied less than 1% with different assumed prey. However, because prey vary in caloric content, the estimate of net energy assimilated varied widely depending on the assumed prey. Prey consumption, both amount and energy content, was calculated for a hypothetical diet consisting exclusively of squid or pollock (Table 5.6). These projections indicated that a squid diet would yield less energy than either an all-capelin or an all-pollock diet, and that the latter two would not differ in assimilated energy. From these results the assimilated food energy was calculated for a hypothetical diet of 66% pollock and 34% squid (Table 5.6).

With one exception, lactating females increased their body mass while at sea; the average increase was 0.54 kg d^{-1} or 1.8% of body mass per day (Table 5.6). When the mass gain was normalized to body mass (% body mass d^{-1}; Table 5.6) foraging females gained equivalent mass in both 1981 and 1982, despite the differences noted in water influx.

The CO_2 production rates at sea differed significantly in 1981 and 1982 (t-test; $t = 3.857, v = 8, p > 0.99$). Assuming a diet of 34% squid and 66% pollock, the assimilated food energy was also significantly greater in 1982 (t-test; $t = 2.015, v = 9, p > 0.95$). However, the mass increase after a trip to sea was equivalent for both years (Table 5.6).

Comparing instrumented and control trips for the same individuals, the metabolic rate increased an average of 19% on trips with a TDR (Table 5.7). However, because individual variation was greater than the changes in metabolism and water flux, instrumented animals as a group were not significantly different from uninstrumented animals in these parameters. Note the differences in water flux (Table 5.7) for females 1789 and 542, which had a very different dive pattern compared to females 579 and 540 (Table 4.1).

Sea water was apparently not ingested by the three juvenile males fed in sea-water pools, since water influx was within -2.3% of the measured food intake. Therefore, the assumption was valid that

TABLE 5.4. Fasting metabolic rate of lactating and nonlactating northern fur seal females.

Condition of female	Initial mass (kg)	Water influx (ml kg⁻¹ d⁻¹)	Fat oxidation (g kg⁻¹ d⁻¹)	Metabolic rate* (W kg⁻¹)
Lactating (N = 7)	42.7	11.4	10.5	4.67
SE	3.6	0.6	0.6	0.30
Nonlactating (N = 4)	44.1	11.8	10.8	4.77
SE	2.3	1.7	1.6	0.72

* Metabolic rates were derived from measurements of water flux, since metabolic water is derived almost entirely from fat oxidation in a fasting fur seal. These rates were not significantly different for the two groups.

TABLE 5.5. Changes in mass of female and pup northern fur seals as a function of pup sex during the initial 7-day perinatal period.

Sex	Female mass				Time	Female mass loss		Pup mass		Pup mass gain		
	Pregnant (kg)	Placenta (g)	Post-partum (kg)	Initial departure (kg)	(days)	Rate (kg d⁻¹)	% Mass per day	Initial (kg)	Final (kg)	Rate (kg d⁻¹)	% Mass per day	% Female mass per day
Male pups	52.5	561	42.3	33.4	6.41	1.44	3.83	6.23	7.59	0.21	2.98	14.34
SE	3.6	36	3.1	3.7	0.33	0.13	0.16	0.27	0.30	0.03	0.34	1.06
N	8	7	8	6	6	6	6	8	6	6	6	6
Female pups	49.7	555	40.4	31.8	7.03	1.28	3.54	5.10	6.27	0.16	2.87	12.84
SE	1.6	33	1.1	1.05	0.24	0.06	0.16	0.11	0.17	0.01	0.15	0.77
N	8	5	11	7	7	7	7	11	7	7	7	7

TABLE 5.6. Food and assimilated energy consumption for lactating northern fur seal females in 1981* and 1982.

Female no.	Water ml kg⁻¹d⁻¹	Food intake g kg⁻¹d⁻¹	Assimilated food energy W kg⁻¹[a]			CO₂ Production mlg⁻¹h⁻¹	¹⁸O Metabolism W kg⁻¹	Stored energy[c]			Increase in mass[d]	
			Squid	Mixed	Pollock			Squid W kg⁻¹	Mixed W kg⁻¹	Pollock W kg⁻¹	kg d⁻¹	%BW d⁻¹
542	149	161	5.77	8.23	9.5	1.15	8.09	-2.32	0.14	1.41	0.36	3.90
1791	264	285	10.22	14.57	16.81	1.48	10.47	-0.25	4.10	6.34	0.79	2.30
1797	171	184	6.59	9.40	10.85	1.55	10.9	-4.31	-1.50	-0.05	0.06	0.20
1789	246	266	9.55	13.58	15.65	—	—	—	—	—	0.64	1.50
579	160	173	6.20	8.83	10.18	1.16	8.19	-1.99	0.64	1.99	0.27	0.72
540	274	296	10.61	15.09	17.40	1.60	11.30	-0.69	3.79	6.10	0.97	2.20
582*	117	126	4.56	6.47	7.46	0.92	6.49	-1.93	-0.02	0.97	-0.21	-0.21
1134*	208	224	8.04	11.47	13.23	1.15	8.14	-0.10	3.33	5.09	1.12	3.00
1136*	140	151	5.43	7.73	8.92	0.77	5.43	0.00	2.30	3.49	0.59	2.00
578*	126	136	4.89	6.94	8.00	0.82	5.81	-0.92	1.13	2.19	0.95	2.00
580*	165	178	6.40	9.08	10.47	0.99	6.98	-0.58	2.10	3.49	0.53	2.00
Means from 1982												
X̄	211	228	8.16	11.62	13.40	1.39	9.79	-1.91	1.43	3.16	0.52	1.80
SE	23	25	0.90	1.28	1.09	0.10	0.69	-0.71	1.08	1.29	0.14	0.54
Means from 1981												
X̄	151	163	5.86	8.34	9.62	0.93	6.57	-0.71	1.77	3.05	0.60	1.76
SE	16	18	0.60	0.90	1.04	0.07	0.48	-0.34	0.57	0.69	0.45	0.53
Both years												
X̄	184	198	7.0	10.13	11.68	1.20	8.18	-1.31	1.60	3.10	0.55	1.78
SE	17	18	0.6	0.93	1.07	0.09	0.67	0.42	0.58	0.98	0.12	0.36

* Data from 1981 field season.

[a] Values were derived from the measured water turnover rates using hypothetical diets consisting of entirely squid, mixed (i.e., 66% pollock and 34% squid), and entirely pollock.

[b] Derived from the at sea CO_2 production.

[c] Stored energy is the energetic benefit of the foraging trip and was calculated as the difference between assimilated food energy and the amount of energy expended for metabolism (¹⁸O metabolism) for the three hypothetical diets.

[d] Increases in body mass are presented as an independent index of the energetic benefit of a foraging trip. BW = body weight.

TABLE 5.7. The energetic liability of carrying a TDR in northern fur seals is shown by comparisons of the food intake derived from water influx measurements, the metabolic rate, and changes in body mass of foraging fur seals with (W/TDR) and without (W/O) TDRs.

Female no.	Water influx		Food intake		^{18}O metabolism		Increase	Mass increase	
	W/O	W/TDR	W/O	W/TDR	W/O	W/TDR		W/O	W/TDR
	$(ml\,kg^{-1}d^{-1})$		$(g\,kg^{-1}d^{-1})$		$(W\,kg^{-1})$		(%)	$(kg\,d^{-1})$	
542	149	241	180	260	8.09	9.98	23	0.36	0.45
1791	264	204	233	221	10.47	12.55	20	0.79	0.06
1789	246	227	266	246	—	—	—	0.64	0.61
579	160	135	183	145	8.19	9.45	15	0.27	0.16
540	274	177	144	191	6.44	7.51	17	0.97	0.66
Mean	219	197	201	213	8.30	9.87	19	0.61	0.39
SE	26	19	22	21	0.83	1.04	2	0.13	0.12

preformed water comes only from the diet. Based on an assimilation rate of 80%, the metabolic rate of these males was 494 kJ kg^{-1} d^{-1}. Herring had a caloric content of 6.74 kJ g^{-1} wet weight and was 73% water.

DISCUSSION

Milk Composition

Declines in fat content of milk occur both during the 7-day perinatal period and during the subsequent 2-day suckling intervals (Table 5.1). The slow rate at which milk fat content recovers to the immediately postpartum levels (requiring at least four foraging trips) suggests that this initial suckling interval is quite demanding. Temporary declines in fat content probably result from a depletion of fat reserves because milk protein content remains stable after the perinatal period is over. If fat were not depleted, we would expect equivalent changes in the fat and protein content as the water content increased. Instead, fat declined in direct proportion to changes in water content while protein content varied little.

This result suggests that during fasting and lactating, fur seals have sufficient water but may be limited by the available fat stores. This pattern is opposite that of phocids, which appear to be limited by water; throughout fasting and lactating the fat content of phocid milk increases and water content decreases (Kooyman and Drabek, 1968; Riedman and Ortiz, 1979; Lavigne et al., 1982). This difference may result from a larger absolute fat reserve in phocids, which allows a more constant lipid supply for milk production. More likely, the difference results from the need of phocids to conserve water during their more protracted fasts (Kooyman, 1963; Kooyman and Drabek, 1968).

The high fat content of northern fur seal milk may relate to the females' attendance pattern, which includes absences of 4 to 8 days followed by a 2-day period onshore (Chapter 3). In 2 days the pup must obtain sufficient energy not only to maintain itself but also to grow during its mother's next absence. A lipid-rich milk with a low water content provides more energy per gram than any other food source. Furthermore, foraging females must store all of the acquired energy and nutrients as efficiently as possible, and fat is the most efficient form of energy storage. Therefore, energy flow in the form of fat may make this attendance pattern possible. Otariids having shorter trips to sea may not be so constrained and may produce milk of a lower fat and higher water content. The existing literature tends to confirm this suggestion (Rand, 1956; Pilson and Kelley, 1962; Poulter et al., 1965; Bonner, 1968).

Milk Ingestion

The quantity of milk consumed by pups varies as a function of the age, mass, and sex of the pup (Table 5.3; Figs. 5.3, 5.4). Of these three factors, it appears that pup mass is a more important determinant of milk intake than either sex or age because male and female pups do not differ when milk intake is plotted as a function of body mass. The effect of body mass would explain the marked sexual difference when milk intake is plotted as a function of pup age, since male pups are larger than females of the same age. The smaller female pups would consume less milk than the larger male pups of the same age.

Female pups have a higher average daily metabolic rate, as indicated by their greater rate of fasting metabolic water production. Average daily metabolic rate can be calculated from the fasting water influx value assuming that the majority of metabolic water is derived from fat oxidation. Assuming that when one gram of water has been produced from fat oxidation 0.4085 W of energy has been released (Schmidt-Nielsen and Schmidt-Nielsen, 1952), then the fasting metabolic rate of male and female pups would be 7.56 and 10.0 W kg^{-1}, respectively. The greater metabolic rate of females would decrease the efficiency with which milk is converted to body tissue because more milk would be catabolized for maintenance. This difference accounts for the different growth efficiencies by sex (Table 5.5).

The energy investment of the mother is greater if she has a male pup, and this investment increases with age of the young regardless of its sex. The quantity of energy invested is estimated as the quantity of milk consumed multiplied by the mean caloric content of fur seal milk (measured to be 19.9 kJ g^{-1}). From this calculation both sexes appear to receive 9.95 MJ d^{-1} during the perinatal period; thereafter, males and females receive 42.5 and 26.4 MJ d^{-1}, respectively. Male pups, therefore, consume 61% more energy than female pups. On this basis we might expect mothers with male pups to spend more time at sea foraging than mothers with female pups. However, analysis of 1982 attendance records shows no difference in feeding-trip duration for twenty-eight mothers of male pups compared to eighteen mothers of female pups (Gentry and Goebel, unpubl. data). We might also expect male pups to spend more time suckling than female pups as evidenced in the Galapagos fur seal (Chapter 11); however, Macy (1982) found no such difference. Therefore, the greater energy transfer to male pups probably results from a greater suckling efficiency.

These results add to a growing number of exceptions to the theory of sexual selection. This theory predicts that mothers should produce more female than male offspring because males cost more and have more variable reproductive success (Fisher, 1930). In red deer, contrary to this prediction, a 1:1 sex ratio was found (Clutton-Brock et al., 1982). The authors suggested that this occurred because the preweaning costs of producing male offspring was offset by the postweaning costs of allowing female offspring to remain with mothers in the prime foraging areas. Northern fur seals also invest more in male pups (this chapter), but nevertheless have a sex ratio of nearly 1:1. Data on behavior and mass change on northern elephant seals suggest a similar exception to sexual selection theory (Reiter et al., 1978). In these two seal species no postweaning investment is made in either sex, so the trade-off cited for red deer does not apply; another basis of exceptions to sexual selection theory must exist.

The female's ability to produce and deliver milk may have an upper limit that is reached when the pup attains a certain size. The age at which this size is reached obviously differs by sex of young, but probably occurs after about 2 months. The evidence that females have such a limit is that the total quantity of energy transferred during the 7-day perinatal period is similar to the amount transferred to older male pups in just 2 days (Fig. 5.3).

During the first few months of the suckling period the milk ingestion rate is limited by the pup's ability to suckle and process milk. Newborns consume milk at a lower rate than older pups even though total milk transferred per female visit is similar (Tables 5.2, 5.3; Figs. 5.3, 5.4). Possibly suckling coordination and efficiency increase over time, or the newborn digestive system requires time to reach maximum capacity and performance, or both.

Lactation Costs

The cost of lactation is primarily composed of the energy contained in the milk since the metabolic cost of milk synthesis appears to be quite small (lactating and nonlactating females did not differ significantly in metabolic rate; Table 5.4). This finding is consistent with similar measurements made on terrestrial mammals (e.g., cotton and house mice; Studier, 1979; Randolph et al., 1977). The average daily metabolic rate of lactating fur seal females is 3.2 times the predicted standard metabolic rate (SMR) for a terrestrial mammal of equal size (Kleiber, 1975) but is only 1.4 times the SMR of nonlactating northern fur seals (Miller, 1978).

Female fur seals transfer milk to the young at a rate comparable to terrestrial mammals, but because of the greater fat content of fur seal milk, the rate of energy transfer is much greater. To compare fur seals and terrestrial mammals by the regression equation for female mass versus milk production (Hanwell and Peaker, 1977) we used a mean mass of 37 kg for a lactating female, derived from the midpoint between parturition and the female's first trip to sea (Table 5.5). The amount of milk ingested by fur seal pups in a 2-day period (1.33 and 2.14 kg d^{-1} for female and male pups, respectively) was similar to the value predicted for terrestrial mammals (1.35 kg d^{-1}). However, the energetic content of this quantity of milk was 4.1 to 6.6 times greater for fur seals than the predicted value for a terrestrial mammal of equal mass (26.4–42.5 MJ d^{-1} for female and male pups versus 6.4 MJ d^{-1}).

Although the attendance pattern of female fur seals is quite different from that of gray and elephant seals, the rate of energy transfer is similar. Energy production in milk can be compared by dividing the daily rate of energy production by the body mass raised to the 0.69 power, a regression exponent derived by Hanwell and Peaker (1977). By this manipulation, milk production in fur seals (2.19–3.52 MJ d^{-1} $kg^{-0.69}$) appears to be slightly greater than for the grey seal (2.06 MJ d^{-1} $kg^{-0.69}$; Fedak and Anderson, 1982) or elephant seal (1.34 MJ d^{-1} $kg^{-0.69}$; Ortiz et al., 1978). However, given the different methods used to calculate values for these species the differences are not striking. The greater fat content of their milk and the considerable energy stored before birth by phocid females are believed to account for the differences between these pinnipeds and terrestrial mammals (Fedak and Anderson, 1982; Ortiz et al., 1984).

Foraging Energetics

Validation studies showed that water influx, measured by the HTO method, accurately estimates the amount of food consumed by free-ranging fur seals if the prey and its water and energy content are known. Sea water is apparently not ingested when seals feed at sea, and estimated food intake agrees well with the actual amounts given during feeding trials. Calculations showed that prey type had very little effect on the estimated biomass of prey consumed, but strongly affected the estimates of assimilated energy (Table 5.6). Since the prey of these fur seals was not known, the values in Table 5.6 are hypothetical.

Despite the fact that fur seals apparently consume more food at sea than previously thought, foraging is not an energetically costly activity for them. The metabolic rate at sea is only 1.8 times the on-shore fasting rate (Table 5.4), and it is only 2.5 times the SMR for fur seals in air (Miller, 1978). Thus foraging increases the metabolic rate of fur seals almost as much as for other marine carnivores (king penguins = 2.8 times SMR, sea otters = 2.9 times SMR; Kooyman et al., 1982; Costa, 1978). These values are in the middle of the range of metabolic rates measured for foraging terrestrial mammals (e.g., 2.0 times SMR for the howler monkey, 4.5 times SMR for the marsupial mouse; Nagy et al., 1978; Nagy and Milton, 1979).

An index of foraging efficiency can be derived from the ratio of net energy stored to the energy expended while foraging. This index was twice the value in 1981 as in 1982 (0.27 versus 0.14; Table 5.6), suggesting that food was harder to obtain in 1982. The change in foraging efficiency was accompanied by an increase in foraging effort in 1982 compared to 1981 (Table 5.6). Nevertheless, the amounts of energy stored and of body mass gained were similar between years, suggesting that fur seals forage at a rate sufficient to obtain a specific quantity of stored energy. Even though increased foraging effort resulted in a larger total amount of food being consumed, an equivalent proportion of this food was used to sustain the higher foraging metabolism. Numerically this relationship can be described as the ratio of assimilated food energy to metabolism at sea; this ratio was similar between years (1981 = 1.27; 1982 = 1.18).

The different foraging efficiencies reported for 1981 and 1982 reflect seasonal differences in energy expenditure; they are not errors due to methodology. The method we used, namely low-level enrichment of the ^{18}O doubly labeled water technique, was recently shown to be accurate for humans to within 2% with a coefficient of variation of 6% (Schoeller and van Santen, 1982). Even if the error for fur seals were greater than 2%, it would have been systematic, resulting in a consistent over- or underestimate. Therefore, we believe that foraging efficiency differed between seasons and that the technique gives a reliable index of environmental variation.

The existence of this small interannual variation does not contradict our earlier statement that the subpolar environment is more predictable than the tropical environment. Northern fur seals compensate for this fluctuation by increasing the intensity of their foraging effort (but without increasing the duration of their trips to sea, as predicted in Chapter 3). Their effort was successful; pup growth and survival were similar in the 2 years. The environment is unpredictable when it fluctuates beyond the ability of the species to make behavioral compensations, a condition that is met more often in the tropical than in the subpolar environment.

The energy and water flux of foraging fur seals were related to their divergent foraging strategies. Table 5.7 shows that females 1789 and 542 (both shallow divers; Table 4.1) had high water fluxes and, therefore, a high food intake in biomass. Female 542 also had the greatest energy consumption of any female. By contrast, females 579 and 540 made fewer, deeper dives and exhibited lower water influx, food intake, and energy expenditure. It appears that a few deep dives demand less energy expenditure than many shallow dives. This conclusion is consistent with our current understanding of diving energetics (Chapter 15). Furthermore, deep divers obtain a smaller mass of food but gain similar body mass during a feeding trip, suggesting that their prey is of higher energy content than that of shallow divers. Some learning or skill factor must be associated with obtaining deep prey, otherwise we would expect more than the observed number of fur seals to exhibit this apparently more efficient foraging strategy.

Overview

The most energetically costly component of lactation is energy bound as fat in the milk (Fig. 5.5). The rate at which this energy is expended differs significantly depending on sex of young and differs within a sex as a function of mass (age). The temporal pattern of this energy expenditure affects the efficiency with which the limited female energy reserves are used. A shorter stay on shore reduces the "metabolic overhead" paid in the form of fasting maintenance metabolism (Fedak and Anderson, 1982), and thus increases the energy available for milk production. Increasing the rate of en-

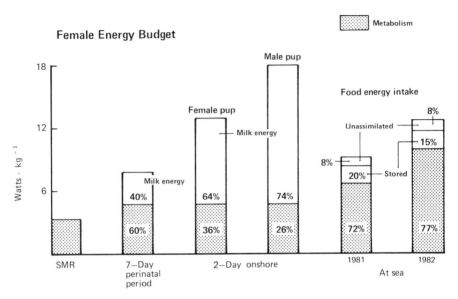

Fig. 5.5. The overall energy budget of lactating female northern fur seals while on shore during the perinatal period, during 2-day visits, and while at sea in 1981 and 1982. Separate values are given for mothers of male and female pups. The proportion of milk energy was taken as the energy contained in the milk ingested by pups. Maintenance metabolism of females was measured only during the perinatal period and was assumed to be equivalent during subsequent 2-day visits. The "At Sea" bars are the total food energy intake based on a hypothetical diet of 34% squid and 66% pollock. Total intake is partitioned into the unassimilated component lost as feces and urine, and the assimilated component stored as tissue energy and expended as the metabolic cost of activity, thermoregulation, and maintenance. The value for standard metabolic rate (SMR) is given for comparison (taken from Miller, 1978).

ergy transfer may be one route by which these stays are shortened because milk production comprises a smaller proportion of the female's total energy budget as the milk ingestion rate declines. For example, milk consumption in the perinatal period accounted for only 43% of the female's onshore energy budget compared to 64%–74% of the budget on subsequent 2-day visits (Fig. 5.5). Reciprocally, maintenance metabolism required 67% of the budget in the perinatal period but only 26%–36% on a 2-day visit. It is therefore advantageous for the pup to consume milk as rapidly as possible, and for the milk to have the highest possible fat (energy) content.

The rate of energy storage at sea (15%–20% of energy acquired) appears too low to accommodate the rate of energy expenditure while on shore (Fig. 5.5). Part of this discrepancy is explained by the fact that the female acquires energy at this rate over a 7-day period and expends it in only 2 days. Another part of the discrepancy may be explained by the fact that foraging measurements were made on females different from those whose pups were used for milk intake measurements, and they were made at different times. Finally, the females may have been consuming a diet higher in energy than the calculations assumed. Therefore, these are very conservative estimates of the energy intake at sea of lactating fur seals.

SUMMARY

The energy budget of northern fur seals was studied as an adjunct to measuring maternal strategies through attendance and dive behavior. Onshore and offshore components of the energy budget were quantified for females and pups from July through August 1981 and 1982, at East Reef rookery on St. George Island, Alaska. Isotopic tracer methods were used to measure changes in milk composition through time, milk consumption by pups, and the energy expenditure of females while on shore and at sea.

Fresh milk was composed of 44% fat, 42% water, and 14% protein by mass at the start of a 2-day suckling bout (N = 22) and 38% fat, 48% water, and 14% protein near the end of such bouts (N = 17). Similar changes in milk composition occurred during the 7-day perinatal period. Milk intake was significantly greater in male pups (4270 SE ± 402 ml milk per 2-day bout, N = 8) than in female pups (2650 ± 262 ml milk per 2-day bout, N = 5). Milk ingestion was positively correlated with increases in pup age and mass. Lactating females fasting on shore did not have a measurably greater metabolism than did nonlactating females (lactating = 4.67 ± 0.3 W kg^{-1}, N = 7; nonlactating = 4.77 ± 0.72 W kg^{-1}, N = 4). Energy expenditure while at sea was only 1.8 times greater than the onshore rate, and 2.5 times greater than the standard metabolic rate for this species measured in air. Higher energy expenditures were calculated for foraging females in 1982 (9.72 ± 0.69 W kg^{-1}) than in 1981 (6.57 ± 0.48 W kg^{-1}), but water influx measurements (1981: 151 ± 16 ml kg^{-1} d^{-1}; 1982; 211 ± 23 ml kg^{-1} d^{-1} suggested that this was compensated for by increased food consumption in 1982. Both groups gained similar mass. Therefore, animals in 1982 foraged less efficiently, spending more energy than animals in 1981 to obtain a similar energy gain.

6 Attendance Behavior of Antarctic Fur Seals ≅ D. W. Doidge,

T. S. McCann, and J. P. Croxall

INTRODUCTION

Over 95% of the Antarctic fur seal population breeds at the island of South Georgia. Very small populations occur elsewhere in the Scotia Arc (Aguayo, 1978; Holdgate and Baker, 1979), at the Prince Edward Islands (Kerley, 1984), Crozet Islands (Jouventin et al., 1982), and McDonald and Heard islands (Budd, 1972).

Following near extermination by late nineteenth-century sealers, pup production at South Georgia rose from a few hundred in the 1930s to 5,000 by 1957, and to over 100,000 by 1976 (Payne, 1977; Croxall and Prince, 1979). The mean annual rate of increase from 1958 to 1972 was 16.8% (Payne, 1977), and the present population probably totals about one million seals.

This rapid population increase was doubtless enhanced by the species' feeding largely on krill, especially *Euphausia superba*, in summer (Bonner, 1968; Doidge and Croxall, 1985), a period when there is no indication that the present population is food limited (Doidge et al., 1984a).

Although long-distance movements away from South Georgia are known (Payne, 1979a), some adult males and juveniles are ashore there throughout the year. No information exists on the distribution of adult females in the vast area of the Southern Ocean during the austral winter, May to mid-November, when they are absent from South Georgia.

South Georgia lies about 250 km south of the Antarctic Convergence and is surrounded by sea water in which icebergs are often encountered; the sea-water temperature fluctuates from 4°C in summer to about − 1°C in winter. Pregnant females begin to come ashore in mid-November, and 50% of the pups are born by about 7 December. Over 90% of births occur in a 3-week period (Payne, 1977). The season of attendance lasts until April when weaning occurs.

This chapter compares the results of seven studies (in five years at three sites) on the patterns of shore attendance by lactating female

Antarctic fur seals. The original study was undertaken to determine whether the pattern of shore attendance correlated with the pattern of fine tooth rings that is visible between the larger, annual growth-increment rings. Subsequently, the work became an essential counterpart to the research on diving behavior, described in Chapter 7. The study also tried to determine whether intersite and interseasonal variations in attendance patterns were a useful index of changes in the marine environment (e.g., changes induced by commercial harvesting for krill) or of increases in the fur seal population size.

METHODS

Female attendance patterns were studied at South Georgia from 1976 to 1981. At each of three sites (Fig. 6.1) a number of females and their pups were individually marked with paint or livestock bleach, and searches were made for them at least once a day. If a female was not found ashore, she was assumed to be at sea feeding, and data were recorded appropriately.

At Elsehul in 1976 (austral summer seasons are denoted here by the year in which they began) searches were made through the entire season (November until April) for twenty-eight marked female and pup pairs. Relocation of the pairs became increasingly difficult over time as some females swam with pups at least 800 m along the beach and/or dispersed far inland to new suckling sites. Consequently, only eight of the original twenty-eight pairs were followed from parturition to weaning. The data from these eight pairs are used to establish the general patterns of attendance. At all other sites and years, data were obtained for approximately the first third of the season.

Data from Bird Island and Schlieper Bay (Fig. 6.1) were used to examine the influence of seasonal and/or site differences on attendance patterns. Bird Island is a long-established breeding site with very high densities of breeding seals; Schlieper Bay is a recently colonized site of much lower density, while Elsehul is of intermediate density and has a rapidly increasing population. Because the duration of observations was different at each site, the data bases were compared according to a fixed number of feeding and attendance cycles to prevent bias from intraseasonal changes in the duration of feeding trips or shore visits. Six feeding cycles per female were used. The number of females and total cycles differed among data sets: Elsehul, 27 ♀, 162 cycles; Schlieper Bay 1979, 8 ♀, 48 cycles;

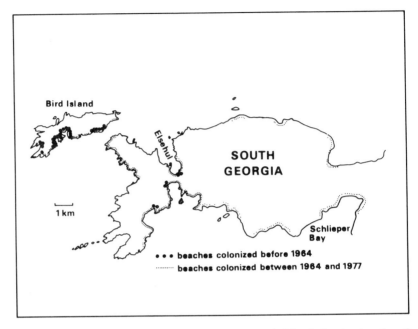

Fig. 6.1. Northwest South Georgia Island, showing location of study sites.

Bird Island 1980, 5 ♀, 30 cycles; Schlieper Bay 1981, 45 ♀, 270 cycles; and Bird Island 1981, 14 ♀, 84 cycles.

RESULTS

The Effect of Parturition on the Feeding Pattern

Pregnant females, which were gregarious while pupping, were ashore for about 2 days before parturition, and for about 7 days

TABLE 6.1. Duration of breeding-season events, female Antarctic fur seals, Elsehul.

Events	Time (d)		Sample size
	Mean	SD	
Haul-out to parturition	1.8	1.0	57
Parturition to estrus	6.0	0.6	7
Copulation to first departure	0.2	0.2	5
Parturition to first departure	6.9	1.9	114
Lactation period	117.0	8.0	8

from parturition until departure on the first feeding trip (the perinatal attendance period; Table 6.1). Thus feeding was suspended
for about 9 days. Females came into estrus 6 days postpartum (Table
6.1) and did not depart on the first feeding trip until after mating.
The interval from copulation to departure on the first trip for five
females ranged from 3.5 minutes to 7 hours (McCann, 1980). Some
females undoubtedly spent more time than this ashore after copulation, but the period was normally less than 1 day.

The duration of the lactation period, from parturition to the last
attendance with the pup, was 117 days. Of this period the total number of days spent ashore before weaning was 41.6 ($\pm$ 6.6, N = 8),
or 34.7 ($\pm$ 6.3, N = 8) if the perinatal attendance period was excluded. This time ashore was divided into discrete visits between
which females were at sea feeding.

Female Visits to Shore After Parturition

For the first few attendance periods, the females fed their pups on
the beach where they had pupped, but from late December onward
increasing numbers moved with their pups into the tussock grass,
Poa flabellata, behind the beaches. As the season progressed the females moved farther inland, and some were found as much as 100
m above sea level and several hundred meters from the shore. Only
a small proportion of the females continued to suckle on the
beaches throughout the season.

As a result of female movements, only counts early in the season
accurately indicated the number of females ashore, or the hours
that the majority of females arrived or left. Females arrived and left
at all hours of the day. Counts made at Bird Island between 0745
and 1745 hours local time (GMT-3) showed no trend in numbers
ashore during this period. No data were collected after 1800 hours
for comparison with northern fur seals (Chapter 3).

The mean duration of each visit ashore to suckle the pup was 2.1
$\pm$ 0.9 days (N = 131; Table 6.2, Fig. 6.2). Postweaning visits to
shore, when the pups were weaned but the females had remained,
lasted 4.2 $\pm$ 1.8 days (N = 8), or twice as long as a normal shore
visit.

Feeding Trips to Sea between Shore Visits

The eight females that were followed to weaning averaged 17.4
$\pm$ 2.2 different trips to sea, and totaled 75 $\pm$ 6 days at sea during
the lactation period. The mean duration of the 139 feeding trips
made by the eight females was 4.3 $\pm$ 2.1 days. The frequency distribution of these trips is given in Figure 6.3.

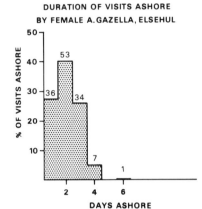

DURATION OF VISITS ASHORE
BY FEMALE A. GAZELLA, ELSEHUL

Fig. 6.2. Duration of visits ashore (excluding perinatal attendance) by female Antarctic fur seals, Elsehul (1976).

TABLE 6.2. Activities of female Antarctic fur seals during pup rearing, Elsehul.

Activity (days)	Mean	SD	Sample size
Time ashore	42.0	7.0	8
Time at sea	75.0	6.0	8
Duration shore visit	2.1	0.9	131
Duration sea trip	4.3	2.1	139
Number of sea trips	17.4	2.2	8

The duration of trips to sea changed throughout the season. The first feeding trip to sea after parturition was significantly longer than the second trip (trip 1 = 4.12 ± 0.99 days, N = 8; trip 2 = 2.62 ± 0.92 days, N = 8; Mann-Whitney U-test, U = 4, P < 0.001). To analyze for further seasonal changes, we plotted the means and standard deviations of feeding-trip duration against trip number (Fig. 6.4). This procedure compensated for differences in parturition dates among females.

Only two of the eight females followed to weaning showed significant increases in feeding-trip duration with trip number (Spearman rank correlation coefficient, r_s = 0.544, p < 0.05, N = 15; and r_s = 0.654, p < 0.01, N = 20). Since a similar relationship did not hold for the majority of females in the sample, it was not possible to combine the data for a grouped regression. However, Figure 6.4 shows that there was an increase in feeding-trip duration for the

**DURATION OF TRIPS TO SEA
BY FEMALE A. GAZELLA, ELSEHUL**

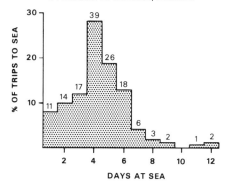

Fig. 6.3. Duration of trips to sea by female Antarctic fur seals, Elsehul (1976).

**MEAN (± S.D.) DURATION
A. GAZELLA FEEDING TRIPS**

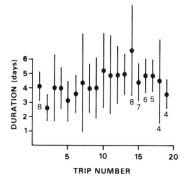

Fig. 6.4. Duration of feeding trips to sea throughout the season by female Antarctic fur seals, Elsehul (1976). Values are means; vertical line represents ± one SD; sample sizes below.

first fourteen trips for which data were available for all eight females. Thereafter, sample size decreased as pups were weaned (average of total trips was seventeen).

Time Spent At Sea

Females spent an average 64.9% (± 13.9) of each feeding and attendance cycle at sea (N = 131 cycles). This value was derived for each female by calculating the time spent at sea as a proportion of the feeding plus attendance time for each cycle. Spearman rank correlations indicated no significant increase or decrease in the proportion of time spent at sea throughout the season.

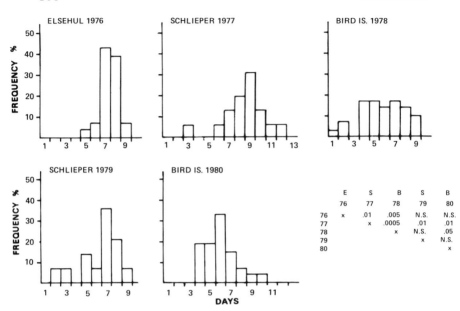

Fig. 6.5. Duration of perinatal attendance periods at each study site.

TABLE 6.3. Duration of perinatal attendance period in Antarctic fur seals.

		Perinatal attendance (days)		
Site	*Year*	*Mean*	SD	*Sample size*
Elsehul	1976	7.4	0.9	28
Schlieper Bay	1977	8.4	2.1	16
Schlieper Bay	1979	6.4	2.0	14
Schlieper Bay	1981	6.9	1.1	56
Bird Island	1978	5.8	2.1	29
Bird Island	1980	7.0	1.5	27
Bird Island	1981	6.8	1.2	28

If feeding-trip duration increased with time but the percentage of each cycle spent at sea did not, then time spent ashore must have increased seasonally. As a group, the eight females did tend to increase the duration of shore attendance during the season. The two females that showed an increase in feeding-trip duration with trip number (Fig. 6.4) also showed an increase in shore attendance during the season ($r_s = 0.719$, N = 14; $r_s = 0.464$, N = 19; P < 0.05).

Effect of Parturition Date

The Elsehul (1976) data were examined for differences in general patterns that might relate to the date of parturition. For eight females that gave birth from November 22 to December 12 (21 days), birth date did not correlate with weaning date ($r_s = 0.193$, N.S., N = 8). This suggests that weaning date was constant and occurred irrespective of birth date. Thus females that gave birth earlier in the season had longer lactation periods than later females (birth date versus length of lactation period, $r_s = -0.80$, P < 0.05, N = 8). No significant relationship (increase or decrease) was found between birth date and percentage of time spent at sea ($r_s = -0.240$, N.S., N = 8).

Seasonal and Site Effects

Despite broad similarities in the patterns shown in different sites and seasons, significant differences were apparent in perinatal attendance periods, shore-attendance duration, feeding-trip duration, and percentage of time at sea (Figs. 6.5–6.8; Tables 6.3–6.5). Perinatal attendance and subsequent shore visits tended to be shorter at Bird Island in 1978 than at other sites in other seasons. Similarly, feeding-trip duration and percentage of time at sea were significantly longer at Bird Island in 1978 than at other sites in other seasons, but in other years and sites they were broadly homogeneous. In the 1981 season, the only one for which data exist for both sites, shore attendance and trips to sea were significantly shorter at Bird Island than at Schlieper Bay (Figs. 6.6, 6.7). Over all seasons, attendance duration was shorter at Bird Island than at Schlieper Bay, but the two sites did not differ consistently in either duration of feeding trips or percentage of time at sea.

DISCUSSION

The period of pup rearing is shorter in the Antarctic fur seal than in any other otariid except the northern fur seal (Chapter 3). This is clearly related to the shortness of the summer season and the severity of the winter. The severe winter causes marked seasonal changes in the abundance of plankton (Foxton, 1956) and thereby the number of plankton feeders. North of the Antarctic Convergence, where waters are warmer and land conditions milder, fe-

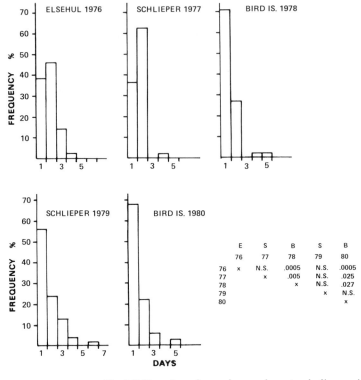

Fig. 6.6. Duration of attendance ashore (excluding perinatal) at each site.

TABLE 6.4. Duration of attendance periods (excluding perinatal) in Antarctic fur seals.

Site	Year	Attendance (days)		
		Mean	SD	Sample size
Elsehul	1976	1.8	0.7	162
Schlieper Bay	1977	1.7	0.5	24
Schlieper Bay	1979	1.7	1.0	48
Schlieper Bay	1981	2.1	0.9	270
Bird Island	1978	1.4	0.6	42
Bird Island	1980	1.4	0.8	30
Bird Island	1981	1.5	0.7	84

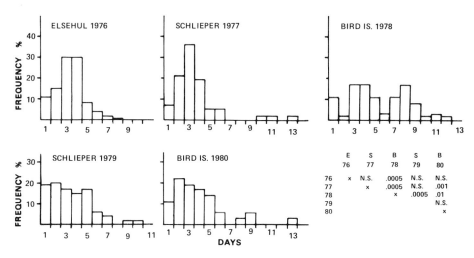

Fig. 6.7. Duration of feeding trips to sea at each site.

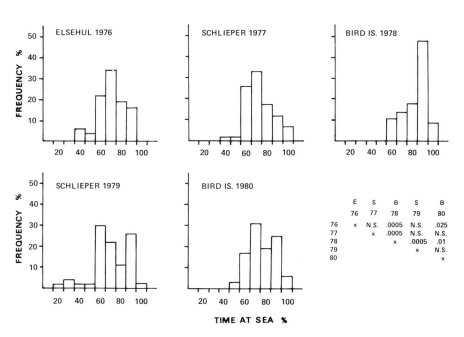

Fig. 6.8. Percentage of lactation period (excluding perinatal attendance) spent at sea at each site.

TABLE 6.5. Duration of feeding periods at sea in Antarctic fur seals.

| Site | Year | Feeding period (days) | | | Time (%) | |
		Mean	*SD*	*Sample size*	*At sea*	*SD*
Elsehul	1976	3.3	1.4	162	63.5	13.6
Schlieper Bay	1977	3.0	1.0	24	63.5	11.0
Schlieper Bay	1979	3.5	1.9	48	65.3	15.7
Schlieper Bay	1981	3.8	1.7	270	62.4	14.1
Bird Island	1978	5.2	2.3	42	76.9	10.4
Bird Island	1980	3.7	2.2	30	70.2	12.5
Bird Island	1981	3.1	2.0	84	64.0	15.8

males of the subantarctic fur seal, *A. tropicalis*, remain around the breeding islands throughout the year. Despite their longer lactation period (8–12 months; Bester, 1977; Condy, 1978), subantarctic fur seal pups are lighter at weaning than Antarctic fur seal pups. Antarctic fur seal pups have a faster absolute, overall growth rate than any other fur seal. Fast pup growth, a short weaning period, and relatively few feeding and attendance cycles are all characteristic of the Antarctic and northern fur seals, the two high-latitude fur seal species.

Because the weaning period was short and fixed, earlier pupping females had a longer lactation period than later arrivals. Older females tended to give birth earlier in the season than younger ones (British Antarctic Survey, unpubl. tagging data), and female weight (though not age) was positively correlated with birth date of male pups at Schlieper Bay in 1981 (Doidge, unpubl.). We expect that pups born early in the season, whose mothers are in better condition and which have a longer lactation period, should reach a greater weaning weight than pups born later.

The seasonal increase in duration of feeding trips to sea may result from increased difficulty in finding food, from greater pup demand for milk, or from a combination of these. Females probably replenish their own depleted reserves during the first few trips to sea when pup demand is low, as with the northern and Galapagos fur seals (Chapters 3, 11). Thus female need may account for the unusually long first trip to sea, but it probably does not explain the seasonal increase in trip duration. The pups' energy needs undoubtedly increase over time as they grow and spend more time in cold water (Irving et al., 1962). Because females do not lose significant body weight during lactation, they appear to meet increasing needs of their pups by extending foraging time (Doidge, unpubl. data). The duration of shore visits increases seasonally partly because the wandering of pups from the feeding sites causes them to reunite less quickly with their returned mothers.

The same factors that determine trip length may also be implicated in the unusual mode of weaning in this species. In most seals, females actively abandon the pups, but in Antarctic (and northern) fur seals, pups leave the island before their mothers do. Pup feces indicate that at least some individuals feed on crustaceans late in the season. Large pup groups (>50) have been seen at sea (Payne, 1979b), where such grouping may enhance the success of krill capture, and may serve an antipredator function against leopard seals, *Hydrurga leptonyx*, which are known to kill fur seal young (McCann, pers. observ.). Perhaps pups satisfy their increasing needs more efficiently by feeding on krill than by waiting for their mothers to return from increasingly long foraging trips.

Despite the variation in sites and seasons, Bird Island and Schlieper Bay differed consistently from each other in female attendance. Bird Island had shorter attendance periods, which may relate to differences in social factors at that high density site. By contrast, the length of feeding trips to sea and the percentage of time spent at sea did not differ consistently between the two sites. Thus the feeding trip data do not support the hypothesis that feeding competition is greater near Bird Island (ca. 150,000 animals) and Elsehul (ca. 270,000 animals), despite their larger populations, than near Schlieper Bay (ca. 20,000 animals). It seems likely that feeding ranges overlap considerably. The mean length of feeding trips was similar among all sites and years (excluding Bird Island, 1978; Table 6.5); nevertheless significant differences did occur.

Several lines of evidence suggest that 1978 was a poor season at Bird Island. Not only was the perinatal period the shortest of all the data sets, but also the amount of time spent at sea was greatest, the time spent ashore with the pup was least, pup weights were the lowest recorded (Croxall and Prince, 1979; Doidge et al., 1984b), and pup mortality was considerably higher (Doidge et al., 1984a). These changes may have related to a lower availability of krill in swarms close to Bird Island, because research and commercial vessels there found only low concentrations that season.

It appears that site-specific differences exist in attendance patterns ashore which may relate to differences in fur seal breeding density, but we do not yet know the mechanisms involved. The length of feeding trips to sea seems to be influenced principally by seasonal rather than site-specific factors. This contention is supported by the strong circumstantial evidence (from fishing catches and sea-bird diets) that there are substantial year-to-year variations in the distribution and abundance of marine resources around South Georgia Island (Croxall and Prince, 1979; Prince, 1980).

SUMMARY

The attendance behavior of Antarctic fur seals was studied at South Georgia Island in the south Atlantic Ocean. The study sites used were Elsehul (1 year), Schlieper Bay (3 years), and Bird Island (3 years). The sites differed in density of seals and rate of population growth. The breeding season extended from November to April. No females attended the breeding sites in winter because they migrated to unknown locations. Males remained in the vicinity of South Georgia in winter. The interval from parturition to weaning was 117 days. The weaning period was short and fixed, and pups weaned themselves. The time of weaning was not related to birth date. Thus earlier-born pups had longer suckling periods. No females suckled yearlings. The prepartum feeding patterns of females were not measured because females arrived on land only 1 to 2 days before parturition. The interval from parturition to copulation was 6 days, during which time females did not go to sea. After parturition females made fourteen to nineteen visits to land, each lasting about 2.1 days. Females spent on average 41.6 days (35%) of the pup-rearing season on land. No data were obtained on the percentage of each visit that pups spent suckling. Females departed to sea at all hours. Foraging trips lasted on average 4.3 days and generally became longer over the first fourteen trips to sea. However, only two of eight females showed a progressive increase in feeding-trip duration throughout suckling. Feeding-trip length was influenced more by seasonal than by site-specific factors and were similar from year to year. No data were obtained on the feeding patterns of nonmothers or on historical differences in feeding patterns.

7 Diving Behavior of Antarctic Fur Seals ≅ *G. L. Kooyman, R. W. Davis, and J. P. Croxall*

INTRODUCTION

This study of diving in the Antarctic fur seal is timely, given the recent history of the species. These animals, which have been relatively undisturbed by humans in recent times, are experiencing a phenomenal, worldwide population increase (Chapter 1). Their food during the pup-rearing period is mainly krill, *Euphausia superba*, a resource that until recently was not exploited by man. Now, however, several countries are developing krill-harvesting capabilities, and soon competition for this resource may develop between man and Antarctic wildlife. Thus it is appropriate to obtain a detailed analysis of the Antarctic fur seal's feeding behavior—particularly that of females caring for pups—now before rapid growth of the seal population ends and commercial fishery grows extensively.

The Antarctic fur seal is the only feeding specialist of the six species we studied, and the behavior of its single prey is well known. In the other five species, the prey taken by a particular instrumented female was not known, even if the range of prey taken by the species was well documented. In the Antarctic fur seal, however, specific correlations could be made between dive patterns and prey movements. Our objectives were to measure the (1) duration of trips to sea; (2) time to reach the feeding area; (3) common feeding depths; (4) duration of feeding periods; (5) dive frequency rates; and (6) preferred feeding times. In addition, we were able to correlate the seal's feeding depths with that of krill depth distribution.

METHODS

The study was conducted at Elsehul, South Georgia Island, in April 1977, and on Bird Island in January and February 1980 (Fig. 6.1). Animals were selected for study from the large population surrounding the field stations at these sites. The nearness of the seals to the station enabled us to identify departures and arrivals, often within minutes.

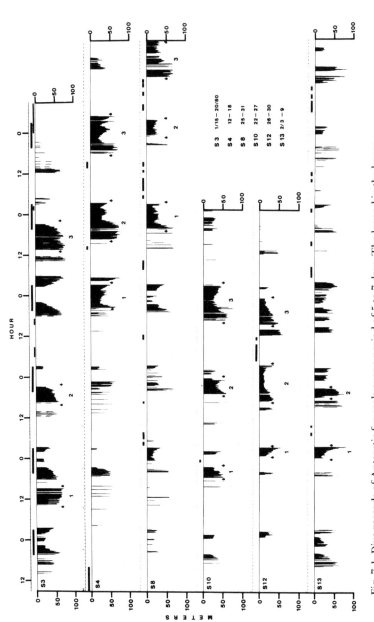

Fig. 7.1. Dive records of Antarctic fur seals over a period of 5 to 7 days. The legend in the lower right gives the seal number, which corresponds to those in the tables. The dates that appear after the seal numbers are for the time period shown on the record. Hour is the local time and the heavy line below the time line is the period between sunset and sunrise. The thinner, heavy line above S3 and all other heavy lines between the time marks and the dive baseline are the periods when the seals rested.

TABLE 7.1. Summary of Antarctic fur seal dive records in 1977 and 1980.

Female no.	Total dives	Record length (h)	Depth Aver. (m)	Depth Max. (m)	Duration Aver. (min)	Duration Max. (min)
1 (1977)	277	128	19	41	<2.0	3.7
2 (1977)	442	225	26	65	<2.0	2.9
1	240	179	12	39	2.4	3.4
2	40	60	26	52	3.1	4.6
3	692	280	42	90	<2.0	3.0
4	828	228	34	83	1.0	4.6
5A	394	308	34	87	—	—
5B	134	120	50	83	0.8	2.3
6A	88	48	38	89	2.4	—
6B	125	25	33	76	2.0	—
8	902	199	27	69	1.0	3.8
9	296	88	18	62	—	3.8
10	576	113	33	85	1.0	4.8
12	612	116	21	66	1.6	—
13	879	246	34	93	—	—
14	147	152	21	101	1.7	—
15	369	144	35	96	1.9	4.9
Total	7041	2659				
Average	414	156	30	75	—	—
SD ±	287	82	9.6	18.7	—	—

Animals were captured with a hoop net and restrained for harness attachment in the usual way. The elapsed time from the selection of the animal to deployment of the TDR was often only 15 to 20 minutes. This procedure caused little disturbance to the rest of the colony. Females rejoined their pups several hours after capture.

Twenty lactating females were captured and released wearing recorders and radio transmitters. From these twenty seals, seventeen records suitable for analysis were obtained. In two instances, seals 5 and 6, the animals were recaptured after a trip to sea and new TDRs replaced the recovered units. Time at sea for the seventeen females ranged from 1 to 13 days, although the female having the 13-day record returned without the recorder. The Antarctic study was one of the most successful of the six diving studies because the seals lacked a flight response, and the short cycles at sea allowed rapid deployment and recovery of recorders.

The assumed swim speeds used in the Discussion to estimate foraging ranges were based on measurements of the minimum cost of transport values obtained for 20–25 kg sea lions swimming in a flume at 1.8 ms^{-1} (Table 15.4a).

TABLE 7.2. Activity patterns for trips to sea for Antarctic fur seals.

Female no.	Dive rate (dives/h)	Rest (%)	Time to first dive (h)	Ashore from last dive (h)
1 (1977)	0.9	—	—	—
2 (1977)	3.7	—	—	—
1	1.2	—	—	—
2	0.3	3	36	14
3	4.9	6	15	8
4	4.9	3	25	21
5A (group 1)	3.7	5	8	20
(group 2)	1.4	7	16	8
5B	1.2	3	10	—
8	5.8	18	9	—
9	4.9	0	16	21
10	5.0	0.5	7	6
12	6.3	5	22	8
13	4.1	14	12	—
14	1.7	0.6	27	2
15	4.1	2	8	—
Average	3.4	5	16	12
SD ±	2.0	5.3	8.9	7.2

Note: All seals made one trip to sea except 5A, which made two—one of 50 hours followed by one of 150 hours.

RESULTS

A total of 7,041 dives was recorded during the equivalent of 16 weeks (2,659 hours) at sea in the seventeen records (Table 7.1). However, these recorded dives may underrepresent feeding effort, since much surface feeding may have occurred. Dive depths showed a steady decline (became shallower) between dusk and midnight, and a consistent increase between midnight and dawn (Fig. 7.1). This pattern correlated well with the vertical movements of krill (Croxall et al., 1985). Gaps between the decline and the increase, and a unique pattern of striation in the baseline during some of these gaps, suggest long bouts of feeding at depths that were too shallow to register as dives.

The average depth of all distinct dives was 30 m (Table 7.1) and the median was 27.9 m. The maximum depth for all seals was 101 m and the average of maximum depths for all records was 75 m. The average dive duration was 1.9 minutes and the maximum dive time for each record ranged from 2.3 to 4.9 minutes (Table 7.1).

The total sea time per trip (average and median) was 5.3 days (±

45 hours; Table 7.2). The seals swam almost constantly and averaged 5% of the time resting (Table 7.2; Fig. 7.1). An average of 414 dives was made per trip, or 3.4 dives per hour over the total time at sea (Table 7.1). After a seal left the colony, the average time it spent swimming before dives began was 16 hours; time spent swimming on return to shore after the last dive was 12 hours (Table 7.2).

The dive-bout criterion for this species was 25 minutes. However, the evidence for surface feeding cited above (especially gaps in the dive record) suggests that "bout" may not have quite the same meaning as in the other species. With that qualification, the average number of bouts per trip was 12.1, bout duration averaged 1.9 hours, and dive rate within a bout averaged 19.3 dives per hour (Table 7.3).

The most frequently attained depth interval for all seals was between 21 m and 30 m (Fig. 7.2), with a nearly exponential decline in frequency at increasing depths. The greatest number of dives occurred between 1700 and 0400 hours (Fig. 7.3). A peak in diving activity occurred between 2000 and 2100 hours with a second, greater peak (including 14% of all dives) between 0200 and 0300 hours. The most frequent measurable dive depth changed with time of day from about 25 m at night to 45–50 m during the day (Fig. 7.4). Dive depths to a maximum of 30 m had a bimodal distribution with peaks at 2000 and 0100 hours (Fig. 7.5). For dives of 31 to 50 m, this bimodal distribution was retained, but the first peak was shifted one hour earlier. Dives between 51 and 70 m occurred mostly before 2100 hours, with a few occurring from 0200 onward into the morning. No dives below 71 m occurred from 2000 to 0200 hours (Fig. 7.5).

DISCUSSION

The distances traveled to the first feeding area and on the whole of the feeding trip can be estimated from assumed swimming speeds. For example, assuming that seals swam in a straight line at an average of 2 ms^{-1} and that diving usually began 8 hours after departure from shore (Fig. 7.6), the distance to the first feeding area would have been about 57 km. Furthermore, since most of the daylight hours were spent swimming at the surface (rest represented only 5% of sea time; Fig. 7.1; Table 7.2), seals could have extended their range far beyond that point during the 4- to 6-day feeding trips. Seal distribution at sea is unknown, but assuming that swim speeds were 2 ms^{-1} and that seals swam for 8 hours each day for 2

Antarctic Fur Seal

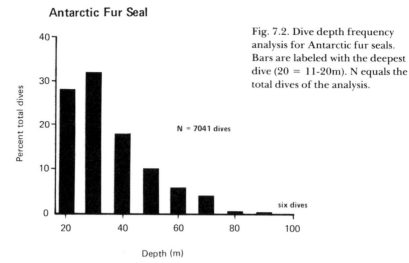

Fig. 7.2. Dive depth frequency analysis for Antarctic fur seals. Bars are labeled with the deepest dive (20 = 11-20m). N equals the total dives of the analysis.

Antarctic Fur Seal

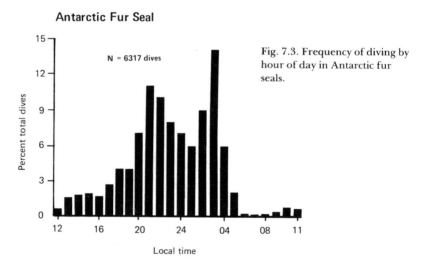

Fig. 7.3. Frequency of diving by hour of day in Antarctic fur seals.

or 3 days before returning to the island, a maximum range from the colony of 150 km (beyond the continental shelf; Fig. 7.6) would be possible.

Based on the occurrence of repetitious diving, feeding appears to begin in the late afternoon or early evening, well before sunset at 1930 hours (Figs. 7.1, 7.3, 7.5) when most deep dives (50–100 m)

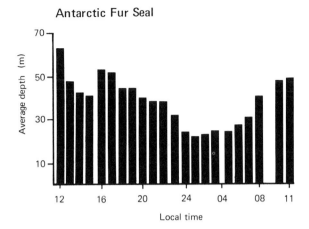

Fig. 7.4. The most frequently attained dive depth relative to hour of day for Antarctic fur seals.

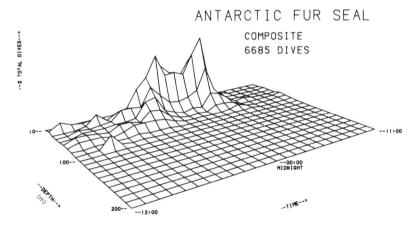

Fig. 7.5. Three-dimensional frequency analysis of dive depth, hour of day, and number of dives for seventeen Antarctic fur seal records.

occur (Figs. 7.4, 7.5). In January and February, when these records were obtained, the seals feed exclusively on mature krill (Croxall and Pilcher, 1984; Doidge and Croxall, 1985). No data are available for the vertical migration of mature krill except in early March when, from midday to 1500 hours, most of the krill are below 50 m (Croxall et al., 1985). If the vertical distribution of krill in January

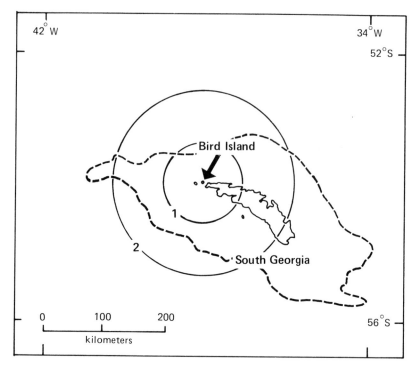

Fig. 7.6. Estimated foraging ranges of Antarctic fur seals from Bird Island. (1) Equals the 57 km range to the first dive 8 hours after leaving the island, assuming a swim speed of 2 ms^{-1}. (2) Equals the maximum range (150 km) for a 4- to 5-day foraging trip, assuming a swim speed of 2 ms^{-1} directly away from the island for 8 hours each day. The dotted line represents the continental shelf edge. (Revised from Croxall et al., 1985.)

and February is similar to this March pattern, the deep dives at that hour of day suggest that the seals begin feeding on krill well before it reaches the surface.

The correlation of krill depth and seal dive-depth frequency is shown in two different ways (Figs. 7.1, 7.7). The seals often started a dive bout in late afternoon (especially seals S3 and S4; Fig. 7.1) with dives >50 m. As night fell, and presumably as krill approached the surface, the dives became progressively shallower until all diving apparently ceased. We suggest that between 2300 and 0200 hours krill were at the surface and that feeding was continuous. That is, the bimodality of the 0–50 m dive depths resulted from shallow dive

Table 7.3. Dive-bout characteristics for the Antarctic fur seals.

Female no.	No. of bouts	Bout duration (h)		Dives/h in bouts	
		Mean	SD	Mean	SD
1	19	1.2	0.8	21.5	8.7
2	4	0.6	0.4	18.3	14.7
3	11	1.5	0.8	17.4	8.2
4	11	3.6	4.1	18.0	6.8
5A	16	1.4	0.8	19.1	11.3
5B	8	1.9	1.2	8.6	3.3
6	4	1.9	1.0	15.2	5.2
8	18	2.1	1.8	17.6	8.3
9	7	1.7	0.8	25.9	7.3
10	10	2.5	2.8	23.2	9.6
12	9	2.9	3.3	22.6	7.1
13	28	1.6	0.9	20.0	9.4
Population average	12.1 ± 7.0	1.9	1.9	19.3	9.2

activity of <10 m depth (Fig. 7.5). Unfortunately, the sensitivity limit of the recorder does not permit us to verify this assertion, which, nevertheless, is testable. The dives from 0200 hours onward may have become progressively deeper because seals followed the descending krill until about 0400 hours, when they abruptly stopped diving (Figs. 7.1, 7.3, 7.5).

Because of the midnight gaps in the dive records, conservative estimates of feeding success can be based on the number of dives made during a feeding period. We assume that in a feeding period, which lasts 10.3 hours and consists of 230 dives (Fig. 7.1), the seal must capture 15% to 20% of its body weight (based upon results from northern fur seals, Chapter 5). Since female Antarctic fur seals weigh 33.5 kg on average, they require 5.7 kg of food per day. Mature krill taken by fur seals weigh 1 g each; therefore, 5,700 *E. superba* must be caught per night of feeding. Since the seals probably feed on krill swarms, in which every dive is likely to produce prey, the average capture rate for each of the 230 dives would be twenty-five krill per dive. With an average dive duration of 1.9 minutes (Table 7.1), this rate is equivalent to catching one krill every 4.6 seconds. If the unknown surface activity between 2300 and 0200 hours were active feeding, and if the dive rate were the same, then 19 krill would be taken per dive.

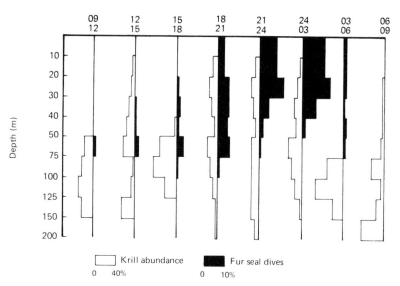

Fig. 7.7. Diving depths of Antarctic fur seals in relation to krill depth distribution over a 24-hour day. Krill abundance is the proportion of total krill in each stratum of the water column. Fur seal dives are the proportion of the period total terminating in each stratum. The krill data are from Croxall et al., 1985.

SUMMARY

Diving behavior of the Antarctic fur seal was studied at Elsehul in April 1977 and at Bird Island in January and February 1980 (both sites are at South Georgia Island). One record was obtained for each of seventeen females. Foraging trips of instrumented females were longer than for uninstrumented females ($\bar{x}$ = 5.3 versus 4.3 days). The outbound transit time on foraging trips was 16 hours, and the return time was 12 hours. The mean number of dives per trip was 414, but the range was 40 to 902. The feeding pattern was distinctly bimodal, with peaks between 2000 and 2100, and between 0200 and 0300 local time. These peaks matched well with the nocturnal rise of krill, the major prey in summer. Most (81%) dives occurred at night. The dive-bout criterion was 25 minutes. Females averaged 12.1 dive bouts per trip and bouts averaged 1.9 hours in duration. The dive rate within bouts was 19.3 dives per hour. The portion of bouts spent submerged was not calculated. All dive bouts were shallow; a break between evening and morning bouts suggested extensive surface feeding too shallow to measure. Depth changed continuously with time during a dive; seals did not spend measurable amounts of time at the greatest depth attained. Dives lasted on average 1.9 minutes, and the maximum duration was 4.9 minutes. The mean depth of all dives was 30 m, with a maximum of 101 m. The most frequently attained depths were 21–30 m. No calculations were made of the relationship between depth and duration of dive, or between surface interval and dive depth. The activity budget at sea was 5% resting, 60% swimming, and 35% diving. The daily pattern of rest bouts was not calculated.

8 Attendance Behavior of South African Fur Seals ≅ *J.H.M. David and*

R. W. Rand

INTRODUCTION

South African fur seals are distributed around the southeastern and western coasts of southern Africa, from Algoa Bay (lat. 34° S, long. 26° E) in the southeast to False Cape Frio (lat. 18°30' S, long. 12° E) in the northwest. Twenty-three discrete breeding colonies occur along this 3,000 km of coastline, of which seventeen are situated on small, rocky, islands, and six (including the four largest) are on the mainland. This distribution is probably related to the northward flowing Benguela current on the west coast and the southwestward flowing Agulhas current on the south coast (Rand, 1967).

Regular migratory movements apparently do not occur in this species (Rand, 1956), although tagged individuals have been recovered over 1,500 km from where they were marked. Some animals have been sighted at least 185 km from land, but the general foraging area appears to be over the continental shelf, usually within 95 km of the shore.

Pupping and mating take place during the summer months (November and December). Females with pups return regularly to the rookery throughout the year, since most pups are probably weaned shortly before the birth of the next pup.

The present report is based mainly on work by the second author, R. W. Rand, conducted at Sinclair Island (Fig. 1.7) during the breeding seasons of 1947 and 1948. A few of these data have been published (Rand, 1955, 1959, 1967), but the majority are analyzed here for the first time. Despite the age of these data, they are included here because they are the only systematically collected data for this species that are comparable to the other attendance chapters. Furthermore, it is likely that present attendance patterns are very similar to these older patterns; Chapter 3 showed that the duration of northern fur seal feeding trips has not changed in 26 years. Finally, the historical value of these observations is considerable as they precede the development of the commercial fisheries (Lucks et al., 1973) off South West Africa (Namibia), which have caused major changes in the abundance of some prey species (Butterworth, 1983).

METHODS

Observations were made at two colonies, Sinclair Island and Van Reenen Bay (Fig. 1.7). Sinclair Island (lat. 27°40′ S, long. 15°31′ E) is a small, rocky islet (3 ha in area) approximately 500 m offshore, where about 12,000 pups are born annually. Preliminary observations were made there in the 1947 season. The data presented here were collected from 1 August 1948 to 26 February 1949, when branded females were available.

The sample consisted of thirty-six females branded either before the start of the 1948 breeding season (females 251, 432, 471, and "L"), on the day of pupping, or within one or two days afterward (the remaining thirty-two females; Rand, 1950a, 1955). Observations were made daily for a variable number of hours from two hides (blinds). The presence, absence, and behavior of marked females were recorded on an opportunistic basis for up to 100 days postpartum. Observation periods normally included the cool, early morning and evening hours when seals were most likely to be present. Females that were seen on land once in a day were scored as spending all day there, and those that were not seen were counted as being absent.

The Van Reenen Bay colony (lat. 27°25′ S, long. 15°19′ E) is on the mainland of South West Africa (SWA), about 37 km north of Sinclair Island; 4,000 to 5,000 pups are born there each year. A small study area, approximately 21 m x 12 m, overlooked by a cliff, was established there in 1977. The study area was about 40 m back from the shoreline, and was completely shaded by the cliff in early morning and late afternoon.

Systematic observations of seal activity and behavior were made there for 12 hours per day for at least part of each breeding season from 1977 onward. Additional winter (July) observations were made in 1982 at the same colony but outside the study area, which was utilized by seals only during the breeding season. No night observations were made at either colony.

Seal harvests occurred for many years at Sinclair Island before 1948, both in the winter for pups and in the summer for adult males. During 1948, however, no sealing occurred on the island. So far as is known, the colony at Van Reenen Bay has never been exploited.

RESULTS

Duration of Suckling

The duration of neonate dependency was quite variable, lasting 8–18 months (Rand, 1959). However, disparate lines of evidence suggest a peak of weaning occurred around 9 to 11 months. Normally, if the pup had not already become independent, it was forcibly weaned at the birth of the new pup. If the new pup died (e.g., females 251 and "L"; Fig. 8.6; Rand, 1950b), suckling sometimes continued into the second year. At least one tagged animal was found with milk in its stomach at 21 months of age, although this was perhaps a rare event (Best and Shaughnessy, unpubl. data). More typically, the rate of weight increase declined from 9 to 11 months, which may have indicated the switchover from milk to solid food (Best and Shaughnessy, unpubl. data). Likewise, a marked decline in blubber yield occurred in animals taken at 11 to 12 months of age (Rand, 1956). Finally, the incidence of cestode parasites in the large intestine, an indicator of solid food intake, increased rapidly from 7 to 8 months, and leveled off at 8 to 10 months (Best and Shaughnessy, unpubl. data).

The weaning process appeared to be gradual. Pups were observed supplementing their milk diet by limited foraging at 5 to 6 months, about 3 to 4 months before most weaning occurred. The gradual onset of cestode parasite infestation further confirmed that self-feeding began before weaning.

Seasonal Pattern of Attendance

Because of the long period of dependency, lactating females visited the rookery regularly throughout the nonbreeding season (January through October). This meant that the rookeries were never deserted, since young of the year, adult females, some adult males, and immature animals were always present.

Despite year-round occupation, the population at breeding sites showed marked seasonal fluctuations. At Van Reenen Bay colony the number of females on the study area was counted daily at 0800 hours from the beginning of the breeding season. The population rose sharply in late November, peaked in the first week in December, and then declined slowly thereafter (Fig. 8.1), probably because lactating females were absent on feeding trips. This pattern correlated with the peak season of births in the last week of November and first two weeks of December.

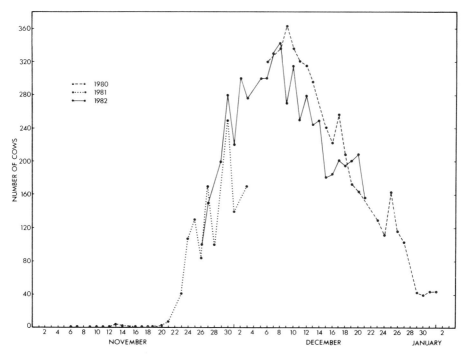

Fig. 8.1. Number of female fur seals in Van Reenen Bay study area at 0800 hours during the breeding season.

Daily Pattern of Attendance

The numbers of seals onshore changed hourly throughout the day. At Van Reenen Bay numbers were high in the early morning, dropped to a minimum in the middle of the day, and tended to rise to another peak late in the afternoon (Fig. 8.2). The drop in the middle of the day was probably related to the rise in direct insolation and the consequent need for thermoregulation at sea. This daily movement pattern did not reveal when females actually fed, especially as feeding excursions usually lasted several days.

During winter the hourly mean movement pattern was quite different. Data from Van Reenen Bay (July 1982) showed a variable flow of females to and from the sea throughout the day, rising to a peak in the early afternoon and declining to a minimum in the early evening (Fig. 8.3). The daytime seaward movements were probably associated with warm temperatures, just as in summer. During win-

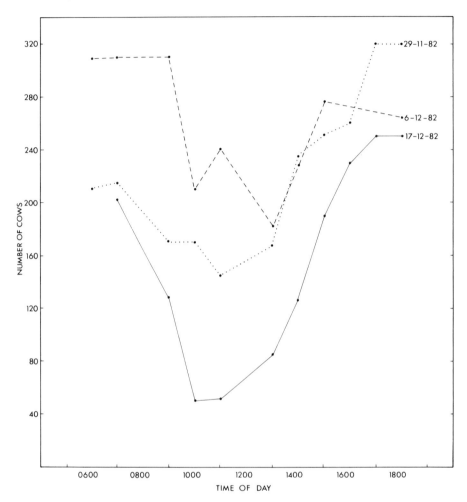

Fig. 8.2. Number of female fur seals in Van Reenen Bay study area throughout the day on 2 days during the peak and on 1 day late in the breeding season.

ter the seals spent most of the time inactive (sleeping) on the beach. Pups suckled as the females slept.

Effects of Parturition on the Feeding Pattern

PREPARTUM. Attendance, based on a sample of two females, increased markedly following parturition, compared to attendance in

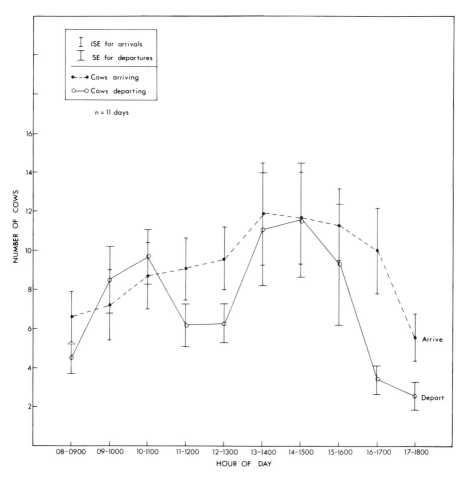

Fig. 8.3. Mean number of female fur seals arriving and departing to sea per hour at Van Reenen Bay colony in July 1982
(winter).

a comparable period before parturition. During the 3 months immediately prepartum, female "L" was present for 3, 3, and 8 days
(total 14 days), and female 251 was present for 9, 10, and 6 days (total 25 days; Figs. 8.4, 8.5). These total attendances (14 and 25 days)
compare with attendances of 48 and 41 days for the same females
during the 3 months immediately postpartum (Fig. 8.6). The mean
attendance for twenty-three other marked females in the 3 months
postpartum was approximately the same ($\bar{x}$ = 41.0 days, range 19–

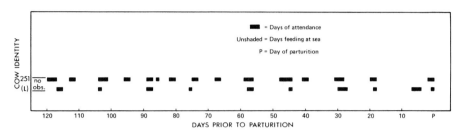

Fig. 8.4. Attendance patterns of marked, pregnant, female fur seals prior to parturition at Sinclair Island, 1948–49.

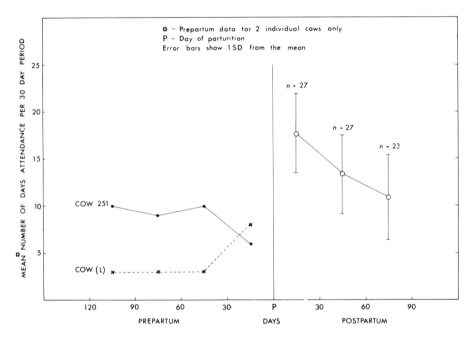

Fig. 8.5. Attendance (in days) of marked, pregnant, female fur seals per 30-day period pre- and postpartum at Sinclair Island during the breeding season of 1948–49. Prepartum data are for two individuals only. Postpartum data are mean values for 27 females.

55 days; Table 8.1). The increased amount of time spent away from the rookery prior to parturition (from June onward) may have resulted from the increasing energetic requirements of the rapidly growing fetus, and may have stimulated the dependent pup to begin foraging for itself.

POSTPARTUM. Females arrived at the colony shortly before they gave birth. At Sinclair Island, female 251 arrived 2 days before parturition and was absent for 16 days prior to that; female "L" arrived 1 day before parturition and was absent for the 3 previous days (Fig. 8.4). At Van Reenen Bay six of ten females arrived 1 or 2 days before pupping (Table 8.2). However, females there may have arrived earlier and spent time onshore in the larger rookery beyond sighting distance of the study site.

The mean duration of the first visit to the rookery, counting day 0 as that on which parturition occurred, was 4.3 days with a median of only 3.0 days (N = 31 females; Fig. 8.7). One female remained with her pup for 13 days but the next longest stay was only 9 days. Thus the initial visit was rather brief, with feeding interrupted for only a short time.

BIRTH TO COPULATION INTERVAL. The mean interval from parturition to observed copulation was 6.0 days (range 5–7 days, N = 6 at Sinclair Island, N = 2 at Van Reenen Bay; Tables 8.2, 8.3). Three of the six Sinclair Island females were absent (presumably at sea) for at least 1 day during that period. Rand (1959) concluded that females did not leave land until they mated, which occurred an estimated 5 days postpartum. However, since only 39% of the thirty-

TABLE 8.1. Total attendance per month of South African fur seal females rearing pups at Sinclair Island.

Month[a]	Total postpartum attendance (days)		
	Mean	SD	N
1[b]	17.6	4.24	27
2[c]	13.3	4.18	27
3	10.9	4.47	23
3 mo. combined	41.0	10.8	23

[a] Months are 30-day periods.
[b] Month 1 vs. 2: t = 3.753; DF = 52; p < 0.001.
[c] Month 2 vs. 3: t = 1.960; DF = 48; p < 0.1 > 0.05.

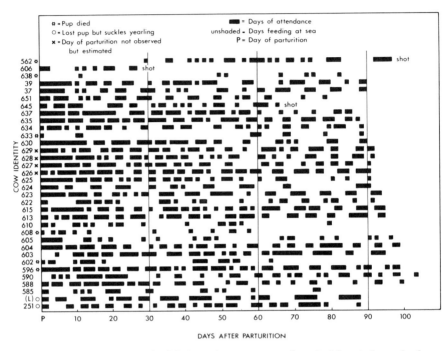

Fig. 8.6. Attendance patterns of marked female fur seals after pupping at Sinclair Island, November 1948 to February 1949.

TABLE 8.2. Arrival, parturition, and copulation dates of marked female South African fur seals at Van Reenen Bay in 1982.

Female no.	Date first observed	Date of parturition	Arrival to parturition (days)	Date of copulation	Birth to copulation (days)
13	Dec 6	Dec 8	2	—	—
49	Nov 29	Nov 30	1	Dec 7	7
90	Nov 30	Dec 1	1	—	—
126	Dec 9	Dec 9	0	—	—
131	Nov 27	Nov 29	2	Dec 5	6
140	Nov 28	Nov 29	1	—	—
192	Nov 26	Nov 26	0	—	—
203	Dec 1	Dec 1	0	—	—
225	Nov 22	Nov 27	5	—	—
229	Nov 29	Dec 1	2	—	—

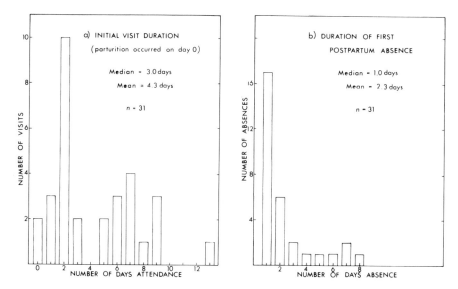

Fig. 8.7. Duration (in days) of (a) the first visit to land, and (b) the first postpartum absence from Sinclair Island colony by marked, pregnant, female fur seals in 1948. The duration of the initial visit is counted from the day of parturition (= day 0).

TABLE 8.3. Duration of first visit to land by pregnant South African fur seal females at Sinclair Island.

Components of visit*	Mean	SD	N
Arrival to parturition	1.5	—	2
Parturition to copulation	6.0	0.63	6
Parturition to first departure	4.3	3.27	31

* Attendance units are days.

one females with a known day of parturition remained continuously with their pups for at least 6 days (i.e., until after the estimated date of mating), and since the mean initial visit lasted only 4.3 days, it appears that the majority of females did not remain on land continuously until they mated. The mean duration of the first postpartum absence was only 2.3 days, with a median of 1.0 days (Fig. 8.7). Presumably feeding could have occurred on this first absence, i.e., before estrus.

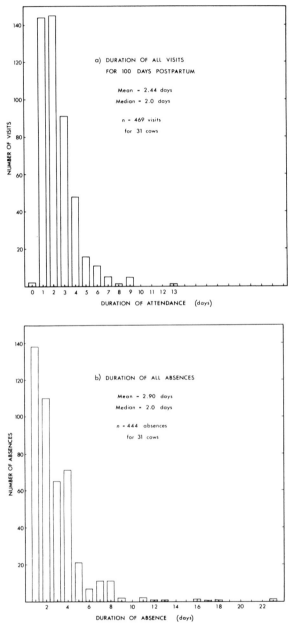

Fig. 8.8. Duration (in days) of (a) all visits to land, and (b) all postpartum absences from Sinclair Island colony by marked female fur seals during the 1948–49 breeding season. Only females with dependent pups are included. Some females were observed for up to 100 days postpartum.

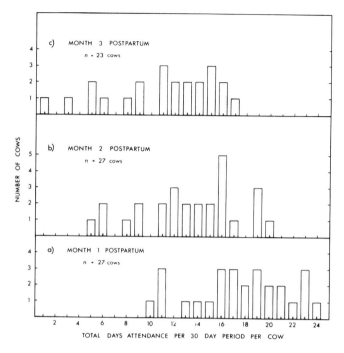

Fig. 8.9. Total attendance per month (in days) for up to 3 months postpartum by marked female fur seals with pups at Sinclair Island, 1948–49. A month is calculated as 30 days.

TABLE 8.4. Duration of postpartum visits and absences by South African fur seals at Sinclair Island.

Type of observation	Month[a]								
	One			Two			Three		
	Mean	SD	N	Mean	SD	N	Mean	SD	N
Visit duration[b]	2.8	1.94	166	2.2	1.14	159	2.2	1.24	123
Absence duration[b]	2.2	1.74	155	2.8	2.33	164	4.0	3.33	118

[a] Months are 30-day periods; all means are in days.
[b] Results of the Mann-Whitney U-test for duration of visit and of absence were as follows:

	Visit duration		Absence duration	
	Month 1 vs. 2	Month 2 vs. 3	Month 1 vs. 2	Month 2 vs. 3
U	16906.5	not sig.	14925	6486
p	0.0005	—	<0.01	<0.0005

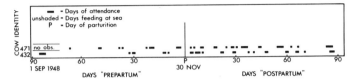

Fig. 8.10. Attendance patterns of two nonpregnant fur seal females for a 6-month period before and during the breeding season at Sinclair Island, 1948–49.

TABLE 8.5. Attendance patterns of females known or assumed to have lost their pups, for three 30-day periods, Sinclair Island.

Female no.	Pup lost (days postpartum)	Days attendance (postpartum)			
		Month 1	Month 2	Month 3	Total
562	0	1	12	12	25
596	6	22	19	16	57
602	4	9	9	1	19
608	11	6	6	0	12
633	0*	3	2	5	10
638	0*	1	2	4	7

* The fate of the pups of females 633 and 638 is unknown, but from the very long absences of these females it is assumed that the pups must have died.

Duration of Shore Visit

Following the initial visit during which the pup was born, females regularly alternated between visits to the rookery and feeding trips to sea (Fig. 8.6). The mean durations of 469 visits to shore was 2.4 days, and of 444 absences was 2.9 days (Fig. 8.8). The visits were significantly shorter than the periods at sea (Mann-Whitney U-test; $U = 95857$, $p < 0.05$, $N_1 = 444$, $N_2 = 469$). This is in contrast to the initial visit (Fig. 8.7), which was significantly longer than the first feeding trip (Mann-Whitney U-test, $U = 240$, $p < 0.0005$, $N_1 = 31$, $N_2 = 31$). No information is available on the total number of days spent ashore between parturition and weaning because of the length of this period. However, females spent 45.6% (41.0 days) of the first 90 days postpartum ashore ($N = 23$ females).

Both the total number of days of attendance per month and the mean duration of each visit changed as the season progressed, being highest in the first month after parturition and declining progressively thereafter (Tables 8.1, 8.4; Fig. 8.9). The decline in total days ashore between months 1 (17.6 days) and 2 (13.3 days) was highly significant, and the decline between months 2 and 3 was very close to significance at the 95% level of confidence. The decline in the mean duration of visits in the first 2 months was highly significant, whereas there was no decline between the second and third months (Table 8.4). The hypothesis that females spent more time at the rookery during the first month postpartum because of the greater nutritional needs of the pup cannot be tested due to a paucity of data on pup growth rates.

Duration of Trips to Sea

The mean duration of feeding trips, although somewhat variable (Fig. 8.6), increased progressively in the first 90 days postpartum; monthly differences were statistically significant (Table 8.4). These durations were considerably shorter than the 10-day absences reported previously (Rand, 1967). In fact, only 8/444 (= 2%) of absences exceeded 10 days (Fig. 8.8). The first trip to sea ($\bar{x}$ = 2.3 days; Fig. 8.7) was not shorter than subsequent trips in the first month. The total trips to sea that females made before weaning is not known, but a sample of 27 females made an average of five trips per month during the first 90 days postpartum.

Behavior of Females Lacking Pups

Females without pups spent approximately half as much time ashore as did mothers. The total attendance from December to February (equivalent to 90 days postpartum for mothers) was 22 days for female 432 and 26 days for female 471, both of which failed to give birth. This compared with a mean attendance of 41.0 days for females with pups (Table 8.1). Furthermore, the days ashore per 30-day interval also averaged fewer for nonmothers than for mothers (female 432 = 4, 2, 4, 10, 5, 7, total 32 days ashore in 6 months, and female 471 = 4, 7, 9, 11, 6, total 37 days onshore in 5 successive months). Postpartum attendance records for six other females that lost, or appeared to lose, their pups soon after birth resembled those of females 432 and 471 in having long absences, of up to 45 days in some cases (Figs. 8.6, 8.10) and averaged only 7 to 25 days total attendance (Table 8.5). Only female 596 maintained an attendance pattern typical of a female with a pup. Although the sample is small, this evidence suggests that the behavior of females with and without pups differed considerably, and that only the former were in regular attendance at the rookery.

DISCUSSION

The South African fur seal is nonmigratory presumably because the environment is relatively constant and an adequate food supply remains within foraging distance throughout the year. The seals feed mainly on the abundant fish and cephalopod populations associated with the rich Benguela ecosystem. This reliable food supply apparently permits neonate dependence to fill the interval between successive births. This pattern is unlike the highly seasonal subpolar fur seals in which pups are intensively fed for a short period and experience rapid initial growth, then are made independent and desert the breeding sites within 17–18 weeks (Chapters 3, 6). Limitations of space imposed by the seals' former habit of breeding on small offshore islands may hitherto have prevented overexploitation of local food resources. The more recent development of large mainland breeding sites may change this situation.

The brief duration of the feeding trips, usually ≤4.0 days by 90 days postpartum, may indicate that most females found food fairly close at hand. However, the considerable variation (Fig. 8.8) may indicate that not all females found food so readily. Nevertheless, very few trips lasted 10 days or longer. The reason for the seasonal increase in duration of feeding absences is not known, but could be related to increased nutritional needs of the growing pup over time. In northern fur seals, females delivered increased amounts of milk per visit over time (Chapter 5). However, this may not apply to the South African fur seal, which has a much longer period of dependence and may have a slower, more uniform growth rate over time.

The number of days of attendance by the female was greatest during the pup's first month of life, indicating the pup's greater need for parental care. Although the mean duration of each visit was also longest during the first month (2.8 days), the visits became shorter by a small but significant amount by the third month. These relatively brief durations may indicate that shore visits function solely to feed the pup, and that as soon as milk is exhausted the female returns to sea.

Several lines of evidence indicate that reproductive status, specifically lactation, determines the onshore-offshore movement pattern. Only females with pups visit the rookery regularly and are absent for brief periods. Females without pups may be away at sea for over 45 consecutive days, and are far less predictable in their movements.

SUMMARY

The attendance behavior of South African fur seals was studied in 1948–49 at Sinclair Island off the coast of South West Africa (Namibia), and from 1977–82 at Van Reenen Bay on the mainland of Namibia. The sites differed in population size (Sinclair Island was larger). The breeding season extended from early November through December. Lactating females visited the rookery throughout the nonbreeding season to feed their pups, which suggests that no definite migration occurs. Weaning occurred at 9 to 11 months, although some young continued to suckle into the second year. Weaning was initiated by the mother, and appeared to be a slow process. The females spent long periods away from the rookery during the 1 to 3 months preceding parturition. The interval from parturition to copulation was 6 days, and females made a brief trip to sea in this interval. The total number of visits to land from birth to weaning was estimated to be fifty to sixty. The mean duration of the first visit, counting from the day of parturition, was 4.3 days. Visits to land after copulation averaged 2.4 days in duration. The mean duration of visits was greatest during the first month postpartum at 2.8 days. Females stayed ashore 41 days (45.6%) of the first 90 days of the pup's life, but the total number of days ashore from birth to weaning was not measured. The proportion of shore time spent suckling was not measured. The numbers of females onshore during the breeding season fluctuated throughout the day, being highest in early morning and late afternoon and lowest in the middle of the day when high temperatures obliged animals to go to sea. In winter the animals went to sea less predictably but at any hour. The mean duration of absences was 2.9 days. The mean duration of feeding trips to sea increased progressively in the first 90 days postpartum, and was 4.0 days by the third month. A mean of five feeding trips per month occurred in this period. Females without pups spent approximately half as much time ashore as did mothers. Females that lost their pups soon after birth showed a similar attendance pattern, being ashore relatively little and having long absences of up to 45 days.

9 Diving Behavior of South African Fur Seals ≅ *G. L. Kooyman*

and R. L. Gentry

INTRODUCTION

The purpose of this study was to test the newly developed TDR system and to obtain data comparable to that described in previous dive chapters. We selected the South African fur seal because, as the largest of the fur seals, we expected it to dive more deeply than the northern fur seal, the only other species we had studied by 1977 when this project began. The proximity of deep water to the breeding sites was also promising because one of our goals was to test bourdon tubes having greater maximum depths than those used in the northern fur seal work. This test was a necessary precursor to deploying the TDRs on truly deep divers, such as the Weddell seal.

The study site, at the DeBeers diamond mining town of Kleinsee, was on the west coast of South Africa in one of the world's five major upwelling systems (Fig. 9.1.). Recent increases in the fur seal population there (Chapter 1) have been linked to the richness of this upwelling system. The coastal waters were cold as a result of the upwelling and because of the Benguela current that carries waters northward from the south polar seas.

Because this site is at the edge of the Namaqualand desert, seal movements, and therefore our capture attempts, were strongly affected by solar radiation. The skies were usually clear except for an occasional morning fog. By midday the sun was intense; temperatures in sheltered rocky areas exceeded 30°C, and seals moved to the water's edge or into the sea, apparently seeking thermal relief. As evening approached, fur seals moved landward, eventually resting high up on the rocks and beaches where they remained in unusually dense masses (for fur seals) until late morning. Two disadvantages of this study were that it was not coupled with ongoing measures of attendance behavior at this site, and no observation facilities were available there.

The study was hindered by behavioral traits unique to this species. For example, because this site is harvested for pelts in winter, animals on the breeding beaches were alert to any movement from

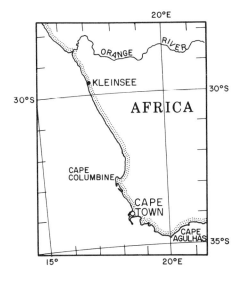

Fig. 9.1. The study site was located within a few kilometers of the diamond mining town of Kleinsee, on the Atlantic coast of South Africa.

landward, and they stampeded easily. Furthermore, after an animal was captured once, usually high up on the beach in early morning, it would thereafter remain close to the water's edge, often some distance from the original capture site (unlike other species in this monograph). This tendency made relocating instrumented seals extremely difficult, as did the rugged beach relief and our failure to use radio transmitters on the TDRs.

Captures were also difficult because the females were large, aggressive, closely grouped, and, unlike other fur seals, they would not be herded. In their dash to the sea during captures, the impression was that they would run over any person in their path who failed to yield. Their behavior at capture was more like that of sea lions than other fur seals.

METHODS

The study site was a broad, rocky beach with many gullies, cracks, and tide pools. Between beaches, a few rocky promontories, about 10 m high, fell away as sheer cliffs to the water, but on the shoreward side they gradually graded into the sandy Namaqualand desert. The study occurred during 3 weeks in January 1977.

Six females, estimated to weigh between 70 and 80 kg, were captured and instrumented using methods described in Chapter 2. Four seals were recaptured, but only two recorders yielded useful

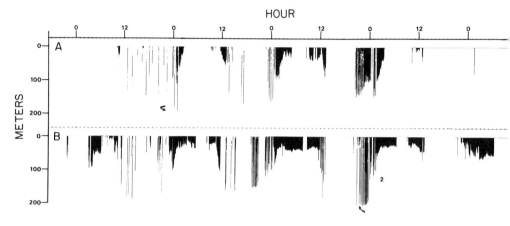

Fig. 9.2. A plot of all dives made on one trip to sea by two South African fur seal females (A is seal 1, B is seal 2). Time was estimated from the geometric constant of the changing spooling rate.

TABLE 9.1. Overall summary of South African fur seal dive records.

Female no.	No. of dives	Record length (h)	Depth		Duration	
			Aver. (m)	Max. (m)	Aver. (min)	Max. (min)
1	313	194	49	191	2.5	7.5
2	968	252	41	204	1.7	6.4

data (the others malfunctioned). Of the two other females, one failed to return from a second feeding trip. The other animal returned twice from feeding trips, but in both cases we failed to recapture her because she remained wary and close to the water in inaccessible places. In one desperate effort, we swam a 20 m channel, through hundreds of pups and adults, to a rocky islet only to miss in our attempt to net her.

The TDRs used on this species differed substantially from those used on other species. The bourdon tube pressure transducer was rated at 450 psi maximum pressure, rather than at 300 psi used elsewhere. This difference caused a loss of detail in the baseline, which obscured not only the hours at which entry into and exit from the sea occurred, but also the periods of rest while at sea. Furthermore, unlike later models, the instrument had no timing circuit, so time on the abscissa was estimated from a constant (see Chapter 2). Small-scale features, such as dive durations and interdive intervals, were less affected by this estimated time base than were larger features, such as the placement of dives in 24-hour blocks. For these reasons, some comparisons among South African fur seals and other species either cannot be made or can be made with poor confidence.

RESULTS

For the two dive records obtained, the number of dives per trip varied by a factor of 3 (Table 9.1), but the difference in mean depth of dives (49 and 41 m) was not significant (at alpha = .05; Mann-Whitney U-test, p = 0.001; medians were 36 and 31 m). However, the difference in median dive durations (seal 1, 1.7 min; seal 2, 1.4 min) was significant (Mann-Whitney, p = 0.001). The maximum depth attained by each, 191 m and 204 m, respectively, was similar, and deep for fur seals. The duration of the trip to sea could not be calculated because entry into and exit from the sea were not reada-ble on the records. For much of the record length (Table 9.1) seal 2 was ashore; therefore, the actual period at sea, about 5 to 6 days, was nearly the same for both (Fig. 9.2).

The grouping of dives was noteworthy (Fig. 9.2). The dive-bout criterion for this species was 18 minutes, with an arbitrary minimum of five dives per bout (Chapter 2). By this definition seal 1 had fewer diving bouts than seal 2, and had a smaller number of dives per bout (Table 9.2). The duration of bouts, dives per hour within bouts, and percentage of bouts spent underwater were similar for the two ani-mals. The proportion of bouts spent underwater did not differ be-tween deep and shallow bouts (ANOVA, p = 0.50), as it did with the northern fur seal. This finding was more attributable to extreme variation in the shallow bouts (range 13%–94%) than to the small number of deep bouts (N = 3). The diving rate (dives per hour) in deep bouts appeared to be slower than in shallow bouts, as in the northern fur seal, but this difference was not tested because of the variation in shallow bouts and the paucity of deep bouts. Both rec-ords showed evidence that the depth of dives within a bout changed over time, suggesting that the prey were moving vertically (Fig. 9.2).

Dive duration correlated well with dive depth; the deepest dives were the longest. The r^2 value for the regression of dive duration on dive depth (Fig. 9.3) was 77.6%, indicating good ability to predict duration as a function of the depth attained. The r^2 value for the dives of seal 2 was 70.6%.

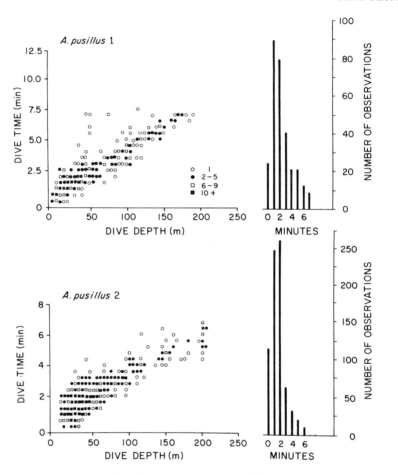

Fig. 9.3. Linear regression of dive duration on dive depth for two South African fur seal records. The histogram shows the distribution of dive durations used in the plot. The number of observations at each locus is indicated by symbols in the key.

Some of the scatter in Figure 9.3 resulted from the seal's tendency sometimes to spend brief periods at the greatest depth of the dive. A profile of two 200 m dives (Fig. 9.4) shows how dive time was partitioned. The descent was rapid, requiring about 1 minute. Then the seal spent about 1.5 minutes at the greatest depth, and she spent the greatest portion of the dive ascending from depth. Such deep dives of more than 150 m represented less than 10% of all dives. For both seals the majority of dives went to depths of 50 m or less

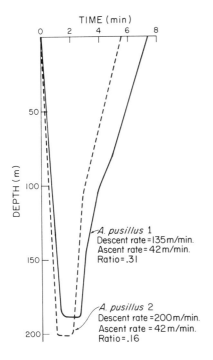

Fig. 9.4. Time and depth profile for two 200 m dives for South African fur seal females. The arrows in Figure 9.2 indicate the dives selected for this plot.

(Fig. 9.5). Sixty-six percent of the 313 dives of seal 1 were in that depth range, 30% were between 50 and 150 m, and only 1% were >175 m. The pattern was only slightly different for seal 2, for which 79% of dives were ≤50 m, and <2% were >175 m. This single peak in depth frequency (<50m) was typical of other species in this volume, except for the northern fur seal.

Both seals showed a bimodal distribution in the frequency of diving at different hours of the day; they differed only slightly in the hours when peak dive frequency occurred. Because of the estimated time base (see Methods), the placement of these peaks relative to dawn and dusk was uncertain (Fig. 9.6). Seals 1 and 2 made 49% and 55%, respectively, of their total dives during the major peak, and 36% and 29%, respectively, in the minor peak. The records suggest that most shallow diving occurred sometime during the night, that some shallow diving occurred in the day, and that deep diving could occur at any hour (Fig. 9.6), as in the northern fur seal.

These results suggest that dive effort varied greatly between individuals. Both seals were at sea for about the same period of time,

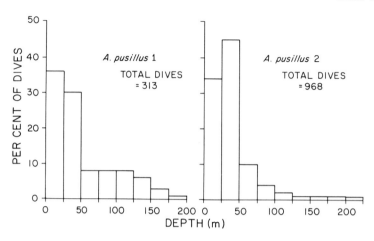

Fig. 9.5. Frequency distribution for depth of dive in 25 m increments for two South African fur seal females. Bars are labeled
with the deepest dive (50 = 26–50m).

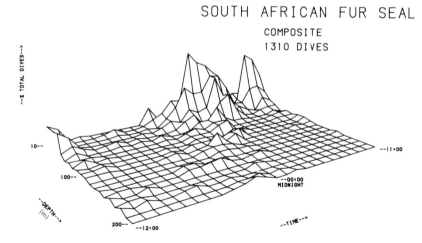

Fig. 9.6. Three-dimensional representation of dive frequency
relative to depth and time of day. Because time is estimated, the
plot shows only relative placement of the peaks, rather than absolute placement relative to dawn and dusk.

TABLE 9.2. Dive-bout characteristics for South African fur seals.

Female no.	No. of bouts	% Dives excluded*	Dives/bout		Bout duration		Dives/hr. in bouts		% Bout underwater	
			x̄	Range	x̄ (h)	SD	x̄	SD	x̄	SD
1	10	9	30.1	6–78	2.1	1.4	18.2	9.0	60	21
2	14	4	67.4	5–165	3.6	2.4	15.3	7.1	61	15
Both combined	12 (2.8)	6.5 (3.5)	51.9	(50.4)	3.0	2.2	16.5	7.9	60	17

Note: Values in parentheses are SDs.
* Dives excluded from bout analysis by the 18 minute dive-bout criterion.

TABLE 9.3. Summary of dive effort.

Female no.	Dives/24 h	Ashore after last dive (h)
1	76	24
2	217	3

Note: Based on an analysis from the first to the last dive.

but the number of dives for the trip to sea and for any 24-hour period were much different (Tables 9.1, 9.3). Finally, seal 2 continued to dive until she was near shore, making the last dive about three hours before her observed landing (Table 9.3).

DISCUSSION

Information on South African fur seal food habits is sparse and was not collected concurrent with this dive study in space or time. According to Rand (1959), the seals depart in small groups. Once at sea, they disperse and usually feed individually except on a concentrated food supply. One such concentration is fish in purse seines where fur seals may fill the net by leaping over the cork line to "steal" fish (Shaughnessy et al., 1981). This habit has caused much enmity with fishermen.

We observed that the seals returned to shore as single animals and as small groups. The swimming rate of these groups was notably high and the animals "porpoised" to breathe. They did not seem to deviate their path from when we first sighted them on the horizon until they reached shore.

Rand (1959) concluded from stomachs of animals shot at sea that feeding activities occupied only a fraction of the feeding trip. However, our data, especially for seal 2, disputes this conclusion since this animal was diving much of the time it was at sea. Rand also concluded that the seals had about three large meals for their 5 days at sea. Again, the dive records show that seals appeared to be diving in earnest at least twice daily (Fig. 9.2).

Rand (1959) concluded that the seals fed exclusively during the day. He was unable to observe or collect at night, but he did find a bimodal distribution of empty stomachs, with one peak at 0800 to 1100 hours, and another at about 1400 hours. Our work confirms that a bimodal pattern of diving occurs, but because of the uncertain time base we cannot determine whether these peaks coincide with Rand's.

Rand (1959) analyzed 245 stomachs of animals collected 150 to 300 km south of our study area. He found that 45% were empty, and that of full stomachs 79% contained fish, 83% had squid, and 19% had crustaceans. Numerically, squid predominated, but by volume fish were the most important (67% fish, 21% squid, *Loligo* spp., and 2% crustaceans). However, Rand cautioned that the estimate of squid volume from beak size was tenuous.

We suggest that seals were taking different prey at different hours and depths. The preferred diving depths of this species was 50 m or less, but frequent dives were made to depths as great as 100 m (Fig. 9.5). The changing dive depths within bouts suggest that at night seals were taking advantage of the vertical migration of prey, such as squid and hake, toward the surface. The daytime shallow dives may represent feeding on shoaling fishes such as pilchards, *Sardinops ocellata*; anchovy, *Engraulis japonicus*; or maasbankers, *Trachurus trachurus*. Daytime deep dives may have been made to take squid or hake that descend during the day.

Most deep dives preceded a diving bout of extended duration (Fig. 9.2). The seals' strategy may have been to make a few deep search dives to select the best depth distribution of prey, after which the prey was followed as it changed depths. Bout 2 of seal 2 (Fig. 9.2) is a striking example. In this bout, seal 2 made eleven consecutive dives to 200 m and then over the next 2 hours gradually shifted to depths of less than 50 m. She continued diving in this range for another 4.5 hours.

Such a deep-dive strategy agrees with the time partitioning of deep dives. The seals descend rapidly and then ascend at a much slower rate (Fig. 9.4). This slow ascent might allow them to search for prey from below. Viewed from that angle, prey are silhouetted against the back-lighted surface water. Direct observations have shown that other species of otariids capture prey by this means (Hobson, 1966).

If the size of the prey is known, some estimate of success rate can be made. In Rand's study (1959), the average weight of fish in seal stomachs was nearly 1 kg. The squid taken often weighed 200 g, but some as small as 3 g were found. If we assume that the fur seals must consume 10%–20% of their body mass per 24 hours to maintain body weight, then 8–15 kg of fish or squid are required. If we use Rand's figures of 1 kg fish or 200 g squid, then eight to fifteen fish or forty to seventy-five squid would be required each day. If seal 1 fed exclusively on 1 kg fish, then only about 10%–20% of the dives were successful. If the seal fed on squid only, its catch rate would have had to be at least one squid per dive. By the same calculation, seal 2 must have failed to capture fish or squid on at least 60% of its dives, and very likely the failure rate was much higher (i.e., 90% if the seal had been feeding exclusively on 1 kg fish).

Finally Rand (1959) found that the two most common types of bony fish in his study were pilchard and maasbankers. In the 20 years since his study, pilchards, anchovy, and horsemackerel stocks have declined precipitously because of increased take by commercial fisheries (Shaughnessy, 1979; Burger and Cooper, 1984). During this same period the fur seal population expanded and is presently growing at a rate of about 3.9% per year (Butterworth et al., in press). The rise in this commercial fishery may partly explain the differences between Rand's (1959) findings and our dive records some 20 years later.

SUMMARY

Diving behavior of the South African fur seal was studied in 1977 at Kleinsee, a large mainland colony in the Republic of South Africa. Two records, one for each of two individuals, were obtained. The duration of foraging trips was longer for instrumented than for uninstrumented females ($\bar{x}$ = 5–6 versus 2.9 days, Chapter 8). The transit times could not be calculated because the baseline did not show landing and departure times. The total dives per record varied from 313 to 968. Feeding occurred in two peaks daily. However, the time of these peaks, including the portion of dives that occurred at night, could not be determined precisely because the time base on the instruments was estimated. The dive-bout criterion was

18 minutes. Females made on average twelve dive bouts of 3 hours duration on a trip to sea. The dive rate was 16.5 dives per hour, but rates as great as 40 dives per hour were recorded. Animals spent about 60% of each bout submerged. Most dives were continuous descent and ascent, although on some dives the animals spent 1.5 minutes at the greatest depth attained. Dives lasted on average 2.1 minutes, with a maximum of 7.5 minutes. The mean depth of all dives was 45 m and the maximum depth was 204 m. The most frequently attained depth was 50 m or less, but dives to 100 m were common. The correlation between depth and duration of dives was good (r^2 = 70.6%). Surface intervals were longer after deep dives, and were highly variable after shallow dives. The activity budget at sea could not be analyzed because the baseline did not show details such as resting.

10 Attendance and Diving Behavior of South American Fur Seals during El Niño in 1983

≅ *F. Trillmich, G. L. Kooyman, P. Majluf,*

and M. Sanchez-Griñan

INTRODUCTION

When we studied the diving and attendance behavior of the South American fur seal in Peru in January and February 1983, the strongest El Niño (EN) in over 100 years was in progress (Cane, 1983). Sea surface temperature (SST) at Punta San Juan, our study site, averaged 22.4 ± 0.8°C (mean ± SD; range 21.0–24.5°C; Pesca Peru, unpubl. data), while in normal years average January SST is 15.5°C and February SST is 16.0°C (Zuta et al., 1978). These high temperatures resulted from a massive influx of warm water coming from the west.

The warm water influx results from a decrease in the atmospheric pressure gradient between the eastern subtropical Pacific and Indonesia. This gradient change relaxes the trade winds and generates a gigantic Kelvin wave that crosses the Pacific in less than 2 months. When this wave reaches the South American coasts, the sea level rises, the thermocline is depressed, and the mixed surface layer becomes thicker. Coastal upwelling continues, but the water transported to the surface is warm and poor in nutrients (Cane, 1983; Kerr, 1983; Fonseca, 1983).

Phytoplankton, which is homogeneously distributed in the mixed layer, is directly affected by these changes. When the thermocline and the mixed layer are deep, the nutrients and light available for photosynthesis decrease. The resulting reduction in primary productivity causes proportional reductions in growth and the reproductive success of zooplankton, fish, and all organisms in the higher trophic levels of the ecosystem (Barber and Chavez, 1983; Fonseca, 1983), including sea birds (Murphy, 1936; Idyll, 1973; Boersma, 1978; Schreiber and Schreiber, 1983). It also brings economic crisis to the Peruvian fishing industry; the fish either disappear or cannot be caught by normal methods (Paulik, 1971; Schaeffer, 1970).

Data from echo soundings (IMARPE, unpubl. data) show that fish that normally live near the surface or migrate toward it during the night stay down in cold subsurface waters below the thermocline and away from intolerably high surface temperatures. To indicate the extent of this effect, the 14°C isotherm was 300 m deep at long. 85°W (off Peru; Toole, 1983) in October 1983, whereas it is normally at about 175 m (Meyers, 1979).

Such drastic changes must affect the hunting success of nightly feeding fur seal mothers and may lead to a negative energy balance. Thus collection of data on fur seal feeding behavior in 1983 constituted a unique natural experiment on the effect of varying food availability on maternal behavior. This study provides the first data on the effect of EN on a marine mammal, and shows that many fur seal females under such conditions were unable to obtain enough energy to support themselves and a dependent young.

MATERIALS AND METHODS

This study was made at the guano bird colony at Punta San Juan (lat. 15°22' S. long. 75°11' W) between 10 January and 12 February 1983. Fur seals are protected inside the guano bird reserve, but are nevertheless frequently disturbed by people and are easily stampeded. To avoid massive disturbances during the attendance study, we chose to observe animals in a cove with about 60 m of shoreline that was made inaccessible by steep cliffs all around.

Censuses were made from the cliff top with 8× or 10× binoculars. Adults and 1- or 2-year-olds could easily be distinguished, but the sexes were usually impossible to distinguish among young fur seals and were sometimes uncertain for adults of intermediate size.

For marking, blown eggs filled with a commercial hair bleach (Clairol Born Blonde) were thrown at the seals from the cliff; four pups and four females (not related to each other) were marked in this way. The study area was searched for marked animals at least five times daily. All females suckling pups were always carefully checked. Adults that were not seen were assumed to be absent, and marked pups that were not found were assumed to be without their mothers. On many days observation in the study area was almost continuous. The durations of presence and absence of females were measured to the nearest half day.

All dead animals were noted during the checks for attending females. Within one day, carcasses of pups were either opened by vultures or were visibly bloated. After about 3 days the carcasses had disintegrated completely. Double-counting of carcasses was thus avoided.

Activity budgets of females with pups or older young were recorded using instantaneous sampling as described in Chapter 11. Time budget observations were made from a distance of 20–50 m using binoculars whenever necessary. Mothers with pups were observed for 35 hours, mothers with yearlings for 40 hours, and mothers with older young for 8 hours.

The body condition of pups was recorded subjectively. Pups were judged to be in poor condition if the bones of the pelvic and shoulder girdle were protruding. In well-nourished pups these bones were deeply embedded in fat.

A TDR, radio transmitter, and flipper tags were placed on one adult female that lacked a pup. The animal was first stalked, hoop netted, and then restrained following the procedures described in Chapter 2. The TDR was on the animal from 15 to 28 January. Drug-induced immobilization was used for recapture because of the fur seals' wariness to approach and the difficult terrain at the recapture site. A telinject 3 ml syringe was shot at the animal from about 30 m distance. The dart contained 300 mg ketamine, 20 mg xylazine, and 150 IU hyaluronidase. Within 2 minutes the animal was immobilized. The seal was mobile again within 2 hours and remained in the area for the next 24 hours.

Blood samples were collected to determine whether blood conditions were measurably affected by the ongoing EN. Samples were taken from eight pups, one immature, and three adult female fur seals. Blood from pups was collected by cardiac puncture. Blood from adults and the immature were drawn from the rear flipper or from the iliac sinus. Samples were immediately capped and placed on ice until they were analyzed one hour later. Standard procedures were used to determine hematocrits and hemoglobin concentration. Oxygen dissociation curves were obtained for whole blood by the mixing method (Edwards and Martin, 1966; Lenfant et al., 1969; Scheid and Meyer, 1978). The blood gas equilibrations were performed in an Instrumentation Laboratory IL 237 tonometer at 37°C. Partial pressures of carbon dioxide (pCO_2) and oxygen (pO_2) were determined in a Corning pH/blood 161 Gas Analyzer at 37°C and calibrated with two humidified gas mixtures. One gas mixture

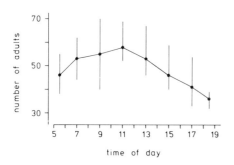

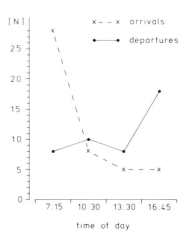

Fig. 10.1. Daily fluctuation in number of adult fur seals in the study area. Averages and ranges from five censuses on 13, 21, 28 January, and 4 and 12 February.

Fig. 10.2 (at right). Distribution of arrivals and departures of females during daylight hours grouped into four time blocks: 0715 = 0530–0900; 1030 = 0901–1200; 1330 = 1201–1500; 1645 = 1501–1830. Arrivals, N = 44; departures, N = 44.

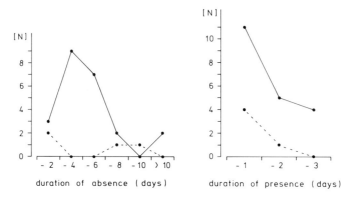

Fig. 10.3. Distribution for duration of (left) absence and (right) presence of females. Solid lines: mothers of pups. Broken lines: females without young.

contained 10% CO_2 and nitrogen, and the other contained 5% CO_2 and 12% CO_2 in nitrogen. Blood pH was measured in a Radiometer PHM 4 pH meter and glass E5021 Ultramicroelectrode.

RESULTS

The Period of Dependence of Young

Most likely, pups were weaned when they were between 1 and 2 years old. At Punta San Juan, fur seal pups are born between October and December. Many females without pups were observed suckling yearlings in December 1979 (Trillmich and Majluf, 1981), and again females were suckling yearlings in January and February 1983. Occasionally mothers were observed with a pup and a yearling simultaneously; such pups were always in poor condition. In our main study area, a pup and yearling pair was observed in a single case out of the sixty mother-and-pup pairs counted on 1 February. The pup later died of starvation. One female simultaneously suckled a male young estimated to be 2 years old, and another male of about 3 to 4 years. Young of about 2 years and older that were still suckling appeared to represent a minority of their age groups.

Daily Fluctuations in Numbers Ashore

Most adult fur seals arrived in the study area in the early morning. The numbers of adults peaked either in the 0900 or the 1100 hour census and then declined toward the evening (Fig. 10.1). This pattern of daily fluctuation in numbers agreed well with direct observations of female arrivals and departures. Arrivals showed a pronounced peak in the morning while departures had a more even distribution and peaked in the evening (Fig. 10.2).

The Female Feeding Pattern

Females with pups spent 23.5% of their time ashore and 76.5% at sea (140 female-days). One female without young and one female that had lost her pup spent 17% of their time ashore and 83% at sea (24 female-days). The distributions of the durations of presence and absence are shown in Figure 10.3. Females with pups stayed ashore for a median duration of 1 day (mean = 1.3 days; N = 26), while females without young stayed slightly shorter periods (median = 0.5 days; mean = 0.8 days; N = 5; Fig. 10.3). This difference approached significance (p = 0.057; Mann-Whitney U-test). Females with pups stayed at sea about as long per trip (median = 4.0 days; mean = 4.6 days; N = 23) as females without young (me-

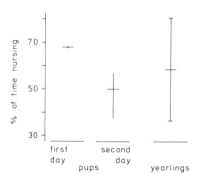

Fig. 10.4. Percentage of time ashore spent suckling by mothers of pups and of yearlings. For pups mean and range of observed values are given. First day (of female attendance): observations on two pups for 20 hours total; second day: observations on three pups for 15 hours total. Yearlings: mean ± SD of 40 hours observation on seven mother and yearling pairs are given.

dian = 4.5 days; mean = 4.9 days; N = 4). No difference was detectable in our small sample (p = 0.5; Mann-Whitney U-test).

Of all seals one year old or older that were ashore at the time of the census, on average 13% were together with their mothers; in pups this was 15%. For a median stay ashore of 1 day for a given mother, this percentage attendance leads to a calculated average stay at sea of 6.1 days, slightly higher than the measured mean duration at sea. Perhaps this indicates that mothers with older young tended to stay at sea for slightly longer periods than mothers of young pups.

Female Time Budget Ashore

Similar to the Galapagos fur seal (Chapter 11), South American fur seal mothers spent most of their time ashore lying and sitting (91.0 ± 8.5%). For thermoregulation they moved to wetted shoreline (walking = 0.7%) or into the water (in water = 0.2%). Thermoregulatory movements led to most interactions, and these accounted for 0.6% of the females' time on land. Aggressive interactions with their own young comprised an additional 0.3% of the females' time.

The proportion of time on shore spent suckling varied with the age of the young and the duration of the shore visit. Mothers of pups estimated to be 2 to 3 months of age and mothers of yearlings suckled for nearly 60% of their time ashore (Fig. 10.4). In contrast, the mother of a 2-year-old spent only 28% of its time ashore suckling (8 hours of data). The marked pups suckled 68% of the time on the first day of their mothers' attendance and only 50% of the time on her second day ashore (Fig. 10.4). Similar effects could not be evaluated for yearlings since we observed no marked mother and yearling pairs and could therefore not determine the mothers' previous attendance time.

Body Condition and Mortality of Young

During our study period most fur seal pups were in poor body condition. In early February only 8% of the pups were judged to be in good condition, 25% were in intermediate condition, and 68% in poor condition (N = 170). Pups in poor condition weighed on average 5.5 ± 1.2 kg (N = 4).

Many of the pups in poor condition died during our study period, and one of the marked pups died after a 10-day continuous absence of the mother. Of about seventy pups in the study area, at least 29 (41%) were found dead on land during 22 days. This number did not include dead young washed out to sea. The mortality rate appeared to increase during the observation time; during the first 11 days twelve pups died, while during the subsequent 11 days seventeen died. During the same 22-day period four yearlings out of forty yearlings and 2-year-olds (average of fourteen morning counts) were found dead from starvation.

Diving Behavior

Table 10.1 summarizes the three trips to sea by the single female from which dive data were obtained. Each successive trip was longer than the previous one, and most information came from the third and final trip, on which 698 of the 968 total dives were recorded. The first trip was not only unusually brief, but also the average dive

TABLE 10.1. Summary of three trips to sea for one South American fur seal female.

Trip no.	Total dive	Trip length (h)	Depth Aver. (m)	Depth Max. (m)	Duration Aver. (min)	Duration Max. (min)
1	85	24	63	170	3.3	5.0
2	185	47	39	81	2.8	3.7
3	698	116	27	90	2.3	7.1
Total	968					

TABLE 10.2. Activity budget for three trips to sea of one South American fur seal female.

| Trip no. | Rest (%) | Dives/h | Transit times | |
			Outbound[a] (h)	Return[b] (h)
1	4	3.5	11.0	6.0
2	0	3.9	8.0	1.5
3	2	6.0	7.5	1.5

[a] Time from departure to first dive bout.
[b] Time from end of last dive bout to return onto shore.

TABLE 10.3. Characteristics of South American fur seal dive bouts.

Trip no.	Dive bouts	Average bout duration (h)	Dives/h within bout
1	2	2.4	14
2	5	1.5	15
3	14	3.1	14

depth was more than twice that of the following two trips. The deepest dive (170 m) was also made on the first trip. Dive durations overall averaged 2.5 minutes and the maximum dive time was 7 minutes. When removing the TDR, we noted that the animal had lost about 5 kg body weight since the instrument was attached.

When the seal went to sea, she swam continuously for 7.5 to 11 hours before diving (Table 10.2). For the remainder of her time at sea, she remained active almost constantly. Even on the longest trip of 4.8 days, she was swimming or diving all but 2% of the time. In all trips the rate of dives per hour for the whole sea period ranged from 3.5 to 5.5. The interval from the last dive to the return ashore ranged from 1.5 to 6 hours.

The dive-bout criterion for this animal was 12 minutes. The average bout duration ranged from 1.5 to 3.1 hours, and the dive rate within a bout averaged fourteen dives per hour for all three trips (Table 10.3).

The most frequently attained dive depths were between 11 and 20 m, and between 21 and 30 m (Fig. 10.5). About 55% of all dives were within these ranges. Dive frequency declined rapidly at greater depths, with fewer than 1% of all dives to depths greater than 90 m. Almost all dives occurred between 2000 and 0700 hours

South American Fur Seal

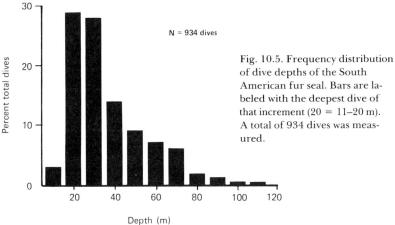

N = 934 dives

Fig. 10.5. Frequency distribution of dive depths of the South American fur seal. Bars are labeled with the deepest dive of that increment (20 = 11–20 m). A total of 934 dives was measured.

South American Fur Seal

N = 934 dives
Night = 1900–0600

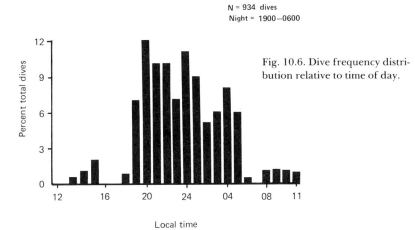

Fig. 10.6. Dive frequency distribution relative to time of day.

(Fig. 10.6). After 2000 hours diving activity rose sharply and remained elevated until 0700 hours, when a sharp decrease occurred. During the night hours the most frequently recorded depth interval was 21 to 30 m, while during the day dive depth was highly variable (Fig. 10.7). The sudden increase in dives and the predominance of deep dives in the early evening compared to other hours are shown in Figure 10.8.

South American Fur Seal

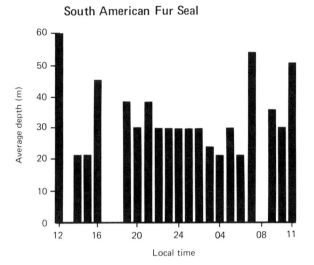

Fig. 10.7. The most frequently attained dive depth relative to
the time of day for the South American fur seal.

TABLE 10.4. Hematological parameters for South American fur seals during EN conditions.

	Pups	Older pups[a]	Immature[a]	Adult females
Sample size	7	1	1	3
Age (months)	2–3	4–5	18	—
Weight (kg)[b]				
Mean	5.4	8.4	17.5	30–40
Range	4.7–6.5	—	—	—
Hemoglobin (g%)				
Mean	14.5	14.0	9.0	16.8
Range	12.4–18.1	—	—	16.5–18
Hematocrit (%)				
Mean	44.1	40.0	24.0	49.3
Range	39–53	—	—	46–51

[a] Captured 24 April 1983. All others captured between 15 January and 11
February 1983.
[b] Weight estimated by eye.

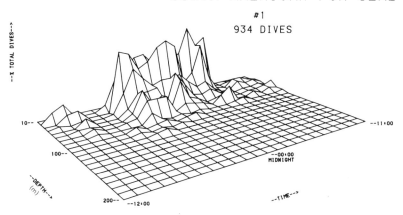

Fig. 10.8. Three-dimensional plot of dive depth, time of day, and number of dives for 934 dives, including all 3 trips to sea of one South American fur seal female.

Blood Chemistry

Table 10.4 gives the mean values for hemoglobin concentration and hematocrit for the fur seals. The half saturation (p 50) value for the adults was 26.0 torr (Fig. 10.9).

DISCUSSION

The South American fur seal is another nonmigratory species in which the period of maternal investment lasts for a year or longer (see Chapters 11 and 13), thus buffering the pup's early ontogeny against slight accidents and environmental uncertainties.

Censuses during daytime (Fig. 10.1), arrival and departure times (Fig. 10.2), and the dive record (Figs. 10.6 and 10.8) taken together prove that this species forages mostly at night, as do most other fur seals. In comparison to the closely related Galapagos fur seal during normal years, these females spent many consecutive days at sea, suggesting that travel costs to and from the foraging areas were high relative to the nightly gain from foraging activity. Although we have no data on foraging-trip duration in normal years, we would expect it to be much shorter, since fish are usually available close off-shore (Johanesson and Vilchez, 1980). Neither duration of shore visit nor the time spent suckling when ashore (Fig. 10.4) indicated

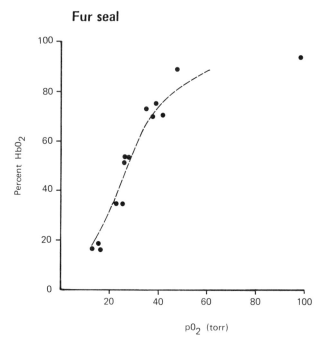

Fig. 10.9. Oxygen dissociation curve for three South American fur seals at pH = 7.4, pCO_2 = 45 torr, temperature = 37°C.

that these long absences were in any way compensated by increased milk transfer from mother to pup during attendance periods (compare with the similar data for the Galapagos fur seal, Chapter 11). The poor body condition and high mortality of pups corroborate this conclusion and suggest that, unlike the northern fur seal, the pup-rearing behavior of this species is not adapted to long periods of maternal foraging. Apparently the quality of milk and the uptake and storing abilities of the young become insufficient if mothers repeatedly remain at sea for more than 5 days.

Strong EN events apparently led to reduced foraging success of females and disrupted normal periodic patterns of female attendance and foraging. At least two factors contribute to this breakdown of the system: (1) absolute density of prey items in the surface layers may be strongly reduced; (2) prey at great depth can only be caught at high energetic cost (long diving time, reduced success rate per dive). These and perhaps other factors may change the benefit to cost ratio of foraging and may induce females to rest in the foraging area during daytime instead of returning to the colony. Overly long stays at sea and/or reduced milk quality and volume may then quickly lead to loss of the pup.

The dive data obtained from a single, nonsuckling female may not accurately characterize the shore and sea cycle of lactating females. However, the duration of stays ashore or at sea did not differ significantly between females with and without pups (Fig. 10.3a, b). Presumably, the dive behavior would also be similar since the means of finding and catching fish would be the same for suckling and nonsuckling females. This assumption is based on the premise that similar durations at sea mean the animals forage in areas where fish distribution and abundance would be the same.

If we assume that the female swam at 2 m per second (Chapter 15), then the feeding areas may have been as much as 50 to 80 km from the colony. However, the interval from the last dive to arrival ashore (1.5 hours) may better reflect the usual distance from the colony. A 1.5-hour swim time would correspond to about 11 km distance. The 7-to 11-hour interval between departure and the first dive may represent searching within this 11 km range for prey that, due to the EN, was difficult to find. We interpret the female's obvious weight loss over the 11 days from release to recapture as evidence of low success in finding food. Her lean condition was similar to that of many other adult and immature seals in the colony.

Despite weight loss and possible poor hunting success, the female adhered strictly to nocturnal hunting rather than attempting to feed throughout both day and night (Figs. 10.6, 10.8) The deepest dives occurred early in the evening (Fig. 10.8) and may have represented initial feeding attempts prior to the vertical migration of fish to the surface. Once feeding began, the diving frequency and dive depth (about 30 m) remained relatively constant throughout the night (Figs. 10.6, 10.7, 10.8), suggesting that the distribution and abundance of fish remained uniform. Because of the EN conditions, we suspect that dive frequency and depth were both greater than normal. However, the dive depths were not as great as we expected them to be; the female did not make any exceptionally deep, serial dives such as northern and South African fur seals make. This result is surprising since the fish population had probably moved to greater depths and, based on her observed weight loss, she had been unsuccessful in obtaining adequate food within the depth range she used.

The steady loss of weight by the female may not have had much effect on her dive abilities. The blood samples obtained from pups and adults showed O_2 capacity, hemoglobin, hematocrit, and dissociation curves to be approximately the same as those measured for other otariids (Ridgway, 1972; Wells, 1978; Lenfant et al., 1970), suggesting that the diving female probably had a normal blood condition despite her weight loss. If so, then as discussed in more detail in Chapter 15, her blood O_2 stores were probably normal and her aerobic dive limit was not affected. Consequently most of her dive capacities, such as dive depth, duration, and frequency, should have been normal.

SUMMARY

Attendance and diving behavior of the South American fur seal were studied at Punta San Juan, Peru, in January and February 1983. This population faces a tropical environment, quite unlike the more temperate environments experienced by other populations of this species. The study was conducted during EN conditions. We found that many females were unable to support themselves and their dependent young. Low foraging success apparently led to extended trips to sea, acute malnutrition, and eventual starvation of pups and yearlings. Pups were born from October to December. Animals attended the breeding sites throughout the year; there was no evidence of an annual migration. The interval from parturition to weaning was 12 to 24 months. Weaning was slow and not always complete; some females suckled a yearling and a newborn simultaneously. The animal that initiated weaning was not determined. No data were obtained on the attendance pattern before parturition, the interval from parturition to copulation, trips to sea before copulation, or number of visits to land prior to weaning. The duration of most visits to shore was 1.3 days. In the study period females spent 24% of their time on shore, and they spent a maximum of 60% of this time suckling, depending on the age of the young. Females departed for sea in the evening and arrived on shore in the early morning. Foraging absences lasted 4.7 days, but because this was an EN year, such durations may have been longer than normal. No data were obtained on increases in feeding-trip duration throughout the season. Nonmothers had slightly shorter stays on shore than did mothers (0.8 days), but trips to sea were about equal in length.

Blood oxygen capacities, hemoglobin, hematocrit, and dissociation curves appeared to be normal for otariids. Nevertheless, due to the presumed scarcity of food caused by EN, 70% of the pups were in poor condition and pups suffered a 42% mortality over 22 days of observation.

Diving records were obtained for three trips to sea for one individual. Two trips were short and one trip (4.8 days) was about as long as for uninstrumented animals. The transit times were 7.5 to 11 hours outbound, and 1.5 to 6 hours returning. The number of dives per trip to sea varied greatly, depending on trip duration. Diving activity occurred throughout the night (88% of all dives occurred then), with no dawn or dusk peaks. The dive bout criterion was 12 minutes. The female had an average of seven dive bouts per trip, with durations from 1.5 to 3.1 hours, and a dive rate of fourteen dives per hour. The portion of dive bouts spent submerged was not calculated. All dive bouts were shallow. Dives were continuous ascent or descent with no time spent at maximum depth. Dives lasted on average 2.5 minutes with a maximum duration of 7 minutes. The mean depth of all dives was 29 m and the maximum was 170 m. The most frequently attained dive depths were between 11 m and 30 m. No correlations were made between depth and duration, nor between surface interval and depth of dive. Females spent 2% of their time at sea resting, but time spent swimming and diving was not calculated.

11 Attendance Behavior of Galapagos Fur Seals ≅ *F. Trillmich*

INTRODUCTION

Galapagos fur seals permanently live close to the equator. They are the only fur seals that experience constant day length and minimal fluctuations between seasons. Tropical conditions are ameliorated by the influx of a cold surface current from the east, by the Peru or Humboldt current, and by an upwelling of the Cromwell countercurrent on the west coasts of the archipelago. Strong east winds along the coast of South America drive the Peru current, and this in turn induces the flow of the Cromwell countercurrent. Massive influx of these cooler waters is restricted to the so-called *garua* (drizzle) season, from approximately June to December. From January to May these currents are weak or absent, and surface water temperatures then rise throughout the archipelago (Houvenaghel, 1978).

On land the fur seals live at the edge of a hot lava desert, where during the day they are forced to retreat into shade or the water. Rock surface temperatures may reach 60°C and sea temperatures are unusually high for a fur seal environment. One of the coldest places of the Galapagos is Cabo Hammond, on the exposed west coast of Fernandina Island, where sea surface temperatures averaged 19 ± 2°C (1977, measured every 5 days during the cold season, between 15 August and 13 November) and never dropped below 15°C. The highest sea temperature measured near a fur seal colony was 25°C at Pinta Island in May 1978.

Since the fur seals remain near their breeding colonies all year, they must cope with these high temperatures. Due to reduced upwelling, primary productivity is lowest during the warm season (Maxwell, 1974), and very likely the abundance of fur seal prey is also low.

I began to investigate the Galapagos fur seal to determine whether this species would show peculiar adaptations to its low latitude environment. I hoped that the study of this special case, through contrast with the better-known subpolar species, might produce insights into the feasibility of adaptive shifts in life history patterns.

Fig. 11.1. Female Galapagos fur seal with yearling on a balance mounted in the shade of a wooden tunnel.

METHODS

This study was done at Cabo Hammond (long. 91° W, lat. 0°28′ S) on the southwest corner of the westernmost island of the Galapagos archipelago (Fig. 1.12). The coast in the study area consisted entirely of lava—either lava flows or large boulders smoothed by wave action. Two small sand beaches interspersed in this lava were never used by adult fur seals.

Observations were made in 1977, 1979, 1980, and 1981 during the reproductive seasons, which lasted from approximately mid-August until mid-November. Individually marked female and pup pairs were followed for up to 72 days. A long period of dependence and movements out of the area by females with young of 60 days or older made it impossible for us to follow a mother and young pair continuously for the whole suckling period. Instead, the behavior of mothers with known-age pups, yearlings, and 2-year-olds was sampled during the reproductive periods. In 1979 observations were made on (1) four females with pups for 192 female-days (mean = 48 days; range = 34–72 days); (2) four females with yearlings for 161 female-days (mean = 40 days; range = 36–47 days); and (3)

TABLE 11.1. Amount of time budget data on fur seal females
with young of various ages.

Age of young	Total observ. time (h)	No. females observed	Sex of young male: female
1 day	46.7	4	3:1
5 days	47.2	4	4:0
10 days	48.9	5	4:1
ca. 20 days	20.4	2	2:0
ca. 30 days	32.1	2	2:0
ca. 60 days	36.6	3	3:0
1 yr	106.5	8	4:4
2 yrs	117.9	9	4:5

four females with 2-year-olds for 203 female-days (mean = 51 days; range = 30–64 days). In 1980 observations were made on five females with pups for 257 female-days (mean = 51 days; range 42–59 days). In 1981 six females with pups were observed for 221 female-days (mean = 37 days; range = 32–41 days).

Females were weighed by placing wooden tunnels with false bottoms (40 x 120 cm) in the colony. These tunnels provided shade for the female, and the false bottom, which was supported at each end by a scale, gave a measure of the seal's weight. Fur seal females readily accepted these retreats, and some females with pups were weighed repeatedly (Fig. 11.1). Readings were taken when a female was resting in the middle of the false bottom without touching either wall.

Attendance of females was checked at least at dawn and dusk and usually five to ten times in between. On many days observation in the study area was continuous. Females not actually seen arriving or leaving were assumed to have arrived or left in the middle of the interval between observations. This rule was operational but introduced a bias, especially for females leaving or returning at night. Such females were calculated to have returned or arrived at about midnight, whereas limited night observations and the TDR records indicated departures shortly after dusk and returns shortly before dawn.

Activity budgets of females with pups, yearlings, or 2-year-olds were recorded using instantaneous sampling every minute on the minute (Altmann, 1974). Females in constant attendance with newborn pups (<1 week old) were observed continuously during all daylight hours. Females with older young were observed from their arrival until sunset, and again the next day if they were still present. A few protocols were made during moonlit nights. Observations were made from a distance of 2–10 m. As the animals were well accustomed to the observer, this proximity did not cause any noticeable disturbance. Most behavior categories were self-explanatory; "lying down while suckling" was recorded as "suckling." As most suckling occurred while the female was lying down, the category called "lying down" by definition decreased as suckling time increased. Total observation times for females with young of various ages are given in Table 11.1.

RESULTS

Seasonal, Lunar, and Daily Fluctuations of Female Numbers

SEASONAL. Based on four visits to the study colony that occurred outside the reproductive season (December 1976, February and June 1978, and April 1981), no strong seasonal changes were seen in female numbers that would suggest an annual migration. Corrected for the phase of the lunar cycle (see section below), the total number of fur seals ashore was about equal in the 1977 reproductive period as in February and June 1978. Individually known females and their young were observed in the colony on all visits. Some had moved several hundred meters away from the study area, but this also happened during the reproductive period.

LUNAR. On a shorter time scale, numbers ashore showed a strong periodicity that correlated with the lunar month (Trillmich and Mohren, 1981). The data in Figure 11.2 were taken during the first month of the reproductive period. At the second new moon, female numbers ashore were higher than at the first because of the more frequent presence ashore of females with pups. The periodic changes in female behavior which produce these rhythmic fluctuations in numbers are documented below.

DAILY. Daily fluctuation of the shore population of fur seals varied with the lunar cycle. Except at full moon, when 90% or more of the individually marked females were found ashore, female numbers were always highest between 0800 and 1600 hours (Fig. 11.3), indicating that females preferred to be on land during the daylight hours and to forage at night. This pattern was most detectable at new moon and 3 days after full moon. It was hardly noticeable at half moon when minimal numbers were on shore at any hour of the

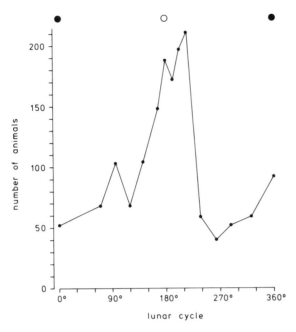

Fig. 11.2. Change in numbers of females over one lunar month (22 August to 20 September 1979). Censuses were made in the morning along 530 m of coastline at Cabo Hammond, Fernandina Island.

day. The full moon census represents a special case. At full moon the number of animals ashore exceeded the number of shaded resting sites; consequently, the numbers ashore dropped near noon as many females spent the noon hours resting near shore. The noontime decline occurred whenever the population was large, except on days with strong winds (the new moon census in Fig. 11.3 was such a day). Thus lunar and daily patterns were influenced by insolarization and wind speed. The full and new moon curves of females ashore were roughly symmetrical around noon, whereas the census of females ashore 3 days after full moon appeared asymmetric.

The Period of Dependence of Young

Births at Cabo Hammond occurred between August and November. Young regularly met with their mothers and suckled until about 2 years old or older. The birth of a new pup did not cause the weaning of dependent yearlings or, in many cases, of 2-year-olds. In such cases the newborn pup either starved to death within about a

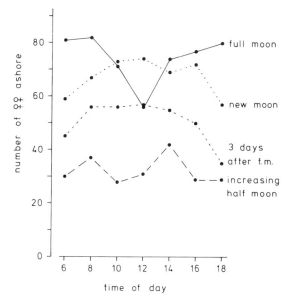

Fig. 11.3. Changes in female numbers ashore during the day-light hours at various stages of the lunar cycle. Counts made between 18 August and 9 September 1980 along 180 m of coastline. The new-moon census was made later in the reproductive season than the full-moon census (second new moon in Fig. 11.2); because of the constant presence of females with newborn pups, the numbers ashore were relatively high at this new moon.

month or was killed by its sibling (in about 5% of the cases). In about 20% of the cases, females temporarily suckled a pup and an older young together, but eventually the younger pup was outcompeted and starved to death. One exceptional case where two young were raised simultaneously is shown in Figure 11.4.

Dependence of the young sometimes extended beyond the second year. In fact, only in 1981 was weaning complete for the majority of 2-year-olds. Other observations indicated that young were often weaned in their third year of life. In three cases of known-age 3-year-olds (one male, two females), the male and one female were weaned before the onset of the reproductive period (at the end of their third year). The other female was weaned in a series of fights with the mother shortly after the latter had given birth again. If a female did not pup at the end of the third year, her 3-year-old sometimes continued suckling sporadically. One 4- or 5-year-old female

Fig. 11.4. Pregnant female suckling a yearling and a 3-year-old simultaneously.

was observed suckling even though it was about equal in body size to its mother.

The Feeding Pattern around Parturition

Before giving birth, females apparently stayed at sea for relatively long periods. One marked, pregnant female without dependent young was absent for 14, 10, and 9 days before coming ashore for parturition. This pattern closely corresponded with the attendance of one nonpregnant female without young, which was absent for 11, 10, and 9 days. Females appeared quite fat when they came ashore for parturition. They stayed in the colony for up to 2.5 days before giving birth.

After birth the females stayed with the newborn for the first 5–10 days (twelve mothers of male pups averaged 7.4 ± 1.2 days, ten mothers of female pups averaged 7.2 ± 1.2 days). During the first 2 days after birth, the mothers remained in almost continuous contact with their pups. Later on they sometimes left the pup for 5–20 minutes to cool off in the near-shore water.

During this time of continuous attendance, one female lost about 14% of her postpartum body weight of 32 kg (Fig. 11.5). This weight loss averaged 2% of body weight per day, or 0.64 kg/day.

After four foraging trips in a fortnight, she had regained 95% of her immediately postpartum weight. Judging from partial records obtained for three other individuals, this weight curve may be typical for females with newborn pups.

Females came into estrus 8.2 ± 1.9 days (N = 25) after birth of the pup. They usually copulated only once with a territorial male. Before copulation most observed females left their pup once for a night of foraging. Females left for these first foraging trips in the afternoon or evening and returned in the early morning. Soon after estrus, females established a regular schedule of feeding trips (Fig. 11.6). Only the first trip to sea and the first two periods of attendance thereafter were significantly shorter or longer, respectively (Table 11.2), than similar measures for females with older young for the same phase of the lunar cycle (see below). The tendency of females to make short feeding trips after parturition may be greater than this analysis suggests, since in some cases the first, short, nightly feeding trip may have gone unnoticed.

Timing of Arrivals and Departures of Mothers

Hourly arrival and departure times of females with pups, yearlings, and 2-year-olds showed no clear correlation with the lunar cycle. The distributions for mothers of pups were not significantly different among all 3 years (Chi-square test; $p > 0.1$) and have therefore been combined (Fig. 11.7A). Similarly, the distributions for mothers of yearlings and of 2-year-olds were indistinguishable (Chi-square test; $p > 0.1$) and were combined (Fig. 11.7B). Females with pups and females with older young, however, clearly differed from each other in their arrival and departure times (Chi-square test; $p < 0.02$ for arrivals; $p < 0.001$ for departures). While both groups of females arrived and departed in maximal numbers in the morning and evening, respectively, mothers of pups showed much broader distributions of arrival and departure times.

This preference for spending the day ashore and the night at sea was borne out again in the analysis of days when females made a choice between land and sea, i.e., days when they either left from or arrived at the colony or did both within one day. In 1979 and 1980 females with pups spent on average 59% of their time ashore in daylight and 41% during the night, whereas they spent 38% of their time at sea in daylight and 62% at sea at night.

This skew in the amount of day versus nighttime spent ashore or at sea was even more marked for females with yearlings, which spent 72% of their time ashore in daylight and 73% of their time at

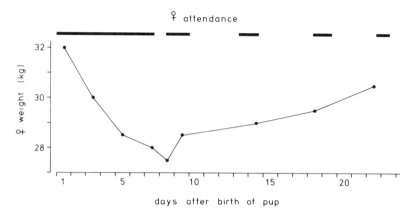

Fig. 11.5. Weight changes of a female over the first 22 days of her pup's life as related to her attendance ashore (days onshore indicated as black bars).

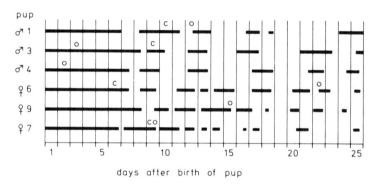

Fig. 11.6. Transition from permanent attendance ashore after birth of a pup (day 1) to the normal foraging routine. Circles are full moon; C is day of copulation (observed in only four cases). Key on the left indicates sex and number of pup.

sea during the night. The difference between females with pups and females with yearlings was significant (Mann-Whitney U-test; p = 0.008 for daytime on land, p = 0.032 for nighttime at sea). The TDR records also showed that females swam and dived most actively during the night (Chapter 12).

Time Ashore and Distribution of Attendance Duration

The partitioning of time between land and sea differed according to year and to the age of the female's offspring. For this analysis only

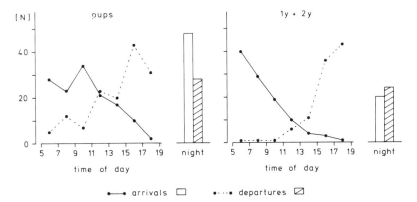

Fig. 11.7. Arrival and departure times of females. (A) Distribution of times for females with pups (data from four females in 1979, five females in 1980, and six females in 1981). (B) Distribution of times for females with yearlings and 2-year-olds (four each, 1979). Times are given as average times for 2-hour blocks (i.e., 6 = 0500–0659 hours). The columns give number of arrivals (a) and departures (d) during nighttime, i.e., between 1900 and 0500 hours.

TABLE 11.2. Relative duration of the first three absences and attendances of females after parturition.

Absence or presence	Compared to average absence			Compared to average presence		
	Shorter	Longer	p	Shorter	Longer	p
First	8	0	0.004	1	8	0.02
Second	6	3	n.s.	1	8	0.02
Third	5	4	n.s.	3	6	n.s.

Notes: The duration is compared to the average duration of absence or presence of females with older pups for the given lunar phase shown in Fig. 11.9 (Binomial test; one-tailed probabilities). n.s. = not significant.

records of females with young older than 10 days were used. In 1979–80 females with pups were ashore for $36.5 \pm 4.4\%$ of total observation time (nine females; 359 female-days), while in 1981 they spent $52 \pm 6.4\%$ of observation time ashore (six females; 161 female-days); this difference was highly significant ($p < 0.001$; Mann-Whitney U-test). In contrast to mothers of pups, females with yearlings and 2-year-olds spent only $31.4 \pm 4.9\%$ of their total time ashore (eight females; 364 female-days). This difference was significant even when only the 1979–80 data for mothers of pups were

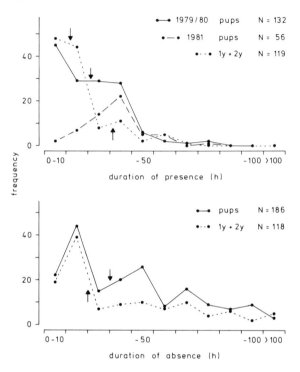

Fig. 11.8. Distributions of durations for attendance (above) and absence (below). For mothers of pups (left) distributions of attendance durations in 1979–1980 and 1981 are given separately. Vertical arrows point to medians of distributions. Total numbers of observations are indicated above the graphs.

tested against data from mothers of older young (p < 0.025; Mann-Whitney U-test).

The differences in time ashore for females with pups, yearlings, and older young were reflected in the distributions for the attendance durations (Fig. 11.8). The distributions for females with yearlings and 2-year-olds were not significantly different (Chi-square test; p > 0.1) and have therefore been combined. A greater sample of mothers of 2-year-olds may, however, reveal some differences. The distributions for females with pups in 1979–80 and in 1981 were very different from those of mothers with older young (Chi-square test; p < 0.001). Also, the median durations for mothers of pups (1979–80 = 21.5 hours; 1981 = 31.3 hours) were greater than for mothers of older young (only 12.0 hours).

Attendance times varied greatly both among mothers of pups (often about a day, but range = 1.5–72.5 hours) and mothers of older young (range = 2.5–59 hours). This great variability was correlated with the lunar cycle (Fig. 11.9). Clearly, all mothers remained ashore longest near full moon and spent the least time with their young at about decreasing half moon. Females with pups stayed ashore longer than females with older young (p < 0.004; randomization test) at all but one time (days 22–24) of the lunar cycle.

Time Absent and Distribution of Absence Duration

Time absent could not be considered a direct measure of foraging effort for these females since observations of absence times did not permit the conclusion that females indeed spent all this time at sea. Females carrying TDRs went ashore elsewhere after foraging in seven (22%) out of thirty-two cases. In four cases (13%) they spent a day resting in the water away from the study colony. Thus, when females were not foraging, they returned to their pups in only 65% of all cases, and rested elsewhere in 35%. Generally, females with pups (1979–80) spent less time away from their young than females with older young (63.5% and 68.6%, respectively; p < 0.05; Mann-Whitney U-test). In 1981 females with pups spent only 47% of their time away from the young, implying differences between years in attendance patterns. Females without young may have stayed at sea for long periods. One such female was observed with barnacles (*Conchoderma virgatum*) attached to her guard hair and vibrissae, indicating an uninterrupted stay at sea of at least 1 or 2 weeks.

Females with pups had a greater median duration of absence (32.5 hours, 1979–80; 30.6 hours, 1981) than females with older young (20.5 hours). This difference was not as clearly reflected in the distribution of absence duration as was the case with attendance times. In fact, the two distributions (Fig. 11.8) were not significantly different, nor were the distributions for mothers of pups in 1981 compared to mothers of older young in 1979 (Chi-square test; p > 0.1).

Since females with yearlings or 2-year-olds spent more total time at sea than females with pups, the latter obviously went to sea less frequently. The average number of foraging trips per 700 hours (ca. one lunar month) was 10.6 for females with pups in 1979–80, 10.3 in 1981, and 13.4 for females with yearlings and 2-year-olds (p = 0.026; Mann-Whitney U-test).

Time at sea also showed a strong phase relationship with the lunar cycle (Fig. 11.9). Females made the shortest foraging trips

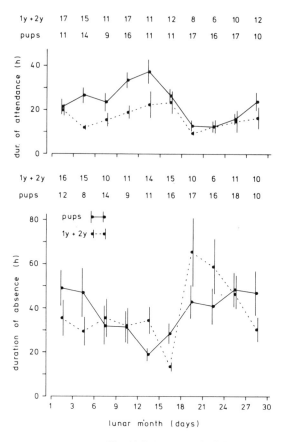

Fig. 11.9. Lunar periodicity in duration of attendance (above) and absence (below) for females with pups and females with yearlings or 2-year-olds. Note the differences in attendance times between females with pups and females with older young. Data were averaged for 3-day intervals. Bars are Standard Error of the mean; numbers above curve are number of observations per 3-day period. Days 1 and 30 are new moon.

around full moon and the longest between decreasing half moon and new moon. In this respect females with pups and with older young were not significantly different.

Female Time Budgets on Shore

Females were essentially resting when on land. Walking occupied 1.7% and grooming 1.9% of their time ashore. Females with young older than about 5 days regularly defecated and, around noon, cooled off in the water. Time in the water amounted to 2.5% of their attendance time. Pups did not accompany their mothers when they went to cool off, but yearlings and 2-year-olds often did. Social interactions with fur seals other than their own young took very little of a female's time (0.9%), attesting to the low density in the colonies. The few interactions between females occurred mostly in competition for preferred resting places in the shade; interactions with males consisted mainly of aggressive defense against subadult males and relatively few interactions with territorial males. No interspecific interactions occurred on land.

Females lay in any position while suckling, but they rarely suckled while sitting. Lying down and suckling accounted for 70%–96% of a female's time ashore. The amount of time spent suckling increased with the age of the young up to 1 year, then declined again in 2-year-olds (Fig. 11.10). Yearling and 2-year-old males suckled consistently more than female young of the same ages (p < 0.025; Mann-Whitney U-test; Fig. 11.11). Suckling time corresponded with average weight, since in both age categories males were significantly heavier than females (t-test; p < 0.02 for 2-year-olds; p < 0.001 for yearlings).

If a female stayed ashore for more than a day, which happened most around full moon, then on the second day ashore time spent suckling decreased (Fig. 11.11). This effect was very obvious among young from 30 days to 2 years of age. On the mother's second day ashore, young pups (15–60 days old) often left their mothers for extended periods, but older young, especially yearling males, remained in almost constant contact with the mother. Second-day suckling bouts for these older young became increasingly shorter and pauses between bouts increased gradually, thus reducing total suckling time.

Despite the enormous suckling time of yearlings, they must have foraged for themselves occasionally since their feces quite often were not the color of pure milk-feces. Two-year-olds often foraged for themselves, suckled much less than yearlings (Fig. 11.11), and separated more often from their mothers. However, a 2-year-old female wounded by a shark regressed to near total dependence on its mother's milk.

DISCUSSION

The observational data on the timing of female attendance (Fig. 11.7) and the direct data on swimming and diving times from the TDRs show that females forage almost exclusively at night. Because

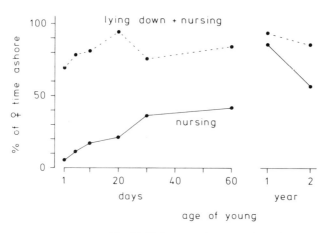

Fig. 11.10. Increase in proportion of time spent suckling with age of the young. Data from male young and from the first day of a female's attendance only.

we know from the TDR records that almost all of this foraging is done near the surface (Chapter 12), two hypotheses suggested earlier (Trillmich and Mohren, 1981) appear to account for the observed relation between lunar phase and time spent at sea (Figs. 11.2, 11.9).

First, food availability might vary due to changing patterns of vertical migration by the fur seal's major food organisms, cephalopods (mainly onychoteuthids; Clarke and Trillmich, 1980) and small schooling fish. Lunar illumination apparently inhibits the upward migration of some commercial fish stocks (e.g., *Trachurops crumenophthalma* in Colombia; F. Köster, pers. commun.) and of the larger larvae of the rock lobster, *Panulirus cygnus* (Rimmer and Phillips, 1979). If prey of the Galapagos fur seal also stayed deeper at higher illumination levels, the benefit of feeding might be exceeded by the metabolic cost of the deep diving and searching effort, thus making a rest ashore the better strategy (Chapter 15). A similar cost to benefit reasoning has been applied to the observation (Chapter 6) that the Antarctic fur seal feeds mostly at night, adjusting its diving depth to the nightly rise of krill (see also Iwasa, 1982).

A second hypothesis is that feeding fur seals silhouetted against the moonlit surface may be in greater danger from shark attacks than seals feeding at new moon. However, the prey of fur seals would also be silhouetted against the surface, making feeding easier. In this conflict situation, constant alertness to potential preda-

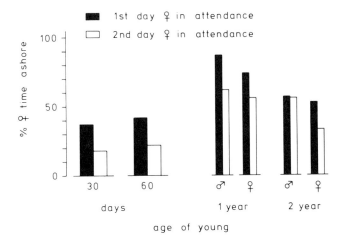

Fig. 11.11. Change in proportion of time spent suckling during the first and second day of a female's attendance with young of various ages and both sexes.

tory attacks might reduce foraging efficiency (Grubb and Green-wald, 1982; Milinski and Heller, 1978) to the extent that staying ashore during moonlit nights might be the better strategy.

Even if these hypotheses, singly or in combination, account for the periodically changing average duration of female attendances and absences, a great variance still exists around the means for each phase of the lunar cycle (Fig. 11.9). This variance must relate to the regulation of foraging effort in response to female needs (e.g., trying to maintain body weight; Fig. 11.5) and to the changing demands of her young when the abundance of prey is variable and its distribution is patchy.

Variability of prey abundance can at present only be inferred. For example, during the second of the two lunar half-months shown in Figure 11.12, many feeding frenzies of Blue-footed Boobies, *Sula nebouxii*, and one massive stranding of *Sardinops sagax* and *Scomber japonicus* were observed. Prey abundance near the colony was probably high. This proximity of food enabled the female to return more frequently to her yearling. Thus short-term increases in food availability apparently induce a female to return more often to her young.

In years of unusually good feeding conditions (such as 1981, when yearlings of both sexes were almost as heavy as 2-year-olds in previous years), females apparently regulated feeding effort by

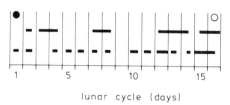

lunar cycle (days)

Fig. 11.12. Attendance (black lines) and absence (open) of one female with a yearling in two consecutive lunar half-months.

staying ashore longer (Fig. 11.8) rather than by shortening their foraging trips. This comparison between years also suggests that females may spend less time ashore and make more foraging trips per month during the warm season (January to May) if the fur seal's food supply is, indeed, lower then (Chapter 15).

Yearlings made greater energy demands on their mothers because they suckled much longer than pups (Figs. 11.10, 11.11) and obtained more milk from their mothers during a given stay ashore (unpubl. data). To facilitate this higher energy transfer, mothers of yearlings shortened their stays ashore, went to sea more frequently, and spent more of their total nighttime foraging, but they did not significantly lengthen individual foraging trips (Fig. 11.8).

In conclusion, females apparently responded to short-term fluctuation of food abundance by adjusting the length of individual foraging trips. They responded to long-term changes either in energy demands of the young or in food abundance at sea by changing the durations of visits to shore.

By extrapolation, a mother weaning her young at the end of its second year will probably have made about 300 foraging trips and spent about 3,000 hours suckling. These are crude estimates because we lack information on the feeding pattern during the warm season, and because age at weaning, which fluctuates between 1.5 and 3.0 years, appears to depend on the sex of the young and on feeding conditions.

Young of the Galapagos fur seal remain dependent longer than young of any other fur seal; the reasons for this are unknown. While the nonmigratory habit of the species makes the mother-young bond easy to maintain, this habit does not explain why young do not become independent earlier. Perhaps a seasonally reduced food level makes it difficult for yearlings or 2-year-olds to find sufficient food independently. However, food abundance in Galapagos waters is unknown. The feeding niche, which is restricted in both time and space (Chapter 12), may also contribute to longer dependence. Finally, predation pressure by sharks might tend to make prolonged maternal investment profitable. By prolonged suckling, females may significantly diminish the need of young to forage for themselves, and thereby reduce the risk of losing young through predation.

SUMMARY

Attendance behavior of the Galapagos fur seal was studied in three seasons between 1977 and 1981 at Cabo Hammond, Fernandina Island, Galapagos archipelago. This colony site is the coldest in the archipelago. The emphasis of this study was on the apportionment of females' time while raising pups, and on the influence of some environmental factors on females' activity budgets. The reproductive season extended from August to November; animals attended the breeding sites throughout the year with no evidence of an annual migration. Weaning occurred at 18 to 36 months of age, depending on environmental conditions, although in one year (1981) weaning was complete for the majority of 2-year-olds. The mother initiated weaning, which was a slow process. Some mothers suckled older young and newborn pups simultaneously. Before parturition, females stayed at sea for several long periods (9–11 days each). The interval from parturition to copulation was 8.2 days, during which time females usually made a brief trip to sea at night. A rough estimate of total maternal effort devoted to raising one young would be about 300 foraging trips to sea and about 3,000 hours of suckling. Postpartum visits to land lasted 0.5 to 1.3 days, depending on the age of the young being suckled. Suckling time increased with the age of the young and reached a maximum of 70%–80% of attendance time among mothers of yearling males. Females departed for foraging trips in the evening hours and returned in the morning. However, this pattern was altered by the lunar cycle; many females stayed onshore during full moon nights. Foraging-trip duration varied as a function of the lunar cycle. It was longest (50–70 hours) around new moon and shortest (10–20 hours) during full moon; stays ashore followed the reverse pattern. Mothers of yearlings spent less time ashore than mothers of young pups (10 days to 3 months) by making more foraging trips per unit time, but individual foraging trips were of about equal duration for both groups of mothers.

12 Diving Behavior of Galapagos Fur Seals ≅ *G. L. Kooyman and F. Trillmich*

INTRODUCTION

The purpose of this study was to determine the offshore feeding characteristics of females which were suckling pups. Since this species is not migratory and is one of the smallest marine mammals, it was of particular value to determine the: (1) duration of trips to sea; (2) time to reach the feeding area; (3) common feeding depths; (4) duration of feeding periods; (5) dive frequency rate within bouts; and (6) preferred feeding times for comparison with larger, migratory species.

The study was done at Cabo Hammond, Fernandina Island (Fig. 1.12), during October and November 1980, the *garua* or drizzle season in the Galapagos. Fernandina, one of the driest of the islands, had only a few mornings of overcast or drizzle. Details about the weather and physical features of the island are described in Chapter 11. Because the dive study was conducted during a single lunar cycle, the powerful lunar cycle effect, seen in the duration of shore visits (Chapter 11), could not be assessed in offshore feeding behavior.

METHODS

Capture and recapture techniques were the same as described in Chapter 2. The Galapagos fur seal, however, showed less response to humans than any other marine mammal in our experience, perhaps because it is fully protected. The females were easily hoop netted, and because of their small size (25–30 kg) we could carry them a few meters away from the colony to attach and remove the recorders. Once this 10- to 15-minute procedure was completed, the seal would return immediately to its pup. Soon thereafter an observer could sit near the seal to determine whether the recorder was well mounted. Captures and recaptures caused little disturbance to the remainder of the colony.

As in all other species, except the South African fur seal, baseline chatter caused by the 300 psi bourdon tube was distinct enough to indicate when the seal went to sea, when it rested at sea, and when it

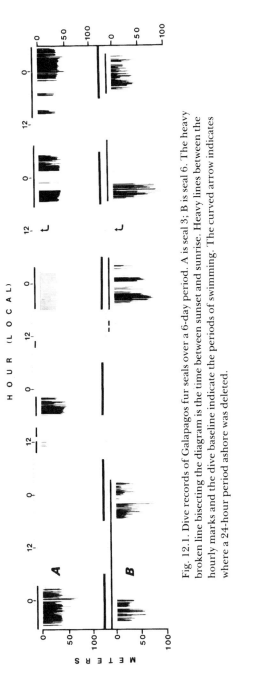

Fig. 12.1. Dive records of Galapagos fur seals over a 6-day period. A is seal 3; B is seal 6. The heavy broken line bisecting the diagram is the time between sunset and sunrise. Heavy lines between the hourly marks and the dive baseline indicate the periods of swimming. The curved arrow indicates where a 24-hour period ashore was deleted.

TABLE 12.1. Summary of Galapagos fur seal dive records.

Female no.	Total dives	Record length (h)	Average depth (m)	Maximum depth (m)	Maximum duration (min)
1	214	78	11	65	3.6
2	209	156	17	68	6.1
3	607	160	36	112	7.7
6	415	161	39	98	3.6
7	1	278	—	110	—
8	81	24	45	99	2.6
9	124	62	58	85	3.9
11	246	120	29	75	3.0
13	358	146	21	115	—
15	211	294	11	35	5.2
16	162	246	19	55	5.0
17	91	98	18	65	2.4
18	53	140	20	75	4.0
20	111	120	16	95	3.0
Total	2883	2083	—	—	—
Average	206	149	26	82	
SD ±	162	78	14.3	23.7	

was ashore (Chapter 2). Thus the TDR records could be partitioned into time spent ashore, resting at sea, swimming at the surface, and diving.

RESULTS

Seals came and went to sea in a routine manner; their dive activity was intense, and swimming and diving patterns at sea were continuous (Fig. 12.1). Of the seals studied, numbers 7, 15, and 17 appeared to have suffered about 10% weight loss while the TDR was attached. A total of 2,883 dives was recorded in fourteen dive records (Table 12.1). Many additional dives, perhaps made during surface feeding, were too shallow (5 m) and too brief (30 seconds) to be resolved by the recorder. The average depth recorded of all distinct dives was 26 m, the median was 24.5 m, and the maximum was 115 m. Most of the dive durations were so brief that a reliable measure was not possible. Therefore, only a few of the maximum durations were measured to derive an upper limit. Maximum dive durations ranged from 2.4 to 7.7 minutes (Table 12.1).

For much of the time that the recorders were attached, the seals were ashore. The total sea time per trip averaged 16.4 hours (not

TABLE 12.2. Activity patterns during trips to sea for Galapagos fur seals.

Female no.	Trips to sea	Trip duration (h)	Dives/trip	Dives/h	Rest (%)	Time to first dive (min)	Ashore from last dive (min)
1	2	11.4	107	9.4	0	192	108
2	2	58.0[a]	105	1.8	26	150	—[b]
3	4	12.5	152	12.2	0	135	129
6	5	10.5	83	7.9	0	39	96
8	1	24.0	81	3.4	0	540	288
9	2	17.0	62	3.6	3	86	—[b]
11	3	20.0	82	4.1	0	50	66
16	5	27.0	30	1.1	2	160	—[b]
17	3	13.0	30	2.3	0	99	100
18	2	21.0	26	1.2	0	180	180
20	1	7.6	111	14.6	0	120	36
Average		16.4	79	5.6	—	159	125
SD		6.4	39.7	4.7	—	13.6	78

[a] Not included in average.

[b] Could not determine from the record when the seal returned ashore.

including the 58-hour trip of seal 2, which was well outside the normal range of 7.6–27 hours; Table 12.2). In some cases a female did not return to shore after a night of diving but continued to swim throughout that night and the following day (seal 6; Fig. 12.1). In other instances seals came ashore elsewhere for short periods. Most seals swam constantly while at sea (Table 12.2; Fig. 12.1) with the exception of seal 2, which rested 26% of its time at sea, mostly during the day.

After the seals departed from the colony, the average time before diving bouts began was 2.7 hours; the average time from the end of the last dive bout until the seals returned to shore was 2.1 hours (Table 12.2). Dive bouts were defined by a log survivor curve (Chapter 2) with the second inflection point at 25 minutes. The probability of ending an interdive interval was significantly correlated with average diving depth ($r^2 = 0.9$; $p < 0.05$; $N = 5$ females), indicating that shallow dives were on average followed by shorter interdive intervals. This effect can be seen even within a single dive bout. For seal 3, dives to more than 60 m were followed by significantly longer surface intervals than were dives to 40 m (Mann-Whitney U-test; $p < 0.001$).

The average dive frequency within bouts was 15.7 dives h^{-1}, and bouts lasted an average of 2.9 hours (Table 12.3). Since on average

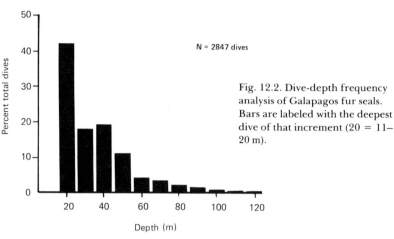

Galapagos Fur Seal

Fig. 12.2. Dive-depth frequency analysis of Galapagos fur seals. Bars are labeled with the deepest dive of that increment (20 = 11–20 m).

N = 2847 dives

TABLE 12.3. Characteristics of Galapagos fur seal dive bouts.

Female no.	Dive bouts	Average bout duration (h)	Bouts/trip	Dives/h within bout
1	3	5.6	1.5	21.4
2	4	2.4	2.0	16.0
3	3	3.7	0.8	21.9
6	8	3.6	1.6	13.7
8	3	1.9	3.0	12.8
9	3	2.1	1.7	13.9
11	5	2.5	1.7	14.2
16	3	3.1	0.6	16.1
17	3	1.5	1.0	13.1
18	1	1.6	0.5	13.1
20	1	4.4	1.0	14.0
Average	3.4	2.9	1.4	15.7
SD	1.9	1.3	0.7	3.1

1.4 such bouts (Table 12.3) occurred on trips to sea that averaged 16.4 hours each, obviously much time was spent at the surface.

The frequency distribution for dive depths showed a single peak at <20 m (40% of all dives; Fig. 12.2), a marked drop and shoulder at depths of 21–50 m (10%–20% of all dives), and another distinct drop in dives deeper than 51 m (10% of total dives).

The frequency distribution for diving by hour of the day showed a strong tendency for nocturnal foraging (Fig. 12.3). Diving began after 1800 hours (sunset) and ended by 0600 hours (sunrise). Diving was most intense between 1900 and 2300 hours.

Three different analyses for the relationship between dive depth and hour of the day showed no marked shifts in dive depths over time (Figs. 12.4, 12.5). Most dives of <20 m occurred before midnight. This was true of dives in all other depth ranges as well, although dives between 31 and 50 m seemed to have a bimodal distribution, with the greatest number occurring before 2300 hours.

DISCUSSION

The swimming speeds of this species are unknown, but based on its size we estimate this velocity to be 2 ms^{-1} (see also Chapter 15). If no surface feeding (i.e., unrecorded dives) preceded the distinct dives and if seals swam directly to their feeding areas, then the average distance to feeding areas was 19 km (range = 4.7–65 km; Table 12.2).

Some of the night swimming in this species may have been related to feeding at the surface. If so, feeding may have begun earlier and continued longer than the distinct dives on the record indicate. These shorter transit times would place the feeding areas closer to the colony than the above estimates suggest. However, four factors argue against the occurrence of daytime surface feeding as a precursor to night feeding: (1) most of the night activity was spent diving—swimming without diving occurred mainly during the day; (2) seals preferred departing to sea shortly before dark and returning soon after daylight (Chapter 11 and Fig. 12.1); (3) if food had been readily available at the surface during the daytime, the local sea lions that dive during the day to average depths of 37 m (Table 14.1) should also have taken advantage of it; and (4) no clearly defined gaps occurred between evening dive bouts characterized by decreasing depths and dawn bouts characterized by increasing depths, as in the Antarctic fur seal (Chapter 7). These observations suggest that (1) the fur seal's hunting strategy resulted in at least 10–20 m deep dives; (2) during the day prey species descended as light levels increased; and (3) the seals' swim activity represented needs other than feeding.

The ratio of time spent at sea to time spent on shore was calculated for each female to estimate the efficiency of feeding and suckling cycles. Seals number 1, 3, 6, and 20, which went to sea nightly and returned to shore the following day, were among the most ef-

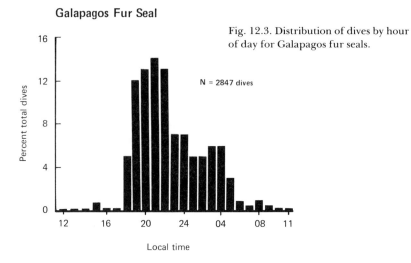

Fig. 12.3. Distribution of dives by hour of day for Galapagos fur seals.

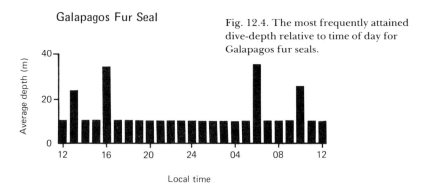

Fig. 12.4. The most frequently attained dive-depth relative to time of day for Galapagos fur seals.

ficient. Another ratio, dive time to time at sea, showed that the same seals were also more efficient than others in sea time spent diving (70% versus 10%–50% ratio for seals 8, 9, 16, and 17). If our arguments concerning surface feeding are correct, then most of the surface swim time of females 8, 9, 16, and 17 probably represented search or transit time during which few prey were captured.

FEEDING BEHAVIOR

Regurgitations collected from seven adult fur seals contained squid and fish remains, but only the squid remains were analyzed.

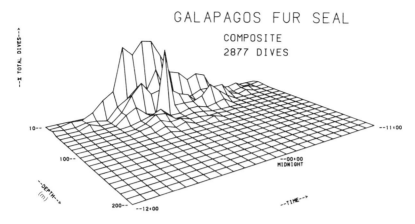

Fig. 12.5. Three-dimensional frequency analysis for depth of
dive, time of day, and number of dives. The figure includes
data for fourteen individual females.

The predominant species by number and mass was *Onychoteuthis
banksi* (Clarke and Trillmich, 1980). The average mass of these
squid, based on beak size, was 12 g. The second most prominent
squid were in the family Ommastrephidae and their average size,
based on beak size, was 150 g. Both species occur near the surface.

The dive habits of the seals probably reflect the most common
depth ranges of the prey species identified (squids). Most dives were
to depths shallower than 30 m and occurred before midnight (Fig.
12.5). Dives between 30 and 40 m were less abundant but were of
nearly uniform distribution throughout the night. If seals hunt by
sight, the occasional dive to these depths may help them locate prey
patches by silhouetting them against the night sky. The rare dives
deeper than 50 m occurred most often between 2100 and 2200
hours, but lacked a clear pattern from which their function could be
inferred. Perhaps these dives functioned to locate prey patches before the seals had completed their ascent to the surface.

The success of prey capture was estimated using several assumptions: (1) dive bouts lasted an average of 2.9 hours and totaled 46
dives per bout; (2) since there were 1.4 bouts per night (Table 12.3),
there were 64 dives per night-feeding session; (3) the energetic requirements of mothers was 17% of body weight per day (this value
is an overestimate for Galapagos fur seals as it is based on northern
fur seals for which pups grow twice as fast, water and air temperatures are much lower, and females spend much longer periods at

sea); and (4) the fur seal's mass was 30 kg. If the food requirement is 17% of body mass, then 5 kg of prey were captured per day.

Based on these assumptions, if food were caught on every dive the average amount taken per dive would be 78 g, an average of seven *O. banksi* per dive or one Ommastrephidae every other dive. However, it is not likely that every dive is successful in producing food. The success rate of king penguins, *Aptenodytes patagonicus*, has been estimated as only 10% of all dives (Kooyman et al., 1982). However, these birds commonly dive to depths >50 m. If the success rate of these fur seals were only 10%, then about 780 g of squid or fish (sixty-five squid if all were *O. banksi*) would have to be caught on each successful dive. For such small prey it seems more likely that the number caught per dive would be smaller and the number of successful dives greater than these estimates. If the prey were Ommastrephidae, then four to five squid per dive on 10% of the dives may have been cost effective, even on deep dives where the chances of failure may be greater.

It is likely that deep dives are less successful than shallow dives because there is less light and the search time is longer. Seals begin deep dives without knowing precisely where the prey is. A search phase would be required during or after descent which would leave little time for pursuit of prey after its detection. Prey that were not captured would have more time to escape before the seal's subsequent dive. Seals may be able to see prey by ambient light or bioluminescence at the start of dives to 20 m or less. The success rate of deep versus shallow dives is discussed in a more detailed, comparative way in Chapter 15.

SUMMARY

The diving behavior of Galapagos fur seals was studied near Cabo Hammond on Fernandina Island, Galapagos archipelago, in October and November 1980. Records were obtained for thirty trips to sea made by fourteen individuals. The average duration of trips, 16.4 hours, was within the range of durations for uninstrumented females (0.5 to 1.3 days). The outbound transit times averaged 2.7 hours, and return transit times averaged 2.1 hours. Females averaged 79 dives per trip to sea but ranged from 26 to 152, depending on trip length. The nightly pattern of diving was not strongly bimodal but tended to have peaks at dawn and dusk. About 95% of all dives occurred at night. The dive-bout criterion was 25 minutes. Females averaged 1.4 dive bouts on each trip to sea. Bout durations averaged 2.9 hours, and the dive rate within bouts was 15.7 dives per hour. The portion of dive bouts spent submerged was not calculated. All dive bouts were shallow. Dives were continuous descent and ascent, with no time spent at the maximum depth. The dive durations were too brief to measure accurately. However, the longest dives were measured to determine maximum dive duration (7.7 min). The mean depth of all dives was 26 m, with a maximum of 115 m. The most frequently attained dive depth was less than 20 m. The relationship between depth and duration of dives was not calculated. However, the shallowest dives tended to be the briefest, and these were followed by the shortest interdive intervals. The activity budget on trips to sea comprised 2.8% resting, 24% diving, and 73.2% swimming. The temporal occurrence of rest bouts was not measured.

13 Attendance Behavior of Galapagos Sea Lions ≅ *F. Trillmich*

INTRODUCTION

Galapagos sea lions live under nearly the same environmental conditions as the Galapagos fur seal (Chapter 11) but cope with these conditions quite differently. Sea lions prefer flat beaches that are sandy or rocky, where they have easy access to relatively calm waters and can spend the hot hours around tidepools or, at some colonies, in the shade of vegetation (mostly *Cryptocarpus pyriformis*). Thermoregulatory problems tend to be less acute for seal lion female and pup pairs than for fur seals because of easy access to calm waters, which are safe even for small pups. Sea lion pups enter the sea when only about a week old, whereas fur seals spend their first 3 to 4 weeks on land. This difference may be due to dangerous breakers and currents along the rugged, rocky coasts preferred by fur seals (Chapter 11). The aim of this study was to provide data for comparing the maternal strategy of the large Galapagos sea lion with that of the much smaller, sympatric fur seal.

METHODS

Most of the work was done on Santiago Island at Punta Baquerizo (lat. 0°16′ S, long. 90°52′ W) during June and July 1977. Whenever no island name is mentioned in the Results section of this chapter, data refer to this 1977 period. These data were supplemented by observations on Santiago Island between 21 June and 21 July 1976, 16–19 November 1977, and 20 January to 3 February 1978. Additional observations were made at Punta Suarez on Española Island (lat. 1°22′ S, long. 89°44.5′ W) from 19 January to 7 March 1977. On Santiago Island, colonies were situated on sand beaches, whereas on Española Island the animals used a flat lava terrace having channels and tidepools.

On Santiago Island in 1976, thirty-nine pups were observed (not all from birth), and in 1977 twenty pups were studied from birth, ten of them for more than 20 days (mean = 31; range = 22–42 days). Five of the latter pups were weighed daily, and the other fifteen were weighed once a week. All were weighed with an accuracy

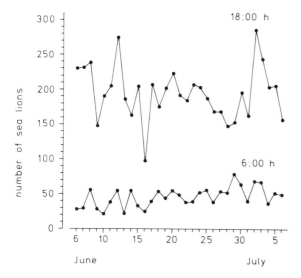

Fig. 13.1. Fluctuation of sea lion numbers in the colony on
Punta Baquerizo, Santiago Island, between 6 June and 6 July
1977. Counts give total number of animals excluding pups. Upper curve: evening counts; lower curve: morning counts.

of ± 100 g. The same twenty pups were observed again in November 1977 and in January-February 1978. Pups were individually
marked by numbers clipped into the hair of their backs with scissors; female were individually recognizable by natural marks on
their skin or by voice peculiarities.

On Santiago Island, presence or absence of females was recorded
every day at 0600 and 1800 hours, and about five times in between.
In 1977 the colony was observed continuously on about 50% of the
days. Regular night observations were impossible to make because
the scissors marks on pups could usually not be recognized at night.
On Española Island, twenty-two pups 5 to 7 months old were tagged
with Dalton Jumbo tags. These tags could sometimes be read at
night by flashlight without causing undue disturbance of the animals. Young of this age moved around much of the Punta Suarez
area. Only eleven of the tagged animals were seen almost daily, but
even they were frequently not found during checks. Because the females usually left before dawn and returned after dusk, no attendance records were obtained at Punta Suarez.

Due to the difficulty of observing known females, the partitioning
of time between land and sea was analyzed only for mothers of the

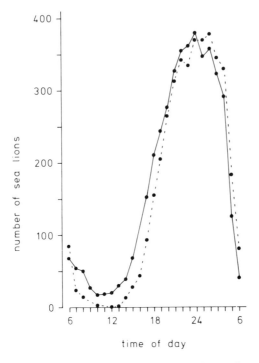

Fig. 13.2. Daily fluctuation of sea lion numbers in the Santiago colony. Counts through 24 hours on two full-moon
days. Circles and dashed lines: 30 June 1977 (reproductive
period, cold season). Circles and solid line: 24 January 1978
(nonreproductive period, warm season).

five daily-weighed pups on Santiago Island in 1977. For these females, unobserved morning departures of animals known to be
ashore the previous evening were assumed to have occurred at
0500; unobserved night arrivals of females not present by evening
were assumed to have occurred at 1900 hours. These hours, 0500
and 1900, represented respectively the midpoints of the decrease
and increase in numbers ashore as observed during the two full-
moon night counts. When both arrival and departure were unobserved, the visit was assumed to last 8 hours. The evidence for such
visits is presented under Results.

Counts were made by walking along the perimeter of the colony.
Hourly counts were made throughout two full-moon nights, one in
the reproductive season and one in the warm season. Animals
younger than a year were not counted. Calling activity—vocal ex-

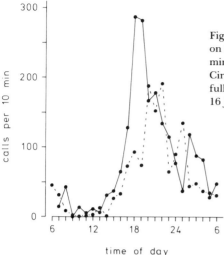

Fig. 13.3. Calling activity in the colony on Santiago. Calls were counted for 10 minutes at the beginning of every hour. Circles and dashed lines: 30 June 1977, full-moon night; circles and solid line: 16 June 1977, new-moon night.

changes that signify reunion of mothers and young—was measured by counting for a period of 10 minutes all calls of adults, immatures, and yearlings that were clearly audible from a fixed position in the colony. Calling activity was used as an index of nighttime arrivals of mothers.

RESULTS

Fluctuations of Female Numbers Ashore

SEASONAL. Sea lions did not appear to migrate in any regular fashion, although some dispersal of yearlings from island to island did occur. Counts on Santiago Island in June and July 1976 and 1977, in November 1977, and in January-February 1978, showed no clear change in sea lion numbers between the cold (reproductive) and warm seasons. Numbers sometimes varied widely from day to day (Fig. 13.1). The average number of sea lions counted in the evenings of June and July 1977 was 173 ± 42 (mean ± SD; N = 52), and in February 1978 it was 149 ± 53 (N = 11).

Individually known females and their tagged young were resighted in all study colonies at all times of the year, which suggests that they stayed there year-round. Also, of about 250 tagged pups and yearlings, more than 95% of the resightings made in the first 24 months of life came from their home colonies. However, some tagged juveniles did show some dispersal. Several yearlings from the Santiago Island colony were seen on Rabida Island, 23 km away, between observations on their birth colony. One yearling tagged on South Plaza Island swam to Santa Fe Island, where it was observed with its mother. A week later the same yearling was seen on Floreana Island, thus having traveled about 76 km. Such wide dispersal seems to be the exception; its exact extent cannot be assessed due to uneven sighting effort.

DAILY. Sea lions were away from the Santiago Island colony during the day and returned between 1600 and 2200 hours (Fig. 13.2) at a rate of about 70 animals per hour (18% of maximum number). They left at a greater rate of 125 animals per hour (33% of maximum number) before sunrise, between 0400 and 0600 hours. The maxima of animals ashore during the two full-moon counts were identical, further demonstrating that sea lion numbers did not change significantly between the warm and cold seasons. However, in the warm season fewer animals spent the day ashore than in the cold, reproductive season (Fig. 13.2).

Calling activity in the colony was roughly correlated with the number of sea lions present during the daylight hours (Fig. 13.3). This correlation broke down at night. Calling peaked in the evening when many females returned and reunited with their young. Thereafter it decreased greatly. A second peak of calling activity occurred between 0100 and 0400 hours—before the major exodus of animals from the colony. When most sea lions actually left the colony—between 0500 and 0600 hours—they called very little (compare Figs. 13.2 and 13.3).

LUNAR. Partial counts on one new moon and two half-moon nights (one decreasing and one increasing half moon) showed roughly similar patterns. Neither these daily fluctuations in numbers nor the counts every morning and evening over two months showed any unequivocal signs of a lunar rhythm of numbers ashore which was so obvious in the fur seals (Trillmich and Mohren, 1981).

Period of Dependence of Young

The breeding season of Galapagos sea lions was much longer than for the sympatric fur seal (Chapter 11) or for California sea lions on the California coast. The reproductive period of Galapagos sea lions shifted slightly from year to year and from island to island. For example, on Santiago Island pupping started around mid-May in 1976, and in 1977 the first pup was born on 15 June. The breeding season started earliest in the west of the archipelago (Fernandina Island: March) and latest in the southeast (Española Island: July-August). In 1977 pups were born on Santiago Island over 6–7 months, between June and November-December.

Pups molted when 4 to 5 months old and subsequently began to feed partly for themselves, as evidenced by the changing consistency of their scats. Normally pups did not appear to forage jointly with their mothers. However, in January-February 1978 pups at Santiago Island were sometimes observed returning to the colony with their mothers. On Española Island young were often observed leaving the colony with their mother but returning ashore alone shortly afterwards.

On average, female sea lions could successfully pup every year. All young suckled regularly when 6 months old, and the majority of them were weaned before 1 year of age. However, yearlings and even 2-year-olds often continued to suckle if their mothers failed to give birth that year. Of forty females for which accurate observations were made on Santiago Island in 1976 and 1977, eight (20%) were still accompanied by an older young (seven yearlings, one 2-year-old male) when giving birth again. In five of these cases the older young was driven off shortly after the new birth. In two cases the females allowed the older offspring (including the 2-year-old) and newborn to suckle simultaneously; the yearling suckled simultaneously with its younger sibling for at least one year. In the last remaining case, direct competition and fighting between the two young, possibly for milk, led to the death of the newborn.

The Feeding Pattern around Parturition

Females on Santiago Island, for which we have the best data, hauled out 1 or 2 days before parturition and gave birth in rocky parts of the colony or close to rock outcrops. They defended an area of about one body length around the newborn and frequently barked at and attacked approaching sea lions. They remained with their pups continuously for 6.8 ± 2.1 days after giving birth (N = 20). Estrus apparently occurred about 3 weeks after parturition because the females then became very attractive to small males. But as no copulations were observed for individually known females, the exact time between parturition and copulation is unknown.

Timing of Arrival and Departure for Mothers

Following the perinatal attendance, females established a routine schedule of spending the day at sea and the night ashore. Sea lions

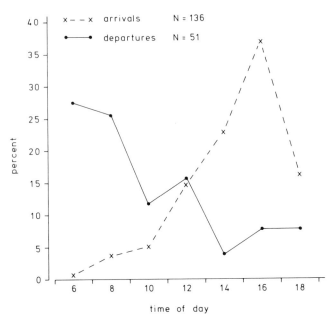

Fig. 13.4. Percentage of total arrivals and departures observed during daytime for 2-hour intervals. Note that daytime departures represent only 29% of total departures. Data from ten pups on Santiago, 1977.

of all ages and sexes (except pups) returned to the colony in the evening, many of them after nightfall, and left in increasing numbers from about midnight until dawn (Fig. 13.2). Females with pups followed much the same routine except that, in contrast to the animals in general, 84% of their arrivals occurred during the afternoon hours (Fig. 13.4). Unlike arrivals, daytime departures were rare and represented only 29% of total departures. Night observations, as well as the data in Figure 13.2, suggest that females left usually between 0400 and 0600 hours (Fig. 13.4).

Arrival and departure times were known for only a few presences and absences because mothers of pups often left before the early morning census. Of eighteen such stays ashore, females spent 66% of the time at night and 34% during the day. Of twenty-six such absences they spent 40% at night and 60% during the day. This difference was significant ($p < 0.05$; Wilcoxon test).

Some seasonal differences were found. During the warm season females on Española Island spent most of the daytime at sea and usually came ashore after dusk. The mothers of eleven regularly observed 5- to 7-month-old pups were in attendance on only 15% (N = 59) of the mornings and 14% (N = 160) of the evenings on which the young were found. In contrast, during the cold, reproductive season (June and July) the mothers of six pups on Santiago Island were in attendance on 22% of the mornings (N = 163) and on 55% of the evenings (N = 166).

The Normal Feeding Pattern

At Santiago Island the five females of daily-weighed pups spent an average of 48% (range = 38%–51%) of the total observation time ashore. Individual stays ashore, calculated by the assumptions discussed under the Methods section of this chapter, lasted between 6 and 34 hours, with a median of 13.75 hours. The time at sea, similarly calculated, varied between 6 and 58 hours, with a median of 12.0 hours. Eighteen presences with known arrival and departure times averaged 12.0 ± 7.6 hours in duration, and twenty-eight such absences averaged 17.9 ± 10.6 hours. The distributions of presence and absence durations (Fig. 13.5) were significantly different from each other (absences showed a distinct tail of long stays at sea) despite their similar medians (Chi-square test; p < .025). A cycle of attendance plus absence lasted more than 24 hours (N = 86) in only 22% of the observations. On average, females returned to their pups every night but would remain at sea every fifth night. In 42% of cases when a female was seen neither arriving nor departing, the pup gained weight overnight, proving that she had been ashore overnight. This conclusion was valid because females suckled their own pups exclusively (Trillmich, 1981).

Attendance data on females at Española Island during the warm season were hard to obtain because mothers usually returned after sunset and left before dawn, a behavior that was rare during the cold season. In nightly checks (between 2000 and 0400 hours) mothers were present in 55% of thirty-eight sightings of marked young, which suggests that the mothers of these ca. 6-month-old young returned ashore only every other night.

Weight Gain of Pups

Until at least 30 days after the perinatal attendance, male pups grew significantly faster than female pups (Mann-Whitney U-test; p < 0.025; Fig. 13.6). Male pups gained 154 ± 30 g/day; female pups gained 116 ± 40 g/day. Fasting pups lost between 107 and 288 g/24 hours with an average of 181 g/24 hours. These values were ob-

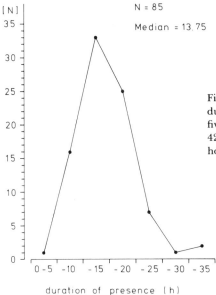

N = 85

Median = 13.75

Fig. 13.5. Frequency distributions of durations of presence and absence for five females with pups between 7 and 42 days of age. Data are grouped into 5-hour blocks.

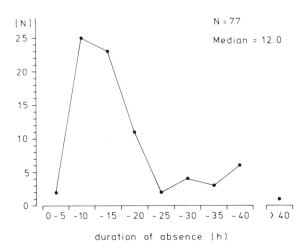

tained from three pups (weights between 6.5 and 9.3 kg) during the second consecutive day of their mother's absences, when the pups were presumably in a postabsorptive state. Pups that had drunk a lot of milk during one attendance (500–1,300 g weight gain) subsequently had increased weight loss (31 g/hour or 740 g/24 hours).

The rate of weight loss correlated with the previous weight gain (r = 0.64; p < 0.05).

The maximum amount gained by a pup during one attendance of its mother was 1.3 kg in 34 hours. This weight gain did not equal the amount of milk transferred since fasting pups lost about 200 g/24 hours. Therefore, this mother must have transferred at least 1.6 kg of milk during her attendance to produce a 1.3 kg weight gain. Sometimes a pup lost weight over 24 hours even though its mother had been with it. In the most extreme case weight loss was 300 g over 24 hours; during 12 hours of this period the mother had been in attendance.

DISCUSSION

Attendance of female Galapagos sea lions was difficult to monitor because arrivals and departures occurred mostly during the night (Figs. 13.2, 13.4). The maximum number of sea lions ashore occurred around midnight, when about twice as many were present as in an average evening count (compare data in Fig. 13.1). The diurnal fluctuation of calling activity (Fig. 13.3) further confirmed that many mother and pup reunions took place after dark. As both arrival and departure may have occurred at night, a female's attendance then may have been missed. Also, for an animal that usually returned in the afternoon, a slight shift in the arrival made mother and young reunion unobservable. Due to the synchrony of decrease and increase of sea lion numbers ashore, slight shifts in average arrival and departure times toward midnight (Figs. 13.2, 13.4) could make a colony appear deserted in the daytime. This effect was very obvious during the warm season on Española Island, where females were rarely in attendance during daylight hours. Day-to-day and even seasonal fluctuations in numbers, assessed by daylight counts, may thus be misleading indicators of actual events in a sea lion colony.

The effects of the lunar cycle, if any, on the number of sea lions ashore were not as obvious as in the sympatric fur seal (Chapter 11). Compared to the full moon counts shown in Figure 13.2, the fewest animals were ashore on one new-moon night and intermediate numbers were present during the moonlit parts of two half-moon nights. However, the data were insufficient to establish any firm relation with the lunar cycle.

The data suggest, surprisingly, that pups did not drink milk at

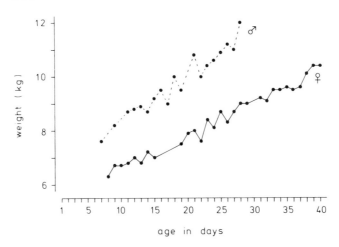

Fig. 13.6. Growth of one male and one female pup gaining weight at close to the average rate.

every reunion with their mothers. Several pups lost weight, one of them 300 g, during 24-hour periods when their mothers were known to be present (see "Weight Gain of Pups" in this chapter). Although slight milk uptake (100 to 200 g/24 hours) might have gone undetected, this seems unlikely to be the whole explanation, given the 24-hourly schedule of weighing and the limited accuracy of the scales (± 100 g). Behavioral observations showed that pups sometimes left their mothers shortly after reunion to play with other pups. Because of the short intervals between female attendances, pups may still have been satiated from milk taken up during the previous night. Mothers with small pups thus apparently formed more milk and came ashore more often than their pups needed. This interpretation is supported by the lack of any correlation between duration of female attendance and weight gain of her pup during that attendance; weight increase of pups was sometimes rapid and at other times gradual (Fig. 13.6).

During the warm season, females on Española Island spent more time foraging and made shorter and less frequent visits to shore than at other sites during the cold season. The different feeding pattern was presumably caused by the increased milk demand of the older and bigger pups. Furthermore, it is just during the warm season, when marine productivity is lowest, that the older pups need more milk for maintenance and growth. This combination may force their mothers to spend more time foraging, leading to shorter and less frequent female attendances.

For a hypothetical pup born in early July and weaned in April or May of the next year, we can roughly estimate the number of feeding trips its mother must make to raise it. Assuming that a female maintains the foraging pattern observed for mothers of young pups, she would make about 150 feeding trips during the cool season, i.e., during the 180 days from July to December. If she returned only every other night from January to April or May, she would make an additional 60 to 75 foraging trips. As young increasingly forage for themselves and demand less maternal investment, close-to-weaning females may make decreasingly frequent visits. Thus about 200 feeding trips may be made from birth to weaning. Time to weaning and number of feeding trips during this interval are much reduced compared to the sympatric Galapagos fur seal (Chapter 11).

Attendance patterns have been little studied in other species of sea lion. Peterson and Bartholomew (1967) found that early in the season—in June—California sea lion females were on land on only 50% of the observation days and that the frequency dropped to 10% of observation days in August. This frequency is certainly too low since even resident pups were observed on only 45% of the days. Early in the season females may have been in attendance every other day. The authors suggested that females attended older pups less frequently than young ones, but no quantitative comparisons with the Galapagos sea lion are possible.

Female Steller sea lions (*Eumetopias jubatus*) left their young overnight and were in attendance during the day (Gentry, 1970). Female absences, not including fifty-seven short overnight absences, averaged 2.3 days. If the overnight absences are included, the absence duration decreases to about 1.9 days. Because absence times of these females lengthened with age of the young, the attendance pattern of Steller sea lion females early in the season may be very similar to that of Galapagos sea lions.

It appears that sea lions have shorter cycles of absence and presence than fur seals. The Central Place Foraging model of Orians and Pearson (1979) predicts that for the exploitation of a patch of given quality, time in the patch should increase as traveling time to the patch increases. Because the larger sea lions swim faster than fur seals (Chapter 15), travel time to a given patch should be shorter for the former. Consequently, the ratio of travel cost to energy gained in the feeding area will be lower for the sea lions, making shorter trips to sea energetically economic. This hypothesis could explain the differences between fur seal and sea lion attendance patterns (see also Chapter 15).

SUMMARY

Attendance behavior of the Galapagos sea lion was studied at Punta Baquerizo, Santiago Island, in 1977, with supplemental observations at Punta Suarez, Española Island, Galapagos archipelago. The Punta Baquerizo site was a sandy beach, while the Punta Suarez site occupied a lava terrace. The breeding season varied in onset and duration from year to year. It usually lasted 16 to 40 weeks between June and December. Adults were in attendance at breeding sites throughout the year, which suggests that no annual migration occurred. Weaning occurred at 11 to 12 months of age. The weaning process was slow and not always total (a few females suckled both a yearling and a newborn). No data were collected on prepartum attendance patterns. The interval from parturition to copulation was about 3 weeks (exact duration unknown), during which time females made trips to sea. The duration of the first visit to land was about 6.8 days. All subsequent visits averaged 0.6 days, and about two hundred such visits were made prior to weaning. No data were collected on the portion of shore visits spent suckling by the pup. Females departed from shore in the morning hours and returned in the late afternoon or after dark. Some visits to shore were made only during the dark hours. The mean duration of absences from shore was 0.5 days. No data were collected on trends in duration of trips to sea throughout the season, but census data suggest that durations increased. No data were collected on the comparative attendance behavior of mothers and nonmothers.

Niche separation between the sympatric Galapagos fur seal and sea lion was more extensive than different habitat choice on land. While fur seals fed mostly at night and at shallow depths (Chapters 11 and 12) sea lions did most of their feeding during the day, thus also avoiding many thermoregulatory problems on land. Sea lion females returned almost daily to their pups and weaned them within one year. During the first month of life, male pups grew significantly faster than female pups. Differences between fur seal and sea lion attendance patterns are briefly discussed.

14 Diving Behavior of Galapagos Sea Lions ≅ *G. L. Kooyman and F. Trillmich*

INTRODUCTION

The general purpose of this study was to compare, for the first time, the diving behavior of two sympatric otariids, the Galapagos sea lion and the Galapagos fur seal. Because of their sympatry, resource partitioning may be critical to the coexistence of these species. Since both species live in a tropical environment where food resources are not likely to be abundant, and since both species live on the same islands and may feed in overlapping areas, competition for food resources has probably shaped different foraging strategies in the two species. We tried to characterize these patterns by collecting the same data for sea lions as previously presented for fur seals. This chapter on sea lions has also been included to suggest some general behavioral differences between sea lions and fur seals.

MATERIALS AND METHODS

The study was conducted in October and November 1980 at a site about 1 km east of Cabo Hammond, Fernandina Island (Fig. 1.12). The physical characteristics of the general region were described in Chapter 11. The sea lion colony, consisting of 300 to 400 animals, was situated on an ancient, exposed lava flow of low relief with many tidepools that were protected by an outer ridge of lava 5 m above sea level. The tidepools graded into a sandy beach mixed with many boulders. Much of the inland area was covered by low shrub, *Cryptocarpus pyriformis*, in the shade of which some animals spent the whole day. Thus the area used by sea lions extended about 200 m inland. Groups of fur seals were found wherever piles of large boulders interrupted the flat relief of this low lava.

TDRs were attached to four sea lion females ranging in mass (estimated) from 50 to 100 kg. Each was suckling a 1- to 2-month-old pup when captured in early morning hours on the inland edge of the colony. Each was drugged to a level of staggering mobility with an estimated dosage of 2–4 mg kg^{-1} of ketamine mixed with 0.3–0.4 mg kg^{-1} xylosine (Trillmich and Wiesner, 1979; Trillmich, 1983). Animals were then restrained with a neck stock and fitted

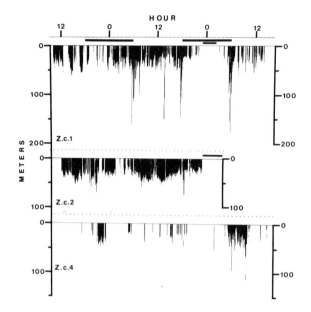

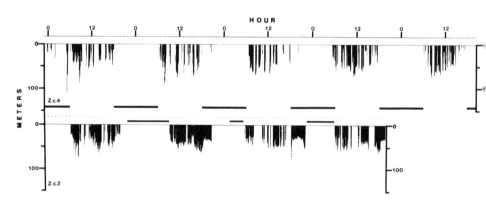

Fig. 14.1. Dive records of the Galapagos sea lion. The heavy broken line above the hourly time intervals is the time between sunset and sunrise. Heavy lines between the hourly time intervals and the dive baseline indicate rest periods.

TABLE 14.1. Summary of Galapagos sea lion dive records.

Female no.	Mass (kg)	Total dives	Record length (h)	Time at sea (h)	Average depth (m)	Maximum depth (m)	Maximum duration (min)
1	60	547	61	56	38	186	6.0
2	50	1,620	142	97	37	146	5.0
3	100	143	11*	10.5	—	20	—
4	90	589	222	145	37	115	6.0

* Recorder leaked after 11 hours at sea.

with a chest harness to which the TDR and a radio transmitter were attached (Chapter 2). The procedure from drugging to release required about 30 minutes, 15 minutes of which were spent waiting for the drug to take full effect.

Returned females were detected and located with a radio receiver equipped with a directional antenna. The instruments were usually recovered at night by carefully stalking to within 1–2 m of the unrestrained animal and cutting the harness off with a knife placed in the curve of a shepherd's hook mounted on a 1.5-meter-long staff.

RESULTS

Females left the colony 1 to 2 hours after harness attachment and usually returned at night. The capture, attachment of the harness, and release disturbed other sea lions only within 25 m of our activities. A few animals showed some interest in the TDR as instrumented females walked past.

The study produced four records, three complete and one incomplete (the TDR of female 3 failed after 11 hours at sea), totaling 436 hours of recording time and 2,899 dives (Table 14.1). The time at sea represented 67% of recording time. The females showed remarkable similarity in the average depth of dives (all at either 37 or 38 m) and maximum duration of dives (5 or 6 min), and only slightly more variation in maximum depths (range 115–186 m; Table 14.1). The average dive durations were <2 minutes. This average excluded many dives of less than 30 seconds which were below the TDR's time base resolution (Chapter 2), and which occurred with such frequency that the end of one dive obscured the start of the next. For such dives we measured depth only.

The activity patterns at sea showed some effects of capture. All first trips to sea after capture were unusually long, and dive episodes were erratic (Fig. 14.1 top). These first trips averaged 47

Galapagos Sea Lion

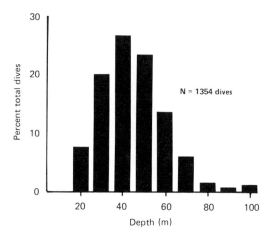

Fig. 14.2. Frequency distribution of dive depth for Galapagos sea lions. Bars are labeled with the deepest dive of the increment (20 = 11–20 m). N is the total dives in the analysis.

Galapagos Sea Lion

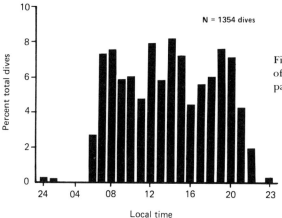

Fig. 14.3. Frequency distribution of dives by hour of day for Galapagos sea lions.

hours, while later trips lasted between 15 and 17 hours (Fig. 14.1 bottom, Table 14.2). The shorter trips, used in all analyses here, were similar in duration to the attendance data from undisturbed females on Santiago Island (Chapter 13).

The diving pattern on these apparently normal trips showed that females made between 90 and 200 dives, or 5 to 13 dives h^{-1} per trip. More than 50% of all dives were to depths of less than 40 m

Galapagos Sea Lion

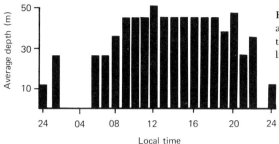

Fig. 14.4. The most frequently attained dive depth relative to time of day for the Galapagos sea lion.

(Fig. 14.2), and almost all diving occurred during daylight hours (Figs. 14.1 bottom, 14.3). Night diving was more common just after sunset than just before sunrise, and all diving activity usually ceased from 2200 to 0500 hours.

Dive depths varied less by hour of the day than for most other species. The most frequent dive depth from 2200 to 0700 hours, when few dives were made, was 30 m (Figs. 14.4, 14.5). Throughout the day and early night (0800 to 1800), when most diving occurred, the preferred dive depth was constant at 45 m. A composite plot of dives by depth and hour of day clearly showed a midafternoon and an early evening peak of activity (Fig. 14.6).

Rest at sea was relatively infrequent. Sea lion 2 did not rest while at sea, and sea lion 1 rested for only 3% of the time (Fig. 14.1). The dive record for sea lion 4 was too faint to partition into resting and swimming periods.

Transit times were very brief. The sea lions began to dive within an hour after leaving the colony, and sea lion 2 began within 10 minutes (Table 14.2). The time between the last dive and the return to shore was about twice as long as the outbound transit time.

Dive-bout criteria, derived as described in Chapter 2, ranged from 12 to 35 minutes (Table 14.3). The average dive-bout durations were between 3 and 4 hours. Sea lion 4 had on average the shortest bouts even though her dive-bout criterion was longest. In all three animals the median dive-bout durations were less than the average durations, showing that dive-bout distribution was skewed toward shorter bouts (1 to 3 hours). In this case sea lion 4's median was less than the median for sea lion 2. Within a dive bout, females made between eleven and twenty-four dives per hour and averaged 2.9 dive bouts per trip (Table 14.3).

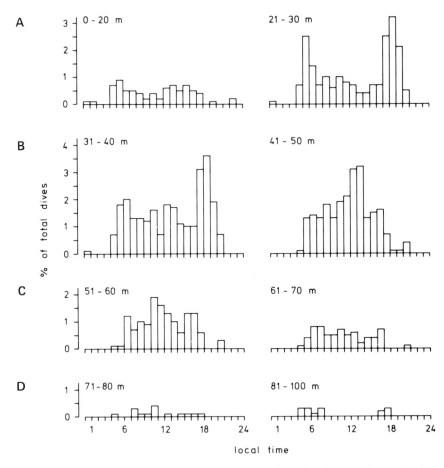

Fig. 14.5. Frequency analysis of dive depth by time of day for Galapagos sea lions.

DISCUSSION

Time Partitioning

Data from the first trip to sea are eliminated from the analysis of time partitioning because behavior was abnormal. Animals on first trips uncharacteristically dived both day and night (Fig. 14.1 top) and stayed at sea abnormally long compared to both later trips and to attendance patterns of undisturbed animals (Chapter 13). We are uncertain whether this unusual behavior resulted because the sea lions had been drugged, or from capture alone. These effects sug-

TABLE 14.2. Activity patterns during trips to sea for Galapagos sea lions.

Female no.	Trips to sea	Trip duration (h)	Dives/ trip	Dives/h	Rest (%)	Transit times	
						Outbound (min)	Inbound (min)
1	2	16 (1)	92 (1)	6	3	51 (2)	120 (2)
2	5	15 (4)	198 (4)	13	0	10 (5)	29 (5)
3	—	—	—	—	—	30 (1)	—
4	6	17 (5)	85 (5)	5	—	54 (6)	133 (6)
Average		15.7	125	—	—	36	94

Notes: Data exclude first trip to sea, which averaged 47 hours and 10 dives/hour for numbers 1, 2, and 4. Numbers in parentheses equal the sample size.

TABLE 14.3. Characteristics of Galapagos sea lion dive bouts.

Female no.	Dive-bout criterion (min)	Dive bouts	Average bout duration (h)	Median bout duration (h)	Bouts/ trip	Dives/h within bout
1	13	12	3.3	1.5	3.4	17.0
2	12	19	3.8	2.9	3.2	24.0
3	—	1	—	—	—	19.0
4	35	18	2.8	2.2	2.1	11.0
Average	—	—	3.3	2.2	2.9	17.7

Note: Data exclude first trip to sea. See note in Table 14.2.

gest that in future studies a few days may be required to eliminate abnormal behavior due to handling.

The distance from the colony to sea lion feeding areas was estimated from assumed swimming velocities. Open sea swim velocities of sea lions are unknown, but a trained 35 kg sea lion at our laboratory (Chapter 15) easily maintained a rate of 2.5 ms^{-1}. Since instrumented sea lions were much larger, we estimated that their swim velocity was easily 3 ms^{-1}, or a relative rate of about 1.8 body lengths s^{-1}. At that rate the elapsed time from departure to the first dive would place the feeding areas about 1.8 to 9.7 km from the colony. The distances would be somewhat greater than these estimates if the first dives were exploratory and did not indicate the usual feeding areas. The final dives before returning ashore were more likely to have ended a feeding bout than initial dives were to begin one. Consequently, return transit times may have given better estimates of the distance to feeding areas than the outbound transit

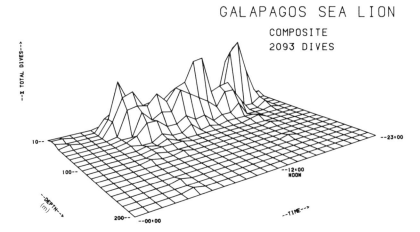

Fig. 14.6. Three-dimensional plot of dive depth, time of day, and number of dives for three Galapagos sea lion dive records combined.

times. Using the same assumptions, these distances were calculated to be 5.2 to 24 km from the colony, or about three times the estimated outbound distances. These distances are similar to those estimated for the Galapagos fur seal (19 km).

Apparently the encumbrance of the harness and TDR did not affect the attendance pattern in this species. The trip durations averaged 15.7 hours (Table 14.2), which was close to the 12-hour sea time in five sea lion females whose departures and returns were continuously recorded. They also approximated eighteen other observations, given in Chapter 13, where average shore time was 12 hours and average sea time (in twenty-eight cases) was 18 hours.

Feeding Behavior

The prey of the Galapagos sea lion is unreported. However, numerous reports exist of food preferences in the California sea lion. Some of these reports deal with the predation of males in the northern parts of their range (Morejohn et al., 1978; Bailey and Ainley, 1981/1982; Ainley et al., 1982). Others have addressed the food habits of animals, mostly females, in the southern parts of their range (Fiscus and Baines, 1966; Antonelis et al., 1984). The latter authors found that among California sea lions at San Miguel Island, squid (*Loligo opalescens*), Pacific whiting (*Merluccius productus*), and juvenile rockfish (*Sebastes* spp.) represented over 90% of the catch.

The average weight of individual fish and squid was estimated to be 45 g, a value we use later in calculating hunting success.

The Galapagos sea lion's preferred dive depth was about two times greater than that of the Galapagos fur seal (Tables 14.1, 12.1). Apparently the sea lion compensated for daytime diving by foraging at greater depths for its prey. Nevertheless, the Galapagos sea lion's dive effort may be less than that of California sea lion females at San Miguel Island, which frequently dive to 200 m and which were active almost continually on 2- to 3-day feeding trips (Feldkamp, pers. comm.).

The strong preference for diurnal feeding in the Galapagos sea lion may indicate a food preference, a temporal change in the type of food available, or some inability (behavioral or physiological) to dive at night. Their diving starts abruptly between 0500 and 0600 hours (Figs. 14.3, 14.6), just before the 0600 sunrise. This well-defined start may indicate hunger, prey accessibility, or a combination of both. Diving activity at this time peaked at the 21 to 30 m interval (Figs. 14.4, 14.5a, 14.6). Diving ended just as abruptly at about 2000 hours (Fig. 14.6).

During the hours when sea lion feeding overlapped with that of fur seals (1900 to 2300 hours; Fig. 12.3) the sea lions fed at greater depths (20–40 m versus 0–20 m; Figs. 14.4, 14.5a, b; Figs. 12.4, 12.5). It appears that although the species overlapped in time they did not overlap in depth. We do not know whether they overlapped in feeding areas or types of prey taken. No information is available on the depth of the deep scattering layer in the Galapagos Islands in the daytime, although in other areas it is usually below 100 m. The tendencies for Galapagos sea lions to dive in the daytime and to attain a median depth of only 45 m suggest that sea lions do not prey on the deep scattering layer. In contrast, the tendency for Galapagos fur seals to dive at night and the correlation between night diving and the lunar cycle suggest that components of the deep scattering layer may be taken when they are near the surface. The Galapagos sea lion and fur seal may compete for prey species only in the evening hours as the deep scattering layer rises.

Deep dives (>80 m) were infrequent in the Galapagos sea lion (3% of all dives; Fig. 14.2), but may have been unusually important, judging from the time of their occurrence. Most deep dives occurred from 0400 to 0800 hours, and from 1600 to 1800 hours (Figs. 14.5d, 14.6), a time of much diving activity. These deep dives may help seals find the horizontal and vertical locations of prey patches.

The dive intensity of the two species was comparable. During dive bouts the Galapagos sea lion dived at a rate of 11 to 24 dives h^{-1} (Table 14.3) compared to 16 dives h^{-1} for the fur seal (Table 12.3). The rate of diving within bouts for sea lions was twice the rate for the entire trip, indicating that about 50% of the sea time was spent in dive bouts. A comparable value for the fur seal was about 6 dives h^{-1} per trip (Table 12.2).

The success rates of feeding trips can be estimated from several assumptions. First, we assume that Galapagos sea lions, like California sea lions, take prey of 45 g, and that a 100 kg female suckling a pup requires 15% of its body weight per day for maintenance. If 15 kg of prey are required, and each item weighs 45 g, then 333 prey items are necessary per feeding trip. If the sea lion makes 100 to 200 dives per 16-hour feeding trip (Table 14.2), and each dive is successful, then it must catch 1.7 to 3.3 fish or squid per dive. This value is close to the 0.5 to 5 prey items per dive calculated for the Galapagos fur seal (Chapter 12).

If Galapagos sea lions make more unsuccessful dives than the Galapagos fur seal, the number of prey captured per dive would have to be greater, and the sea lion should have a higher rate of diving in a bout, longer bouts, more dives per bout, or some combination of these trends. Instead, it appears that the species were about equally successful. The sea lion dive bouts were only slightly longer than those for the fur seal (3.3 versus 2.9 hours), and their dive rate within a bout was also only slightly greater (17.1 versus 15.7 dives h^{-1}). Perhaps a greater absolute breath-hold limit, resulting from larger body size (Chapter 15), has permitted the Galapagos sea lion to dive deeper more successfully and thus work in the daytime. On the other hand, the success of the Galapagos fur seal may lie in its ability to hunt more effectively at night.

SUMMARY

The diving behavior of Galapagos sea lions was studied near Cabo Hammond, Fernandina Island, in October and November 1980. Records were obtained for thirteen trips to sea of four females. The first trip to sea of each female was unusually long due to use of drug immobilization and was thus excluded from analysis. The duration of subsequent trips was 15.7 hours, about the same as the 0.5-day trips of uninstrumented females. The outbound transit times averaged 36 minutes, and return times averaged 94 minutes. Females fed mostly in the daytime (25% of dives were at night), with peaks of dive activity in midday and early evening. Using a dive-bout criterion of 12 to 35 minutes, females averaged 2.9 dive bouts per trip to sea. The bouts had an average duration of 3.3 hours, and the dive rate within bouts was 17.7 dives per hour (with rates as great as 25 dives per hour in some bouts). The portion of dive bouts spent submerged was not calculated. All dive bouts were shallow, around 37–38 m. The number of dives per trip to sea ranged from 85 to 198. During a dive, animals spent no measurable time at the greatest depth attained. Dives were so brief that the durations of shallow dives could not be measured accurately. The maximum duration of deep dives was 5 to 6 minutes. The mean depth of all dives was 37 m, and the maximum depth attained was 186 m. The most frequent dive depth was 45 m during the hours of peak dive frequency (0800 to 1800). The relationships between depth and duration of dives, and between the depth of dives and interdive intervals, were not calculated. The activity budget at sea included 1.5% resting, 35% swimming, and 63.5% diving. Resting occurred with such low frequency that temporal patterns were not analyzed.

15 Synthesis and Conclusions

≅ *R. L. Gentry, D. P. Costa, J. P. Croxall, J.H.M. David,*

R. W. Davis, G. L. Kooyman, P. Majluf, T. S. McCann, and

F. Trillmich*

INTRODUCTION

We now return to the subject of maternal strategies, the main emphasis of this book. As stated in Chapter 1, these strategies cannot be identified from the study of either attendance behavior or diving behavior alone, nor even from a comprehensive study of a single species. We characterize these strategies by comparing six species according to more than forty different measures. In brief, the comparison shows that latitude correlates with broad suites of traits that are related to rearing pups (hence maternal strategies). Despite differences in taxonomic affinity and diet, seals of comparable latitudes share traits that seals of different latitudes possess but express differently. Many traits vary somewhat within a species, suggesting that similarities and differences between species may represent accommodation to local environments more than adaptation through genetic change. However, the distinction between adaptation and accommodation is not crucial to the results that follow.

The comparison is broad but not all-inclusive; eared seals of temperate latitudes are generally underrepresented. The comparative measures are also broad and include aspects of diving and attendance behavior, activity patterns of females at sea, and growth and postweaning development of pups. Because we use the comparative method, we do not identify cause-and-effect relationships or test hypotheses (Stearns, 1977), although we do note some functional relationships between pairs of traits and suggest hypotheses for testing.

In the first part of this chapter we compare the species on a subject-by-subject basis; we collate material appearing in previous chapters and present new information associated with or inferred from the collated material. In the second part of the chapter we dis-

*All authors contributed to the concepts, data, and writing of this chapter; first authorship was assigned on the basis of editorial contribution.

cuss the various strategies and relate these to existing theories; we attempt to identify general principles in behavior, ecology, physiology, and population dynamics of fur seals, and discuss them in a physiological and evolutionary context. We summarize our major findings in the third part of the chapter.

PART 1. SYNTHESIS

Characteristics of Attendance Behavior

We begin by characterizing similarities and differences in attendance behavior among species. In deriving general patterns we are not seeking to de-emphasize the appreciable variation, presented in detail in each chapter, among individuals, between adjacent sites, and over different seasons. This comparison clearly shows that breeding-cycle characteristics are susceptible to significant modification.

The data summarized in Table 15.1 enable us to distinguish two main pup-raising strategies. The first is typical of the two subpolar species, the northern and the Antarctic fur seals. These species have highly synchronous pupping followed by a comparatively short period to weaning, during which lactating females make relatively few feeding trips, each of medium to long duration, alternating with attendance periods that normally last 2 days or more.

In contrast to these, the Galapagos fur seal, Galapagos sea lion, and the South American fur seal in Peru, all of which inhabit tropical and subtropical regions, show lower synchrony of pupping, and pup rearing is prolonged to the extent that consecutive offspring may be simultaneously dependent on their mothers. Feeding trips and attendance periods for these species are seldom longer than one day each, and females complete a few hundred such cycles while rearing a pup.

The latter group is less homogeneous than the subpolar group, perhaps largely because it includes a sea lion. The Galapagos sea lion is distinctly different from the Galapagos fur seal in its very short feeding and attendance cycles, its essentially annual breeding cycle, and its propensity for diving in the daytime. A few of these traits may be general differences between sea lions and fur seals (see discussion in Chapter 13). We are uncertain how different the South American fur seal is from other members of its group. Feeding trips were measured for this species only during EN conditions and may have been unusually long, as indicated by the large-scale death by starvation of pups subjected to this feeding regime.

TABLE 15.1. Data on attendance patterns.

Species	Female migratory	Age at weaning (mo)	Pupping period duration (90%) (wk)	Days female available to pup (%)	Number of trips to weaning	Mean trip length (days)	Fasting female Arr. to part. (days)	Fasting female Part. to 1st trip (days)	Attend. duration (days)
Northern fur seal	+	4	3–4	27	8–12	6.9	1.2	8.3	2.1
Antarctic fur seal	+	4	3	36	14–19	4.3	1.8	6.9	2.1
So. African fur seal		9–11	4–5	39	50–60	2.9	1.5	4.3	2.1
So. American fur seal (Peru)*	–	12–24	4–5	27	?	4.7	?	?	1.3
Galapagos fur seal	–	18–36	10	40	300	1.5	1.5	7.3	0.5–1.3
Galapagos sea lion	–	10–12	16–40	73	200	0.5	1.5	6.8	0.6
New Zealand fur seal	–	10	4					9.0	—
Subantarctic fur seal	–	9–11	4–6					—	—
Guadalupe fur seal	–	9–11	6					—	—
So. American fur seal (Uruguay)	–	8–12						—	—

* Data obtained during El Niño conditions.

Finally, it is important to note that a species may show different trends in different parts of its range. Thus South American fur seals in Uruguay complete a breeding cycle in about a year (Vaz-Ferreira and Ponce de Leon, in press) and doubtless show some related differences, compared to the adaptations of Peruvian conspecifics. The New Zealand populations of the New Zealand fur seal rear pups to weaning in 8 to 9 months (Mattlin, 1978; Miller, 1975), whereas in South Australia some females of this species still suckle pups near the start of the next breeding season (Stirling, 1971).

The two strategies, which we refer to as the "subpolar" and the "tropical" patterns, probably represent the extremes in attendance behavior shown by fur seals. In the interval from birth to weaning, number of trips to sea before weaning, and duration of feeding trips, the South African fur seal seems intermediate between these two strategies. The limited data available on other temperate fur seal species (the New Zealand fur seal: Stirling, 1971; Miller, 1975; and the subantarctic fur seal: Condy, 1978; Kerley, 1983; Roux and Hes, 1984) suggest that these species also may be intermediate between the subpolar and tropical strategies. Bester (1981) made the suggestion, based upon data on the interval from birth to weaning, that among fur seals a cline exists in annual breeding cycles between subpolar and tropical areas. Our data agree with this statement.

Characteristics of Growth

Growth rate of pups is the integrated result of attendance behavior, diving behavior, and milk composition. The growth data on which we compare these seals are mainly from unpublished sources. The greatest absolute growth rates between birth and weaning occur in male South African and female Antarctic fur seals (95 and 76 g d^{-1}, respectively; Table 15.2. See also Doidge et al., 1984b; Payne, 1979b). The northern fur seal lies very close to this value and the ranges of variation for different species overlap (Gentry et al., unpubl. ms.; Rand, 1956; compare with growth rates of the New Zealand fur seal in Crawley, 1975; Mattlin, 1981). The Galapagos fur seal, which has a much longer period to weaning, grows initially at a similar rate but then slows down so that overall its growth rate until weaning is only about 25% that of the other seals (Trillmich, unpubl. data).

A more important finding, however, is that over the first 2 to 3 months relative growth rates are nearly the same among species, despite the other differences. In all species we studied, the median doubling time for birth weight is about 66 days (Table 15.2). Fur-

TABLE 15.2. Comparative growth data for otariids.

Species	Adult ♀ mass (kg)	Birth weight (kg)		Doubling time from birth (days)		Growth over first 60 days (g d⁻¹)		Weight at weaning (kg)*		% Adult ♀ mass at weaning		Milk fat (%)
		♂	♀	♂	♀	♂	♀	♂	♀	♂	♀	
Northern fur seal[a,b]	37	5.8	5.2	81	93	72	57	14.1	11.7	38	32	47
Antarctic fur seal[c,d]	33	6.7	5.7	74	75	90	76	17.1	14.5	52	44	40[e]
So. African fur seal[f,g]	57	6.0	5.5	63	84	95	65	25.0	1	44	37	19[f]
Galapagos fur seal[h]	27	3.9	3.4	66	78	58	43	16.0	14	59	52	25[i]
New Zealand fur seal[j]	~45	3.9	3.3	87	72	45	46	14.1	12.6	~31	~27	—
Galapagos sea lion[k]	80	~6.0	~6.0	40	52	154	116	~25.0	—	—	—	18[l]

* Age at weaning is given in Table 15.1.

[a] Gentry et al., unpubl. manuscript; [b] Costa and Gentry, Chapter 5; [c] Doidge et al., 1984b; [d] Payne, 1979b; [e] Costa, unpubl. data; [f] Rand, 1956; [g] David, in press; [h] Trillmich, in press, a and b; Trillmich, unpubl. data; [i] Trillmich and Lechner, in prep.; [j] Mattlin, 1981, and Mattlin, in press; [k] Trillmich, Chapter 13, and unpubl. data; [l] Trillmich and Lechner, unpubl. data.

thermore, the initial growth rates are similar, namely, 1.3%–1.7% of birth weight per day. After about the fourth month of life, growth rate of the still-dependent Galapagos fur seal drops, as it does in young of the subpolar species, which are by then independent. Finally, the percentage of adult body weight that fur seal pups reach by weaning is roughly similar in all the species (Table 15.2). The differences are hard to interpret, especially given the appreciable intraspecific variation in adult female mass (e.g., 50–110 kg and 20–35 kg, respectively, in the Galapagos sea lion and fur seal), duration of pup-rearing periods, and birth weights.

The major difference in these six otariids lies not in the parameters of growth but rather in the age at weaning, which seems to depend on behavioral and environmental factors that vary with latitude. These relationships are shown graphically in Figure 15.1. The point at which weaning occurs relative to the inflection point in the growth-rate curve depends on the availability of food, seasonality, migration, and environmental predictability. Intraspecific variation in the age at weaning also varies with the same four factors. High-latitude, migratory seals that wean shortly before the onset of migration (Bester, 1981) are the least variable.

How can these species achieve similar growth rates despite widely different attendance patterns? Varying milk composition might compensate for the effects of divergent attendance patterns. The milk of northern fur seals is extremely rich, having a 47% lipid content (Table 15.2). Unlike the milk of northern elephant seals, its composition does not change progressively throughout lactation (Fig. 5.2). Thus females deliver a concentrated volume of energy to the pup and then abandon it for long periods without risking its starvation. Antarctic fur seals are very similar (Table 15.2). Galapagos and South African fur seals have only about 19%–25% milk fat (Trillmich and Lechner, unpubl. data; Rand, 1956), though in the latter species samples are few and small. Delivering milk of low fat content frequently (and perhaps in smaller volumes) could produce the same energy uptake over time as in the high-latitude species. We cannot determine with present evidence whether the correlation between milk-fat content and attendance pattern holds, but the hypothesis is testable.

Characteristics of Diving Behavior

The characteristics of individual dives are remarkably similar among species. For example, the relationship between the depth and duration of individual dives is linear with relatively little variation in northern and South African fur seals (r^2 = 81% and 78%

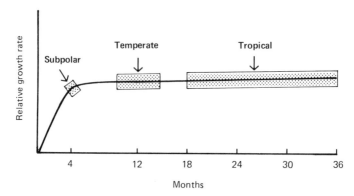

Fig. 15.1. Timing and extent of intraspecific variation in weaning among subpolar, temperate, and tropical otariids (mostly fur seals). All species wean when the pup is ca. 40% of adult female mass. The extent of intraspecific variation (stippled areas) is controlled by food, seasonality, migration, and environmental uncertainty.

respectively; Figs. 4.7, 9.3). This relationship could not be tested for the other species, but it is apparent from examination of the dive traces. Also, the mean and maximum duration of dives showed striking similarity among species (Table 15.3). Except for the northern fur seal, which was discussed in Chapter 4, mean depth of all dives is similar for all species. Maximum depths attained, although differing by a factor of two among species, were not consistently different between the subpolar and tropical groups.

The time of diving is also similar; all fur seals dive mainly at night. The most frequently attained dive depths are shallow at night and deep during the day (Fig. 15.2) in all except the Galapagos fur seal, which has an almost constant median dive depth at all hours. Northern and Antarctic fur seals are also similar in having peaks of diving behavior at dusk and around dawn (Fig. 15.3); Galapagos fur seals may have only a dusk peak. The Galapagos sea lion is different from all fur seals by beginning to dive at dawn, diving throughout the day, and ceasing at dusk or shortly thereafter (Fig. 15.3).

The depth of dives is similar—and shallow—for most seals. The frequency distribution of diving depth shows a single peak, always at 50 m or less, for all species except the northern fur seal (Fig. 15.4), which has two such peaks, one at 60 m and one at 175 m. The second peak gives the species an overall greater average dive depth than the other species (Table 15.3), though this was not evident in

TABLE 15.3. Dive characteristic averages for all otariid species studied.

	Northern fur seal	Antarctic fur seal	So. African fur seal	So. American fur seal	Galapagos fur seal	Galapagos sea lion
Time at sea (days)	7.5	5.3	—	1.0–4.8	0.7	0.7
% time resting (at sea)	17.0	5.0	—	2.0	2.8	1.5
% time swimming	57.0	60.0	—	74.0	73.0	34.0
% time diving	26.0	35.0	—	24.0	24.0	63.5
Time to 1st dive (h)	15.0	16.0	—	8.8	2.7	0.5
Time from last dive (h)	10.2	12.0	—	3.0	2.0	1.5
% dives at night	69.0	81.0	—	88.0	95.0	25.0
Dive-bout criteria (min)	40.0	25.0	18	12.0	23.0	12.5–35
Bouts/trip	15.8	12.1	—	7.0	1.4	2.9
Dive-bout duration (h)	2.3	1.9	—	2.3	2.9	3.3
Dives/h/bout	18.7	19.3	—	14.3	15.7	17.7
Dive duration (min)						
Mean	2.2	<2.0	2.1	2.5	<2.0	<2.0
Max	7.6	4.9	7.5	7.1	5.0	6.0
Dive depth (m)						
Mean	68	30	45	34	26	37
Max	207	101	204	170	115	186

Northern Fur Seal

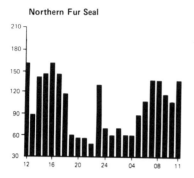

Antarctic Fur Seal

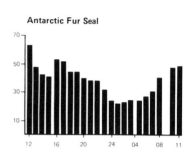

South American Fur Seal

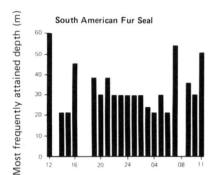

Galapagos Fur Seal

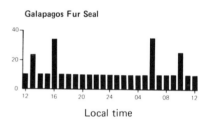

Local time

Galapagos Sea Lion

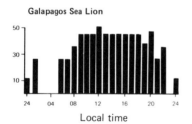

Local time

Fig. 15.2. The most frequently attained diving depths by hour of day for all species except the South African fur seal, for which hour of day was not measured.

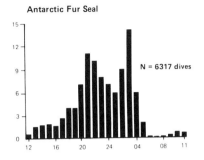

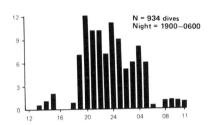

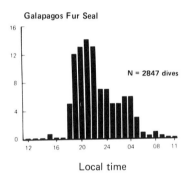

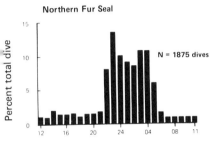

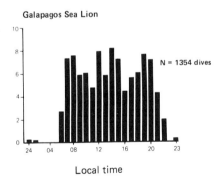

Fig. 15.3. Frequency distribution for dives by hour of day regardless of depth. Data are shown for all species except the South African fur seal, for which hour of day could not be determined.

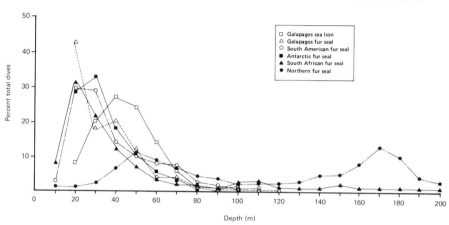

Fig. 15.4. Frequency distribution for dives by depth in 10 m increments, regardless of hour of day. Data are shown for six
species of otariids.

the 1975 data for the species (Kooyman et al., 1976). Because of its
long recovery times from these deep dives, the northern fur seal
also has the longest dive-bout criterion (40 minutes, compared to
12–23 minutes for other species; Table 15.3).

Individual variation within a species for depth, timing, and frequency of dives is not extensive except in the northern fur seal. This
is most evident when comparing the 3-dimensional plots for all species (Fig. 15.5). Northern fur seals have three distinct diving patterns. The composite plots for all other seals (particularly the Antarctic fur seal) resemble only the shallow type of the northern fur
seal.

The mean dive frequency (i.e., dives per hour within bouts) is
similar for all species (Table 15.3). This finding suggests that the
difficulty of locating prey probably does not determine the great
difference in feeding-trip duration between subpolar and tropical
forms. It also suggests a common physiological limit to dive frequency. Because dive frequency depends on the depth of diving
(Fig. 4.6), the northern fur seal, with the greatest variation in depths
(Fig. 15.4), also has the greatest variation in dive frequency.

When pup growth rates and the proportionate weight at weaning
are similar among fur seal species, and the characteristics of individual dives are also similar (but not directly fixed by physiological constraints; see Part 2), then female flexibility in obtaining energy exists only in their onshore-offshore movements to and from feeding

areas, as well as the time of day, location, and frequency with which they perform single dives. We refer to these combined patterns as maternal strategies at sea, implying that both short- and long-term options exist regarding the performance of diving.

Our work shows consistent distinctions in maternal strategies at sea between the subpolar and tropical species. Specifically, the two subpolar species stay at sea for long periods on feeding trips (Tables 15.1, 15.3) and have a large number of feeding bouts (16) per trip (Table 15.3). The tropical species make short trips to sea throughout a lengthy period, and have a small number of bouts on each trip (1–3; Table 15.3). Also, the subpolar seals have longer absolute transit times, implying greater distances to feeding areas (Table 15.3). This combination of long trips to sea, long transit times, and many bouts per trip suggests that, compared to tropical forms, subpolar fur seals need to acquire more energy per trip (discussed above), that their food is more difficult to locate, or that they are exploiting more distant food resources (discussed in Part 2).

In summary, it does not appear that maternal strategies are matched to local environments by alterations in the character of individual dives. These dives, although differing somewhat in depth among species, show no systematic similarities or differences. Instead, the species have altered the patterning of dives within a foraging trip commensurate with the number of foraging trips that are made prior to weaning.

Activity Patterns at Sea

The subpolar and tropical groups also differ in the time spent resting at the surface during trips to sea (5%–17% versus 1%–3%, respectively; Table 15.3). These proportions vary directly with the durations of feeding trips. Species that make short trips, such as the Galapagos fur seal, may postpone rest until they return to shore. Species with long trips rest more at sea, probably because rest cannot be postponed for the 6 to 8 days of the trip. Furthermore, at least in the northern fur seal, rest occurs in bouts that are much shorter than bouts of either diving or activity at the surface. The factors that account for the generally low occurrence of rest at sea in these species, and prevent rest from occurring in more prolonged bouts, are considered in Part 2.

The subpolar and tropical groups show no consistent differences in the proportion of time they spend active at the surface or in diving (Table 15.3). The Galapagos sea lion spends a greater proportion of time at sea diving than all fur seal species (about double their

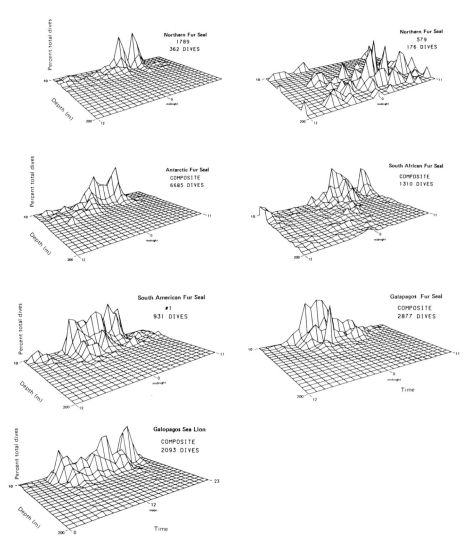

Fig. 15.5. The 3-dimensional relationships of dive frequency, depth, and hour of day compared for six species of otariids. Each species is represented by the combined patterns of all individuals measured except for the Northern fur seal, in which two distinct patterns were recognized.

values), and the proportion of time it spends swimming at the surface without diving is concomitantly smaller (35%; Table 15.3). Undoubtedly, some of the activity at the surface is associated with travel, either to and from the island or searching for prey patches. However, an unknown proportion of surface activity for fur seals is probably devoted to grooming, which is an important activity for maintaining the insulative properties of the underfur (Kooyman et al., 1976).

Development to Weaning

The weaning process, the onset of independent feeding, and survival to reproductive age may differ in the subpolar and tropical otariids. Pups of the two groups differ at weaning in several morphological and behavioral traits. Pups of both subpolar species have a well-developed blubber layer and have molted into their adult pelage by about 3 months. These two attributes aid a pelagic existence in cold water. Shedding of the deciduous teeth begins *in utero* and is complete by 13 weeks (data from the northern fur seal; Scheffer and Kraus, 1964). By 3 months of age Antarctic fur seal pups spend much of their time swimming. Examination of scats indicates that some pups at this time supplement their milk diet by feeding on some crustaceans; by 4 months of age pups of the subpolar species therefore appear to be morphologically (but perhaps not experientially) prepared for total nutritional independence.

At 4 months of age Galapagos fur seal pups have not yet molted or are just beginning to do so. By 4 or 5 months they begin to shed their deciduous teeth, some of which may persist to the age of 1 year. Independent feeding certainly does not play a role in the energy budget of these young before they are 10 to 12 months of age. But by weaning at 18 months they are morphologically as prepared to feed themselves as are subpolar pups at 4 months. At weaning they have the added benefit of extensive feeding experience.

Given such important differences in development and age at weaning, postweaning survival rates may differ for the two groups. Survival in early life appears to be very low for the subpolar species (about 38% survive to age 2 in the northern fur seal; Lander, 1981/82). This low rate may be attributable to greater risk from predation, exposure to parasite infestation via food organisms, starvation during the transition to independent feeding, or exposure to storms and cold in the relatively turbulent waters they inhabit. Since pups of the tropical species are older and more experienced at weaning, data on their postweaning survival are desirable for comparison.

Some Characteristics of the Environments

Given that maternal strategies are divisible into subpolar and tropical groups, how do the environments in which seals breed affect these strategies? The differences in physical characteristics among polar, temperate, and tropical seas are well documented and considerable. The pattern of productivity in subpolar waters ensures a rich but highly seasonal availability of food to northern and Antarctic fur seals. In autumn the main fish prey of northern fur seals migrates south into the open ocean, apparently avoiding the advance of cold water across the Bering Sea shelf (Smith, 1981). The reduced krill population of subantarctic waters overwinters at considerable depth (possibly under the ice edge; Foxton, 1956). Also, the fish populations of the continental shelf are reduced and become largely benthic in habit.

In winter it is thus no longer feasible for females to find food sufficient to continue rearing a pup within a restricted radius of their breeding site. This constraint and the rich resources available in summer presumably combined to favor the compression of the breeding cycle to about 4 months, and the weaning of pups sufficiently early in the year to permit them to acquire the foraging and swimming skills needed to survive the winter. This constraint probably acted through females that are rearing pups. Sufficient resources remain in subpolar waters to support overwintering populations of males.

Temperate and especially tropical fur seals tend to breed close to rich upwelling areas, often associated with cold current systems, in environments of substantially reduced seasonality. The rate of productivity in these areas of upwelling is greater than in surrounding areas of no upwelling, but may not be as great as in polar areas. The absence of migration suggests that food is available on a more sustained basis than in subpolar areas. These conditions have apparently favored the development of a considerably extended pupping season and a much longer rearing period. Contingent on food supply available to the population, pups either wean in the spring following the summer in which they were born, or remain dependent on their mother for a year or more.

From the standpoint of maternal strategies, the most important aspect of the environment is not seasonal stability but rather environmental predictability (Orians, 1969). An environment can be predictable either by being constant at all seasons or by differing among seasons so long as a given season has little variability in successive years (Colwell, 1974). Despite the fact that tropical seals experience less seasonal change than subpolar seals, they may have a less predictable marine environment because of periodic EN conditions. As stated elsewhere, the interval between ENs is unpredictable, as are the severity, character, and biological consequences of each. Seals at the Galapagos Islands and in Peru are most affected by ENs (Limberger et al., 1983), but less severe effects are experienced by seals as far away as California (Antonelis and DeLong, 1985).

By contrast, subpolar fur seals experience far fewer or less intense periodic changes at their summertime breeding areas. Short- and long-term climatic changes do occur in these areas, but they are usually less profound and less stochastic than EN conditions in the tropics. Chapter 1 showed that the yearly means of sea surface temperatures deviated around the overall mean more frequently for the Peru site (Fig. 1.1) than for the Pribilofs. Although temperature changes in subpolar areas probably affect the survival and spawning success of prey stocks, large-scale failures in primary productivity, such as in areas affected by EN conditions, have not been recorded.

In summary, the two groups of seals are affected by the predictability of marine productivity in their breeding areas. Because of EN conditions, tropical seals face seasonally more constant but unpredictable (over the lifetime of a seal) yearly patterns of productivity. On the other hand, subpolar seals face extreme seasonal variation that is highly predictable between years. The latter respond to seasonal extremes by migrating, but their maternal strategies are adapted to a predictable food supply. The few data available for temperate fur seals suggest that they are intermediate between these two groups, although they are somewhat closer to the tropical group.

PART 2. DISCUSSION

The previous section showed two distinct types of maternal strategies and suggested an intermediate form. The two groups did not differ in some aspects of relative pup growth, nor in characteristics of single dives. They did differ markedly in their attendance behavior, patterning of dives during feeding trips, activity budgets while at sea, and in the predictability of the environments in which they breed. Before these pieces are integrated into a larger picture, some further discussion of the previous comparisons is required, includ-

TABLE 15.4. Hypothetical relationships between body mass, O_2 stores, and O_2 utilization in otariids of the approximate size range studied in this monograph.

Mass (kg)	30	40	50	80	100
Muscle mass 0.3 of total M_b (kg)	9	12	15	24	30
Muscle O_2 (l)[a]	0.42	0.56	0.64	1.13	1.41
Blood volume (l)[b]	3.30	4.40	5.50	8.80	10.90
Blood O_2 store (l)[c]	0.53	0.71	0.88	1.41	1.75
Dive lung O_2 (l)[d]	0.23	0.30	0.37	0.57	0.70
Total O_2 (l)	1.18	1.57	1.89	3.11	3.86
Estimated resting $\dot{V}_{O_2}$ (l min^{-1})[e]	0.14	0.18	0.21	0.30	0.35
Swimming $\dot{V}_{O_2}$ (l min^{-1})[f]	0.35	0.45	0.53	0.75	0.88
ADL (min)[g]	3.40	3.50	3.60	4.10	4.40
Most economical swim speed (ms^{-1})	2.00	2.00	2.00	3.00	3.00

[a] Muscle mass 0.035 kg myoglobin kg^{-1} muscle $\times$ 1.34 l O_2 kg^{-1} (Lenfant et al., 1970).

[b] 0.109 l kg^{-1} (ibid.).

[c] (0.33 V_b) ($H_b\% \times 1.34 \times 0.95$) $-$ (0.33 V_b) ($H_b\% \times 1.34 \times 0.20$) + (0.66 V_b) ($CaO_2 - 5$ vol. %); $H_b = 0.165$ l kg^{-1} blood (Kooyman and Sinnett, 1982; Lenfant et al., 1970; data from Chapter 10).

[d] Total lung capacity, TLC = 0.135 M_b $^{0.95}$ (Kooyman, 1973); diving lung O_2 volume = TLC $\times$ 0.5 $\times$ 0.15 (ibid.).

[e] Standard resting $\dot{V}_{O_2} = 0.011$ M_b $^{0.75}$; in l O_2 min^{-1} and kg (Kleiber, 1975).

[f] Estimated from minimum cost of transport values obtained for 20–25 kg sea lions swimming at 1.8 ms^{-1} (Feldkamp, unpub. measurements).

[g] If these values are plotted (Fig. 15.6), the best fit equation is [ADL (min) = 1.57 mass (kg)$^{0.22}$]; this approximates the expected equation where O_2 stores scale to $M_b^{1.0}$ and $\dot{V}_{O_2}$ to $M_b^{0.75}$.

ing mechanisms at the individual level, processes that occur across species lines, theoretical implications, and projections based on calculations.

Physiological Limits: Diving

The previous section showed that dive durations are consistently less than 2 minutes, and that dive depths never exceed approximately 200 m (Table 15.3) in the species studied. Are these limits set by the prey distribution and the strategy of predation, or by physiological limits common to all six species?

If dives are to be functionally useful for predation, the recovery period should be short enough to allow a sequence of dives with brief surface periods. Recovery periods will be shortest when dives are completely aerobic because only blood and muscle oxygen stores need to be replenished between such dives. If the dives are so long that a significant amount of anaerobic metabolism must occur to meet the energy needs of the increasingly hypoxic tissues, then the use of muscle and liver glycogen and blood glucose as a fuel will increase. Combustion of glucose will be incomplete, resulting in lactic acid (LA) as an end product. Clearance of LA is a slow process requiring a much longer surface time for recovery than that needed for completely aerobic dives.

The effects of LA clearance can be seen in data from freely diving Weddell seals. If the blood LA concentration increases 6-fold above resting, the time required to return LA concentrations to normal levels is about 20 minutes (Kooyman et al., 1980). This recovery time is 5 to 10 times greater than for Weddell seals diving aerobically. The crossover between the two types of diving is termed the aerobic dive limit (ADL). This is defined as the longest dive duration that can be endured without the blood LA concentration rising above normal during the dive or during the postdive recovery period.

If many dives in a series exceed the ADL, and if LA is not restored to its resting level during the surface recovery times, then each dive that exceeds the ADL adds more LA to blood and muscles, and a metabolic acidosis will develop. With increasing acidosis, blood and tissue pH steadily decline, lowering blood hemoglobin and muscle myoglobin O_2 affinity. This lowered affinity in turn reduces hemoglobin and myoglobin saturation levels, thereby reducing the total O_2 carrying capacity of blood and muscle. The drop in pH probably reduces enzyme activity as well, which hinders metabolite turnover. The lower oxygen levels and metabolic efficiency result in more rapid depletion of oxygen and energy stores, and loss of muscle power comparable to the loss of stamina in a marathon runner who fails to pace properly.

The above chain of events results when the seal fails to remain within its ADL on serial dives. If the ADL is calculated for fur seals as it was for Weddell seals, where the calculated value correlates closely with the physiologically determined limit (Kooyman et al., 1983b), a prediction can be made of the maximum durations and depths to which different size fur seals can work effectively. The variables used in the calculations are presented in Table 15.4, as are the resulting calculated ADLs. Viewed graphically, it is clear that ADL in animals greater than 100 kg does not increase as rapidly with size as it does in animals of less than 100 kg (Fig. 15.6). A yearling-size animal is at a disadvantage in breath-hold ability compared to adult-size animals. Most dive durations measured for seals in our study are well below their ADL. Only 0.2% of Antarctic fur seals'

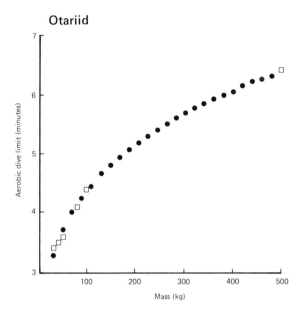

Fig. 15.6. Aerobic dive limit (ADL) calculated as a function of
body mass for hypothetical otariids. The squares represent
known masses of female fur seals and a large South African fur
seal male.

dives and only 3.4% of the South African fur seals' dives exceed this
limit.

Since the great majority of dives are within the ADL for each species, we conclude that serial dive durations are infrequently limited
by the ADL. This conclusion assumes that the surface times were
long enough to replenish O_2 stores completely. This seems a fair assumption because blood and muscle O_2-carrying pigments can be
rapidly saturated. It also assumes that the average swim speed was
not much greater than estimated. Nothing is known of average
swim speeds under natural conditions since these depend largely on
hunting methods. If either assumption is invalid, the estimated
ADLs would be briefer or longer than shown in Table 15.4.

RATE OF ENERGY EXPENDITURE AND DIVE DEPTH. Only a few estimates, and no detailed studies, have been made of swim speed in
fur seals. The rate at which they swim is basic to all aspects of their
behavior at sea, and especially to their energetic requirements. Es-

timates of the most economical swim speeds are made for different size animals (Table 15.4). Based on these values, the power outputs of swimming females are estimated, and these are translated into mass of body stores utilized. Estimates are then made of the rates at which weight must be gained on feeding trips of various duration.

The O_2 consumption rates ($\dot{V}_{O_2}$) during diving are estimated for various size animals from assumed swim rates. When the O_2 stores, which scale approximately to mass to the power of 1, are divided by the $\dot{V}_{O_2}$, which scales approximately to mass to the power of 0.75, the result is an approximation of the maximum breath-hold duration in which the body O_2 stores meet the combustion requirements of metabolism without a net production of anaerobic metabolites. If the aerobic dive limit is a reasonable predictor of working dive durations, then from this calculation and the swim speed, the maximum functional depth limit can be calculated. The two calculations—traveling distance to the feeding areas and dive depth limits—describe the functional foraging range of fur seals in three dimensions.

In calculating the greatest depths that fur seals could theoretically attain, we know the rate of change in depth, but we do not know the angle of descent and ascent, nor the swim speed. If we assume a nearly vertical dive, a swim speed of 2 ms^{-1} for the smaller animals, and a speed of 3 ms^{-1} for the sea lion, then they could theoretically reach depths of about 240 m and 400 m, respectively, and remain within their ADLs. However, descent and ascent rates were consistently below these values in the northern fur seal, a species in which enough deep dives were available to allow these rates to be reliably calculated. For two animals the descent rates were 1.7 and 1.3 ms^{-1}, and the ascent rates were 1.25 and 0.98 ms^{-1}; the durations averaged 4.3 minutes, just at their 4.4-minute calculated ADL (Table 15.5). Therefore, although deep dives were at the ADL, the dives may have ended well short of their theoretical depth limit because the effective descent and ascent rates were slower than predicted. These slower rates may be necessitated by the methods used to capture prey. The seals may also have been under physiological constraints.

We performed calculations to determine whether some physiological limit might prevent fur seals from diving to the theoretically possible depths. For these calculations we assumed that (1) cardiac output is half the resting level due to restricted flow; (2) O_2 consumption remains at 2.5 times the resting level as assumed in pre-

TABLE 15.5. Average descent and ascent rates for two deep-diving northern fur seals.

Female no.	Maximum depth (m)	Average descent rate (m min^{-1})	Average ascent rate (m min^{-1})	Dive duration (min)
1133	195 (13)	103	75	4.2
538	157 (25)	78	59	4.3

Note: Numbers in parentheses equal total dives.

TABLE 15.6. Dive depth, pulmonary shunt, and arterial oxygen tensions.

	Depth (m)	Shunt[a] (%)	Alveolar tension[b] (torr)	Arterial tension (torr)[c]
Descent	100	70	823	57
	170	100	0	45[d]
Ascent	100	70	823	28[e]

[a] $\dot{Q}_s$ = 12.5 + 5.1 P; $\dot{Q}_s$ = % shunt; P = atmos. absolute (Kooyman and Sinnet, 1982).

[b] Assume alveolar O_2 tension is 100 torr at the surface and at 100 m ~ 7.8 × ambient pressure. Assume no gradient between alveoli and pulmonary capillaries.

[c] O_2 solubility = .003 ml O_2 100 ml^{-1} whole blood at 37°C torr^{-1} O_2 pressure. At 823 torr, there is 2.5 ml O_2 100 ml^{-1} blood. Venous tension = 45 torr or 75% sat. (Fig. 10.9). Arterial tension = (75% sat.) (0.7) + (100% sat.) (0.3) + (2.5 ml O_2 100 ml^{-1} × 0.3 ÷ 22 ml O_2 100 ml^{-1} × 100) = 86% sat., or Arterial tension = 57 torr.

[d] At 100% shunt Arterial tension = Venous tension.

[e] See text for explanation.

vious calculations (Table 15.4); and (3) other blood and O_2 conditions are as previously calculated. Additional conditions are noted in the footnotes of Table 15.6.

The calculations are also based on the following brief description of lung function. When the fur seal reaches a depth of about 170 m, lung collapse is complete. At that depth lung volume is nil due to graded compression in which all except absorbed gas has been forced out of alveoli and into rigid, nonexchanging upper airways (Scholander, 1940; Kooyman, 1973, 1981). No further gas exchange occurs until the fur seal ascends to a shallower depth. During lung collapse, as a consequence of no gas exchange in the lung, arterial oxygen tension matches returning venous tension, and it may drop rapidly if oxygen consumption remains at a high level. An important final consideration is that rapid descent incurs an early lung shunt (defined as the fraction of blood that passes through the lung without exchanging gas), thus conserving some pulmonary O_2 until the ascent. As the animal ascends, arterial tension could actually increase (Table 15.6) as the lung begins to reinflate and gas exchange resumes.

The calculations show that at a descent-ascent rate of 120 mmin^{-1}, a dive to 170 m without delay at depth would take 1.4 min. This rate would allow a 35 kg animal to spend about 0.6 minutes at a depth below which 100% shunt occurs and retain tolerable arterial O_2 tensions. During this time the arterial O_2 tension would decline from 45 to about 28 torr (assuming O_2 consumption remains at 2.5 times the standard metabolic rate calculated for terrestrial mammals). The latter is a low tension (humans lose consciousness at about 28 torr). Such low and declining arterial O_2 tensions may prompt the seal to return to the surface.

During ascent the arterial O_2 tension would remain low despite the increasing lung inflation and decreasing shunt because blood O_2 saturation would be only 50% and declining. This is a calculation of the worst possible case in which muscle O_2 is not considered to be in the store available for consumption.

In sum, the calculations indicate that about 200 m may represent a physiological limit for fur seals and sea lions because O_2 consumption would reduce arterial O_2 to a critical tolerance level. Too many unknowns exist in the equation to predict accurately what blood gas tensions may exist in a deep-diving fur seal. Nevertheless, the calculations give some idea of the limited time available at depth before unusually low tensions may prevail.

The predictions from these calculations are supported by behavioral observations. A trained 100 kg male California sea lion descended to a maximum depth of 230 m, in a dive duration of about 5 minutes. The apparently exhausted animal would not dive again without an extended rest period (Ridgway, pers. commun.). Also, female California sea lions of about 100 kg have only occasionally reached 275 m in the course of several thousand dives (Feldkamp, unpubl. data).

Physiological Limits: Thermoregulation

In Part 1 we showed that seals rest at sea in brief bouts, and that rest is the least frequent category of activity at sea for all species studied. Rest may be limited in part by thermoregulatory needs. Studies of captive 35 kg juvenile male northern fur seals show that (1) body temperature decreases if seals remain inactive in water of less than 12°C; (2) the critical temperature in water is about 18°C;

and (3) the metabolic rate increases linearly as the water temperature decreases (Kooyman and Davis, unpubl. data). The average metabolic rate in water of 6°C is 7.7 W kg^{-1}. This value is similar to the free-ranging metabolic rate of foraging mothers (estimated as 8.3 W kg^{-1}; Chapter 5) and is 2.3 times above resting levels in a thermoneutral environment (which is the same as the standard metabolic rate).

Although shivering may be a mechanism that increases metabolism, it is more likely that higher activity levels cause the increase. The captive northern fur seals referred to above spent 60% of their total time in water of 5°C in active grooming, diving, and swimming. But they spent only 21% of their time in water of 25°C in comparable activities. Since mean sea temperature around the Pribilof Islands and South Georgia Island is 5°C or less, the subpolar fur seals may remain active to prevent hypothermia. Such a mechanism appears to operate in sea otters as well (Costa and Kooyman, 1984).

Thermoregulatory factors may also require Galapagos fur seals to remain active despite their being in warmer water. The sea temperature around the Galapagos Islands ranges from 16°–22°C. However, the fur seals have less dense pelage and less body fat than the subpolar forms. As a result, the critical temperature for this species may be higher than the ambient sea temperature. No measurements of the critical temperature in the species exist to test this hypothesis, but individuals observed resting close to shore frequently kept their flippers in the air (just as subpolar fur seals do), apparently to minimize heat loss.

The duration of rest bouts may be affected indirectly by an animal's hunting success and the subsequent process of food digestion. As food is assimilated, it causes an increase in metabolic rate known as Specific Dynamic Action (SDA) that results in increased body heat. Due to SDA, the metabolic rate of fur seals may double in the postabsorptive period compared to fasting periods (based on results from sea otters, Costa and Kooyman, 1984; also see Chapter 5). This increased heat production would supplement their overall thermal budget and increase the duration of rest periods. The extent of this increase may reflect the amount of food captured.

Energy Partitioning

The overriding difference between short and long weaning periods appears to be the temporal pattern in which energy is transferred. Since relative growth rates are the same between temperate, tropical, and subpolar species, we can assume that the relative amount of energy transferred to pups up to 4 months old is equivalent. However, the rate and patterning of energy transferred is strikingly different; the *daily rate* of energy transferred is considerably greater in the subpolar than in the other species. The difference may be mediated by fat content of the milk and by the percentage of the female's energy budget that is devoted to milk production. The northern fur seal has about 47% milk fat throughout lactation, and females devote about 50% of the onshore energy budget to milk production (Chapter 5). We predict that in temperate or tropical fur seals milk-fat content is lower, and that milk production represents a smaller percentage of the daily onshore energy budget than for subpolar species—a prediction that could be tested in the field.

Consistent differences in the energy budgets of foraging females are less obvious. Females of both groups must obtain quantities of energy sufficient to meet their own and their pups' requirements. Even though their foraging patterns are now known, data on caloric value of prey and prey availability, which are necessary to estimate energy acquisition, are not generally available. It would seem that subpolar species devote a greater proportion of the pelagic energy budget to swimming, which suggests that these females would require more prey in compensation. However, tropical seals make a larger number of brief transits between land and feeding areas prior to weaning. Therefore, overall the two groups may expend similar amounts of energy to capture a comparable amount of prey.

Fasting Abilities of Pups

The corollary to the pattern of energy flow, whether pulsed or nearly continuous, is the pups' ability to fast between visits of the mother. Pups of the Galapagos fur seal and sea lion fast for only one-half to 3 days between mothers' visits, but pups of the subpolar species must fast for 4 to 7 days between feedings. Is the ability of these pups to fast periodically for longer intervals based on physiological adaptations?

If the fasting period of the subpolar pups is within their normal physiological ability to maintain metabolic homeostasis by using fuel reserves between feedings, then the Galapagos fur seal and sea lion may also have this ability. Factors that determine the duration of female foraging make long fasts unnecessary for the latter species under normal circumstances. However, Galapagos fur seal pups have been known to survive 2-week fasts when the mother fails to return from sea. These pups can probably recover from and continue normal growth after single fasts of 4 to 7 days, but they may not recover if such fasts are repeated. Young South American fur seal pups did not survive repeated fasts of more than 5 days caused by EN conditions (Chapter 10).

Pups of subpolar species may have enhanced capacity to maintain metabolic homeostasis and grow normally while fasting. Experimental evidence on this point is lacking. One clue to the subpolar fur seal pup's ability to fast repeatedly, acquire fat reserves, and maintain metabolic homeostasis during the mother's absence may be the high fat content of the mother's milk. Because Galapagos fur seal pups feed almost daily, they require smaller fat reserves. A thinner fat layer may enhance the pup's ability to thermoregulate in a warm equatorial climate, but it makes the pup more susceptible to starvation.

Pups of the subpolar and tropical groups appear to differ in the amount of fat they have accumulated as weaning approaches. The northern and Antarctic fur seal pups are weaned after having acquired very large reserves. Immediately after weaning, these pups either fast or obtain energy at a reduced rate as weights decline after weaning. Presumably their extensive fat reserves sustain them while they learn to feed independently. These pups are relatively inexperienced at foraging prior to weaning, and the transition is therefore critical. In contrast, Galapagos fur seal pups suckle continuously for 12 to 18 months, during which they gradually learn to forage at sea. These pups do not acquire large fat reserves, no postweaning fast occurs, and the transition period is perhaps less critical.

In summary, the available evidence indicates that single fasts of less than one week can be physiologically withstood by Galapagos fur seal pups, but that repeated fasts may jeopardize their survival. They are weaned with little excess fat but with considerable feeding experience. In contrast, pups of the subpolar species may be adapted to periodic fasting while simultaneously maintaining normal growth and acquiring additional fat reserves for the postweaning period, which is made critical by their relative inexperience at feeding.

Termination of Feeding and Suckling Periods

We have shown that trips to sea and visits to shore, during which energy is acquired and transferred, end abruptly and are of predictable duration for each species. What mechanisms determine these durations so closely?

Nutritional set points may regulate this system. Mrosovsky and Sherry (1980) showed that birds have hypothetical nutritional states to which they return if they are either starved or overfed. They showed that the state of the adipose tissue depot may regulate the duration of hypophagia. Although body-weight regulation is an active area of research (Rothwell and Stock, 1981; Cioffi et al., 1981), a formal definition of set point is not yet available.

Seals, too, may have a nutritional set point to which they fall during shore visits, and it, too, may be associated with the fat depot. The evidence in Chapter 5 showed that during the first 7 days postpartum, while northern fur seal females are suckling and fasting, the fat content of the milk falls while its protein content remains relatively constant. This pattern suggests that the female's available fat reserves are declining, while the lean body mass is affected less or is unaffected. Thus the fat deposit or the fat-lean ratio may constitute the set point. The set point may be similar in all females because the duration of the perinatal visit to shore is very uniform (Chapter 3).

The duration of the females' subsequent visits to shore appear to be determined by the rate at which energy is removed from the fat stores. Female northern fur seals that were prevented from reuniting with their pups immediately after arrival on shore (hence lost fat at a lower daily rate) spent three to four times longer on shore than when reunion was immediate (Chapter 3). More important, a decrease in the pup's demand for food (by artificially feeding it milk before reunion) lengthened the shore visits. Therefore, the rate at which fat is transferred, which depends on pup demand, appears to determine the rate at which returned females are brought down to the set point, and thereby determines the interval to the female's next departure.

Seals may have a second nutritional set point associated with the amount of fat deposited. We know that fat reserves, lowered by suckling in the postpartum period, are restored over time. Furthermore, throughout lactation subpolar fur seal females continue to store energy in excess of the amount needed to meet pup demand. This excess may be necessary for the female's migration once the pup is weaned. Two studies indicate that the amounts of energy stored and mass gained on a feeding trip may remain the same despite the demands placed on females. In one study (Chapter 5) demand was in the form of foraging effort as measured by ^{18}O. Females with high and with low effort nevertheless gained equal mass and stored equal amounts of energy per trip. In another study (Chapter 5) the demand was in the form of carrying the TDR; instrumented and uninstrumented animals did not differ in mass or energy gained per trip to sea. These results suggest that (1) a set point of "nutritional satiation" may exist, which terminates trips to sea, and (2) the set point may be independent of the energy expended to acquire food. Foraging effort must increase over time to meet the dual demands on a female's resources.

Foraging Ranges and Resource Levels

The transit times suggest that subpolar and tropical seals differ in the distances they must swim to forage. The distances to feeding areas can be estimated from assumed swim speeds. The outbound transit times suggest that tropical species start foraging much closer to shore than do the subpolar seals (Table 15.3). If fur seals swim in a straight line at 2 ms^{-1} and sea lions swim at 3 ms^{-1}, the Galapagos fur seal and sea lion would start diving 20 km and 5.4 km, respectively, from shore, compared with 60 km and 110 km for Antarctic and northern fur seals. These estimated distances roughly approximate the distances to continental shelf edges, where prey are known to be concentrated. At the Galapagos Islands the shelf edge is close to shore and seals should be able to reach it quickly. At Bird Island the travel direction of sixty radio-tracked Antarctic fur seals (Bengtson, unpubl. data) was to the north. The shelf edge in that direction is 55 km, a value close to our estimate of distance to foraging area. At St. George Island the shelf edge is 25 km away at its closest point but extends beyond 110 km, the distance suggested by transit times.

Foraging range need by no means be confined to shelf-edge areas. The two subpolar species with their longer foraging trips may range over much greater areas than their tropical counterparts. Mean maximum foraging ranges (using average trip length and assuming all periods other than rest and diving are active swimming away from or toward the island) are calculated to be 340 km for northern and 220 km for Antarctic fur seals, compared with 44 km and 75 km for Galapagos fur seals and sea lions, respectively. These values should be taken as no more than the magnitude of potential feeding areas available to each species. However, it is interesting to note that lactating northern fur seals have frequently been collected at sea off Unimak Pass, 290 km from the nearest breeding site (Kajimura, 1983).

Foraging-trip duration clearly increases as distance to the foraging area increases. Within a species this trend is most obvious in the northern fur seal. Females from St. Paul Island, 65 km farther from the shelf than St. George Island females, stay longer at sea on all trips (Chapter 3). At 2 ms^{-1} this difference amounts to 9 hours swim time each way. Animals from the Commander Islands, which are 11 km from the shelf edge, stay at sea for only 3.4 days, compared to the 6.9 days for females from St. George (Vladimirov, 1983). Antarctic fur seal females from Schlieper Bay stay at sea longer than females from Bird Island (about 20 km closer to the shelf, the apparent feeding area) in the same season (Chapter 6). These results suggest that distance to feeding areas may have a more powerful influence on differences between subpolar and tropical seals than other differences, such as differential ability to fast.

Under some circumstances, the time animals spend at sea may change with resource level. In 1978 mortality of Antarctic fur seal pups was increased over its previous level, and sea birds suffered almost complete reproductive failure, apparently because krill density around South Georgia was lower than normal (Croxall and Prince, 1979). Under those conditions, time at sea for Bird Island fur seals was 5.3 days on average, as compared to 3.1 and 3.7 days in normal years. Furthermore, during the strong influx of warm tropical waters of the 1982-83 EN, female Galapagos fur seals stayed at sea for 5.1 days (Limberger et al., 1983) compared to 1.3 days (uninstrumented animals) under normal conditions. However, these declines in food stocks were catastrophic. The Pribilof population of northern fur seals has not shown changes in feeding-trip duration in 30 years of competition with commercial fisheries for walleye pollock (Chapter 4). Therefore, trip duration may change only when the species is a feeding specialist, and/or the food reduction is large. Trip duration is not an accurate index of resource levels because location, depth, dive frequency, and prey species taken can change without affecting trip duration.

Our findings that trip duration increases with distance to feeding area and that time at sea may change with resource level agree qualitatively with the predictions of Central Place Foraging theory (Orians and Pearson, 1979). This theory predicts that time spent in a feeding patch should (1) increase with travel time to it, and (2) increase as the quality of the patch decreases, given that travel time remains the same, and that the predator has imperfect information about quality on arrival.

The quantitative relationships among travel time, resource level, and total time spent away from the central place (the breeding colony) cannot be determined because no absolute measures of resource levels exist. However, the existing data show that travel time

TABLE 15.7. Comparison of transit times and trip durations based on species averages.

Species	Transit (h)		Trip duration (h)	% of trip in transit
	Out	Back		
Northern fur seal	15.0	10.2	165	15
Antarctic fur seal	16.0	12.0	128	12
Galapagos fur seal	2.7	2.0	16	29
Galapagos sea lion	0.5	1.5	16	13

Note: Data for the South American fur seal were deleted because they were collected during an El Niño year and probably did not represent behavior during a normal year.

to the feeding areas varies with, and is probably an important determinant of, differences in feeding-trip duration. When the seals carrying TDRs are ranked in order of absolute travel time, the ranking coincides with the rank order of foraging-trip duration (Table 15.7). More important, transit times comprise similar proportions of total sea time (12%–29%) regardless of absolute trip duration (Table 15.7). The subpolar and tropical species do not differ consistently in this trait, but the results for the South American species do not represent a normal year. If transit time is regressed on trip duration for species averages, a good fit results ($r^2 = 76.1\%$). However, if this regression is run for individuals without taking species averages, the fit decreases to only 35.7%. Therefore, transit time may largely determine trip duration for the species, but its effect is partly obscured by large individual variation. This variation may result from the varying success that individuals have in finding prey patches. Again, data on the temporal and spatial distribution of prey are needed.

Can the concept of local resource depletion—depletion caused by fur seals—explain the correlations between travel time and total duration of foraging trips? No evidence for local resource depletion has been found in any fur seal population. It would seem more likely to occur at low latitudes where prey abundance is relatively low and seasonally uniform, and where fur seal populations are sparse. It would seem less likely to occur at high latitudes where a great abundance of prey is available seasonally, and where fur seal populations are dense but migratory. Even if local resource depletion plays a role, and this seems questionable, it could not by itself explain why females spend more days in the foraging area if they have to travel farther to get to a less exploited foraging area. Only the contention that longer travel times lead to longer foraging time in the feeding area explains the observed facts. This contention appears logical, as the benefit derived from a given feeding time at sea must decrease as travel time to the feeding area becomes increasingly costly.

Maternal Strategies At Sea

Most seals in our work dived at night. Peaks in dive frequency and depth occurred around dawn or dusk with a hiatus between peaks. In general this pattern coincides with the nightly vertical migration of prey (Longhurst, 1976) and with the hours of darkness when prey detection should be most difficult. We found two exceptions to this general pattern. A few northern fur seal females dived deeply at all hours of the day, always to similar depths. Also, Galapagos sea lions were mostly diurnal, with peaks of activity around dawn, noon, and dusk, and they generally dived deeper than the sympatric Galapagos fur seal. These patterns are shown graphically in Figure 15.7. How can the economics of diving and the movement pattern of prey explain these basic trends and the exceptions noted?

A considerable amount of work on the economics of foraging in birds and insects has produced the concept of "optimal foraging" (Pyke et al., 1977). Two papers on optimal foraging in mink (Dunstone and O'Connor, 1979a, b) are relevant to fur seal diving. In one study, principal component analysis of foraging behavior showed that 51% of the variance in mink feeding behavior was due to foraging economics (with components such as encounter rate, number of pursuits per bout, etc.), and 23% was due to O_2 constraints (components such as duration of searches and giving up time of the bout). The other study showed experimentally that dive behavior was influenced by prey density. Specifically, it showed that (1) the durations of dive chases were more prolonged at lower encounter rates; (2) dive frequency correlated negatively with encounter rate: and (3) pursuit duration was shorter for high encounter rates.

In fur seals, the deeper the dive, the greater the energy invested. If each dive is treated as a visit to a "patch," then, according to the results for mink (Dunstone and O'Connor, 1979b), the deeper the dive, the richer the patch should be in prey size or encounter rate to repay this investment. If the prey changes its distribution, then the predator should change its behavior. From a cost-benefit standpoint, seals should always reduce their dive time and energy expenditure and maximize energy captured. Cost-benefit considerations may underlie our finding that seals dive predominantly at

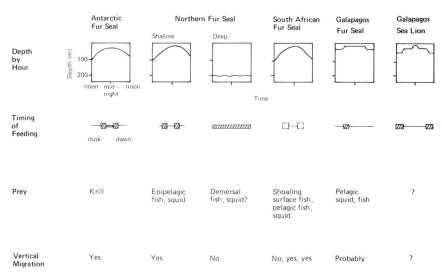

Fig. 15.7. Summary of type of prey, movement pattern of prey, and depth and time of day when eared seals intercept these prey for each species in this study.

night. Not only are vertical distances to the prey less at that time, but diurnal competitors, such as marine birds, are eliminated.

If the economics of foraging dictate that feeding should occur generally at night, then why is feeding not uniform throughout the dark hours? Why are dives deepest and most frequent at dusk and dawn, with a hiatus in the middle hours? Concerning dive depths, we found in northern and Antarctic fur seals that the first dives after dusk and the last dives made at dawn tended to be the deepest of the night, and that between these dives the depths became first shallower, then deeper. Food motivation may partly explain this pattern. Preying mantids stalk their food farther when less food is in the gut (Charnov, 1976a). Perhaps, similarly, the appetite of fur seals causes them to dive deeply at dusk before their prey reaches the surface. An attempt to reach satiation before a day of fasting may motivate them to forage as long into dawn hours as they can obtain a net energy gain. Food deprivation may explain the finding (Croxall et al., 1985) that the cessation of diving at dawn, following a night of foraging, is less variable ($\pm$ 1.1 hours) than the onset of diving at dusk ($\pm$ 3.7 hours) which follows a day of fasting. The dawn foraging pattern would seem to agree with the marginal value theorem of optimal foraging (Charnov, 1976b).

Diving frequency may be greater at twilight than in darker hours because of a greater likelihood of success then. Two factors, singly or in combination, could increase the success of twilight dives: (1) prey silhouetted against brighter surface water at twilight may be detectable farther away than it is at night; detection would depend on the type of prey and whether or not it employed effective bioluminescent camouflage (Muntz, 1983); (2) prey may be more densely clumped during vertical migration (hence more economical to exploit) than later at night when it disperses at or near the surface. No empirical data are available on either point.

The absence of diving in the middle of the night in some northern and Antarctic fur seals constituted as clear a trend as the propensity for diving at dawn and dusk. The following factors may influence this pattern: (1) time may be needed to clear the stomach after the dusk feeding bout; (2) prey may disperse after having risen to the surface; (3) ambient light levels may decrease below the prey detection threshold, thus decreasing the encounter rate with prey; and (4) diving may occur but may be too shallow to detect with the present TDR. We believe the latter factor is most likely, at least for some species. Feeding probably continues but at such shallow depths that dives are not recorded. Thus the hiatus, which was most apparent in the Antarctic fur seal records (Chapter 7), may have been an artifact.

The least likely explanation is that the encounter rates decline because of low ambient light. Light levels are probably never too low for these nocturnal animals to detect surface prey underwater at night. Psychophysical experiments show that when harbor seals, *Phoca vitulina*, are fully dark-adapted, they are capable of detecting moving objects on a moonlit night at 360 m depth in clear oceanic waters (Wartzok, cited by Schusterman, 1981). Furthermore, Schusterman and Balliet (1971) showed that light levels as low as 10^{-4} mL had only slight effects on the visual acuity of California sea lions. They concluded that "the highly specialized pinniped eye is structurally adapted for efficient function in dim light . . . but . . . only under water."

One exception to the general fur seal dive pattern occurred with the few northern fur seal individuals that dived consistently to depths of 150–200 m throughout day and night. Given the general visual capabilities just discussed, these seals should be able to reach the depth of the deep scattering layer (DSL) at any time. The DSL is almost global in occurrence (Longhurst, 1976), usually at depths of 100–400 m. Since it occurs offshore, it is in oceanic waters that are noted for clarity; even on cloudy nights there is enough light at 200 m (10^{-7} μ W cm^{-2}) to permit broad field vision in man (Clarke, 1971, as cited in Smith, 1976). Also, prey capture may be enhanced by seals taking bioluminescent prey. The consistent dive depths of these northern fur seal females suggest that their prey remains at the same depth over time and does not move with the DSL. The grouping of dives into obvious bouts suggests that fatigue or satiation ends the bout, not migration of the prey to deeper depths as for shallower divers. We assume that the energy (biomass) gained per deep dive is on average greater than on each shallow dive. This suggestion stems from the finding that deep divers made one-third as many dives per trip as shallow divers (Chapter 4) yet gained comparable body mass (Chapter 5).

The final exception to the general dive pattern—the differences between Galapagos sea lions and fur seals—may be explained by size differences and associated swim speeds in morphologically similar and closely related species. Sea lions are two to three times larger than the fur seals, and as a result they may swim faster. This conclusion stems from the relative ways in which drag and power output change as a function of size. Surface area scales with length squared, and muscle mass scales with length cubed. Therefore, because drag is proportional to surface area and power output is proportional to muscle mass, power output may increase at a greater rate than drag as size increases. It follows that sea lions should be able to dive to greater depths than fur seals at the same or even lower cost (lower mass-specific metabolism), and that they have a greater ADL (Table 15.4). In addition, because of their larger size, sea lions should be able to handle bigger prey than fur seals can handle. If prey size differs by hour of day, then day diving for large prey would be a more profitable strategy for the larger animal. When they dive at the same hours (night), sea lions dive deeper and possibly capture more small food items on the longer way up.

Differences in size and diving behavior may help reduce intraspecific competition for food. In otariids the breeding males are considerably larger than the females and probably have a greater ADL. This would permit them to dive longer and deeper than females and young of the species, and to feed on different species or year-classes of prey. This hypothesis is testable. Competition is also reduced by the prolonged fasting of adult males during the breeding season, and by the geographic separation of the sexes outside the breeding season. These two generalizations pertain more to migratory than nonmigratory otariids.

In summary, fur seals of the subpolar and tropical groups may usually dive at night because prey species are closer to the surface at that time and shallow diving is more economical than deep diving. The pronounced twilight peaks in diving activity may reflect relatively higher prey availability and capture rates than in the darkest hours of the night, and possibly greater food motivation. Daytime diving is deeper. Galapagos sea lions, because of their larger size and probable faster swim speeds, can economically exploit prey at greater depths than can fur seals, especially if large prey are available. Size differences may act between and within otariid species to reduce competition for food. A more detailed interpretation of seal diving patterns must await better data on the vertical migration patterns of the prey species involved.

Hunting Tactics

In addition to the determinants that shape maternal strategies at sea, other principles or factors may guide the individual dive. We term these collectively "hunting tactics" to denote that they are small-scale actions serving the larger purpose of maternal strategies. We propose and discuss four rules of hunting that are supported by data from dive profiles.

1. *Dive no deeper or longer than necessary.* Since dives are energetically costly, seals should not dive much deeper than where their prey are likely to be. Ideally, search and feeding should occur at the surface because then the entire dive would consist of pursuit and prey-handling time. If the prey are easily captured, then the energy investment in each capture is small and the seal can profitably take small, dispersed prey. As depth increases, prey size or encounter rate should increase. A further advantage of shallow feeding is that the dive-chase is short and O_2 stores need not be completely loaded before the dive begins (Dunstone and O'Connor, 1979b). Also, with short pursuit times at the surface, the influence of O_2 constraints would be small, as it is in mink. Most seals discussed in this work performed some shallow, brief dives (<1 minute) that fit this description. If in fur seals, as in mink, economic factors outweigh O_2 constraints to foraging, then shallow diving would be an economic advantage. Even if prey are dispersed near the surface, capture costs there are small, and each dive could result in a net energy gain.

Even the exceptions to the general fur seal diving pattern—the Galapagos sea lions and the deep-diving northern fur seals—probably follow this rule. However, both of these groups dive day and night, thus foraging for longer continuous periods and returning to

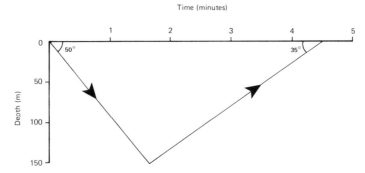

Fig. 15.8. Calculated angle of dive relative to sea surface for fur seals. The angles are calculated from dive depth, descent and ascent rates, and dive durations as measured for northern fur seals using a TDR, and from a presumed swim rate of 2 ms⁻¹.

young sooner. Sea cycles of the Galapagos sea lion are about 12 hours long (Fig. 13.5), compared with 30 to 50 hours for the Galapagos fur seal (Fig. 11.9). Deep diving northern fur seals average 132 hours at sea compared to an average of 199 hours for all other northern fur seals (Table 4.1).

The economics of deep diving may require that the animals be large and experienced. Theoretically, animals of less than about 50 kg could not make extended dives (>4 minutes; Table 15.4) consistently enough to feed effectively at the depth ranges required in daytime (100–200 m). Dive depth changes linearly with the sum of dive plus surface recovery time until the ADL is exceeded, at which point recovery time increases nonlinearly. This causes a decline in the proportion of total time spent diving, which is tantamount to a decrease in foraging efficiency. The dive depth at which this proportion changes is usually deeper for a larger animal when intraspecific comparisons are made.

2. *Search during the descent, and descend as quickly as possible.* The search phase of a dive may occur during the descent or on the ascent as seals approach prey from beneath. In either case the descent should be made as rapidly as possible. This tactic saves time and oxygen stores for pursuit, and it decreases the energy invested in the dive. Therefore, as soon as prey are encountered, or the depth at which they are usually found is attained, the descent should end and pursuit or ascent should begin. This maximum depth, or giving up time, may be determined by the type, size, or density of prey, the encounter rate on past dives, or the food motivation of the fur seal.

If the prey patch is broadly distributed over a uniform depth and is dense enough for the encounter rate to be high, then the dive depths will be uniform or will shift consistently with the prey (some examples are the northern, Antarctic, and South African fur seal dive patterns; Figs. 4.1, 4.2, 7.1, 9.2). However, if prey are less dense, then the pattern will be less consistent, as seen in the Galapagos sea lion (Fig. 14.1).

3. *Search for, pursue, and capture prey on the ascent.* Both the ascent angle and ascent rate suggest that prey capture occurs in this phase of the dive. Search and pursuit may follow a consistent pattern in all dives. But in our records this pattern is clear only in the deepest dives where well-defined profiles were obtained. Profiles constructed from the average descent and ascent rates of northern fur seals give a descent angle relative to the sea surface of between 40° and 60° and an ascent angle of 30°–40° (Fig. 15.8). This result is based on an assumed swim velocity of 2 ms^{-1} without any horizontal deviations. A slower swim rate would increase the angle, and a faster rate would decrease it. With a shallower angle, a longer transect would be searched for prey.

In the South African fur seal, ascent rate was four to five times slower than descent rate (Fig. 9.4), and in northern fur seals it was 1.4 times slower (Table 15.5). In almost all deep dives analyzed, the traces indicate a steady rate of descent and ascent. If burst swimming occurred during pursuit and capture, it was not indicated in descent-ascent rates. Rapid descent may represent direct searching and travel to the patch (see rule 1). The slow ascent may represent

TABLE 15.8. Energy available in food consumed by fur seals.

Food	Energy of food[a] (kJ g^{-1})	Assimilation[a] efficiency	Usable energy (kJ g^{-1})
Herring			
Clupea spp.	7.7	0.93	7.2
Pollock			
Theragra chalcogramma	5.9	0.94	5.5
Squid			
Gonatus spp.	3.7	0.85	3.1
Krill			
Euphausia superba	4.4[b]	0.90[c]	4.0

[a] Miller, 1978.

[b] Clarke & Prince, 1980.

[c] Interpolated from squid and fish.

TABLE 15.9. Prey requirements to meet the energy expenditures of foraging females.

Species	Mass (kg)	At sea W kg⁻¹*	MR MJ day⁻¹	Prey requirements (kg)				Adult weight (%)
				Herring	Pollock	Squid	Krill	
Northern fur seal	37	8.2	26	3.6	4.7	8.4	—	9–21
Antarctic fur seal	34	8.4	25	—	—	—	6.3	18
So. African fur seal	68	7.0	41	5.7	7.5	13.2	—	8–19
Galapagos fur seal	29	8.7	22	3.1	4.0	7.1	—	11–24
Galapagos sea lion	80	6.8	47	6.5	8.5	15.2	—	8–19

Notes: These values do not include the prey energy required by females to produce the milk energy consumed by the pup on shore. MR = metabolic rate.
* Based on cost to a 37 kg northern fur seal (using ^{18}O) of 8.2 W kg^{-1} (Costa and Gentry, Chapter 5), and scaling this in proportion to $W^{-0.25}$ we have the equation MR (W kg^{-1} = 20.2 M (kg)$^{-0.25}$.

more searching and, if prey is encountered, pursuit and capture. This pattern is consistent with Hobson's (1966) observation that sea lions feed on the ascent, silhouetting prey against the bright surface water and capturing prey from below.

4. *Capture only large or energy-rich prey on deep dives.* Those seals that are large and experienced enough to dive deeply (200 m) should do so only if the energy obtainable on a single dive is greater than on a single shallow dive. As the recovery time following deep dives is proportionately longer than for shallow dives (Chapter 4), more energy must be obtained per deep dive, or the rate of energy acquisition would be slower than for shallow dives. Deep-diving northern fur seals apparently found such energy-rich prey because they gained as much mass on a trip as did shallow divers that performed three times as many dives.

Energetic Requirements and Success of Prey Capture

Given that fur seals of the subpolar and tropical groups reduce the effort expended on obtaining energy by adjusting dive frequency to match greatest prey abundance at least depth, do they differ in their energetic requirements or in the success of prey capture? By matching known dive frequencies with estimated energy content of prey, assimilation efficiencies, usable energy (given in

Table 15.8), and estimated prey requirements of females (Table 15.9), we can give approximate answers to this question. These answers are not intended to be absolute, but instead show the range of variation in the species studied. Daily prey requirements for lactating females depend on diet, and range from about 3–8 kg day^{-1} for those eating fish to 7–13 kg day^{-1} for those eating squid. These values represent about 10% of a seal's body weight per day if it takes fish, but about 20% if it consumes squid.

To estimate the amount of prey that animals must capture on each dive, we combined data on prey requirements with information on dive frequency (Table 15.10). Note that daily dive rate is lowest in northern fur seal deep divers, doubles in Antarctic fur seals, and is much greater again in both Galapagos fur seals and sea lions. The amount of prey required per dive is less variable; it is least in the Galapagos fur seal, only slightly higher in the Galapagos sea lion and Antarctic fur seal, and greatest in northern fur seals.

From these estimates we can predict the number of individual prey items that must be captured on each dive if we know the mean size of prey. Data on prey size are scanty except for Antarctic fur seals. The results show that the Galapagos fur seal needs to catch a small number of fish or squid per dive, the northern fur seal's requirements vary widely, and the Antarctic fur seal needs large numbers of prey (Table 15.10). This suggests that on average each dive should be "successful" in terms of capturing some item of prey. The greater number of dives required of tropical species to fill roughly similar energetic needs suggests that their prey may be more dispersed. The Antarctic fur seal may make more dives per day than other species because its prey are so small.

Given that the duration of dives is known for all species, we can calculate the weight and number of prey items that must be captured per minute of each dive (Table 15.11). Note that deep-diving northern fur seals make fewer and longer dives each day than shallow divers of the same species (Table 15.10), but that the required rate of prey capture is very similar for both. This suggests that neither alternative pattern is necessarily more profitable than the other.

In summary, prey capture rates (in weight taken per unit time) during dives are broadly similar among species, reflecting the general similarity in dive durations. The prey capture rates presented here are maximum estimates, as they are based on the assumption that no feeding occurs at the surface. This assumption may not be valid for some species (Antarctic fur seal, Chapter 7) where surface

TABLE 15.10. Estimates of prey required per dive time.

Species	Number of dives per day	Mean duration (min)	Prey needed per dive					
			g min^{-1}			Individuals min^{-1}		
			Herring	Squid	Krill	Herring	Squid	Krill
Northern fur seal								
Deep	26	3.6	38	89	—	0.4	—	—
Shallow	38	2.1	44	103	—	0.4	—	—
Antarctic fur seal	82	1.9	—	—	40	—	—	40
Galapagos fur seal	134	1.0	23	53	—	2.0	4	—
Galapagos sea lion	192	2.0	17	40	—	—	—	—

TABLE 15.11. Estimates of prey required per dive.

Species	Dives		Prey	Prey size		Prey per dive (g)	Mean no. individuals	Range
	h^{-1}	day^{-1}		Mean (g)	Range (g)			
Northern fur seal	1.5	36	Herring			98		
			Pollock	100	10–400	129	1.3	0.3–13.0
			Squid	—	—	228	—	—
Antarctic fur seal	3.4	82	Krill	1	0.7–1.1	70	70	64–100
Galapagos fur seal	5.6	134	Squid	12	—	49	4	—
			Fish	10	—	21–28	2–3	
Galapagos sea lion	8.0	192	Squid	—	—	74	—	—
			Fish	—	—	32–42	—	—

feeding may be of considerable importance. If better data on prey size, abundance, and distribution become available, such calculations could be used to show more extensive ecological differences between species.

Parent-Offspring Conflict

The subpolar and tropical groups differ in the degree of parent-offspring conflict (Trivers, 1974) that develops at weaning time. In both Antarctic and northern fur seals the majority of pups wean themselves. They abandon the beaches to forage for themselves while their mothers are still onshore and available for suckling. The pups of the temperate or tropical species, in contrast, are abandoned or driven off by the female before she gives birth again. In the Galapagos fur seal, pups are sometimes killed by their older siblings or starve to death as a result of competition for access to the mother (Trillmich, in press). What factors account for these different patterns in parent-offspring conflict? To answer this question we must consider the costs and benefits of independent foraging versus suckling for both the pup and the mother.

A pup should only suckle as long as its average expected net energy gain per unit time is greater than it would be if it fed independently. If mothers end shore visits when they reach a lower nutritional set point, energy transfer from mother to pup can be increased only within relatively narrow limits. If the pup forages at sea between its mother's visits, it can reduce the cost of fasting while waiting. As soon as pup foraging success becomes energetically more advantageous (on average) than waiting for the mother's return, the pup should wean itself.

This point should be reached much earlier in the subpolar than in the tropical species since their travel distances (costs) to and from foraging areas are much greater. For them, the cost of travel is much higher relative to the expected benefit from suckling because the feeding cycles of mothers are much longer. Furthermore, the probability of meeting the mother when coming ashore is much lower for these pups. When a northern fur seal pup comes ashore it can expect an average waiting time of about 3.5 days for its mother, whereas a returning Galapagos fur seal young will almost never have to wait longer than a day.

Finally, in the migratory species the probability of the mother's return ashore decreases steeply toward the end of the season. For young of the tropical species, this probability remains high throughout the year (mother is likely to return), so that tropical fur seals can always expect some benefit from returning to shore. In migratory species the mother-young bond breaks at the latest at the onset of migration. Mother-young pairs have not been seen at sea later than that time. Weaning coincides with migration presumably because contact at sea is almost impossible to maintain when solitary hunting is the best foraging strategy.

Differences in parent-offspring conflict also stem from differential effects of suckling on the mother's future reproductive success. In the subpolar species, in which suckling near the end of the short rearing period would not seriously interfere with the mother's next pregnancy, suckling the young until late in the season would presumably cost little. Providing a small or late-weaning young with some extra energy may well benefit the young's survival much more than it reduces the mother's ability to invest in her next offspring. This is not so in the Galapagos fur seal, where the long suckling period reduces the mother's reproductive output by decreasing her pregnancy rate and the survival of her newborns. Therefore, the differences that we observed in mother-young conflict over parental investment are predicted by theory.

Population Dynamics

Chapter 1 showed that the subpolar species each have populations ≥1 million animals, whereas the tropical species number only about 40,000. What combination of factors has led to these differences in population size?

We would expect larger populations to exist in more predictable environments. The seals in this study fit this prediction if we accept the contention in Part 1 that production in subpolar areas is more predictable than in tropical areas that are subject to EN events. The least predictable areas should be the Galapagos Islands, where seals depend on a narrow band of upwelling around islands (Barber and Chavez, 1983). This upwelling would be more severely influenced by EN events, which are centered on the equator, than in coastal areas where upwelling continues, although at a reduced rate. Seals along the coast of South (and North) America should be increasingly less affected (have increasingly more predictable environments) the farther they are from the equator.

The route by which EN conditions affect population size may be through the serial loss of potential female recruits. York and Hartley (1981) showed that loss of potential female offspring following a reduction of adult females in the Pribilof herd of northern fur seals could account for 70% of the decline in pups born after the reduction ended, and that the effect was still measurable 22 years later. Tropical species that experience total or partial loss of some year classes because of the effects of EN events may experience successive waves of this "lag effect" that prevent the population from recovering fast from any given reduction.

The behavioral and demographic studies done to date suggest that the mechanisms that control population size (mainly for subpolar species) act during the pelagic phase of the seals' life history. The space available on land, pregnancy rates, juvenile and adult survival on land, and the behavioral characteristics on land may change, but do so usually as a result of changed population size. Predation may control populations during the pelagic phase, but this is not likely to occur in migratory species of high latitudes. Ultimately, the availability of food must exert some influence on population size. Few data are yet available on absolute resource levels by which subpolar and tropical areas could be compared. However, transit times, trip durations, and time spent swimming suggest that the extent of area available for foraging is much smaller in the tropical forms.

In summary, seal populations with similar maternal strategies share some characteristics of population dynamics. Subpolar seals spend summers at high latitudes where a seasonal pulse of productivity occurs over an area broad enough to support a large absolute population. However, the seasonal nature of productivity requires the existence of rich, winter feeding areas within migratory distances (about 5,500 km one way for the northern fur seal). Because females in such populations produce a new offspring each year, and because no catastrophic reductions in food availability cause the serial loss of female recruits, recovery of such populations from reductions in size can be rapid. Tropical seals depend on marine productivity that occurs over a restricted area. In that area densities in seals per square kilometer of sea may be as great as in subpolar areas, but the areas are so restricted in size that smaller seal populations are supported. The absence of marked seasonality makes migration unnecessary, and the absence of alternative winter feeding areas within migratory distance mitigates against such migration. Because females produce independent young only every 2 to 3 years, and because periodic ENs cause the serial loss of female recruits, recovery from reductions in population size is very slow.

Life History Theory

Life history theory relates patterns in reproduction with environmental variables, and predicts the best reproductive "decisions" that populations should make to solve different environmental problems. Diverse components of reproduction are considered by these theories, such as juvenile and adult mortality schedules, age at first reproduction, reproductive life span, clutch size, size of young, and interbrood interval (Wilbur et al., 1974; Stearns, 1977). A species expresses each of these traits differently, depending on the combination of environmental pressures it has experienced. The combination of its expressions for all traits is termed its life history "strategy."

Two theories have been advanced to explain life history strategies. The r- and K-selection theory predicts that in fluctuating environments, traits leading to fast population growth will predominate. Examples of these traits are maturing early in life, giving birth once in a short lifetime, and producing large numbers of young.

Conversely, the theory predicts that in a stable environment, traits leading to reduced reproductive effort will be favored. Species in such environments will tend to mature late, reproduce repeatedly over a long lifetime, produce few young per brood, and produce larger numbers of broods.

An alternative theory, termed "bet-hedging," predicts different outcomes in a fluctuating environment, depending on whether adult or juvenile mortality is affected by the environment. If adult mortality varies, the bet-hedging theory predicts increased reproductive effort, just as the r- and K-selection theory predicts for fluctuating environments (Table 4 in Stearns, 1976). However, if juvenile mortality varies, bet-hedging predicts that reduced reproductive effort will be favored, the same outcome predicted for stable environments by the r- and K-selection theory.

The maternal strategies of fur seals generally fit the predictions of bet-hedging theory under conditions of varying juvenile mortality. Seals in the more unpredictable environment (tropical areas affected by EN conditions) had lower reproductive effort than seals in the more predictable (high-latitude) areas. They spent longer periods producing each weaned offspring; as a result they probably produced fewer weaned young in a lifetime than females in the more predictable environment. This comparison cannot be extended because important data, such as the age at first reproduction, life span, and juvenile mortality, are not yet available for most fur seal species.

PART 3. CONCLUSIONS

We define a maternal strategy as the long- and short-term options by which females produce the largest number of independent offspring in their lifetime. The choices are graded along a scale from very inflexible to very flexible; all are affected to some degree by environmental and other constraints.

Inflexible traits probably represent adaptation to a general set of conditions that do not change or that change within predictable bounds. Also, they relate more to the total lifetime reproductive output than to rearing of a given young. In our work the two most inflexible traits were that weight at weaning (ca. 40% of adult female weight) and the tendency to bear a single young per year were the same in all species. Presumably these traits are general adaptations to a marine existence, and hence they do not change over time or between species. Another trait specific to the otariid family is that, unlike phocid females, all females in our study alternated between feeding and suckling. Two other relatively inflexible traits are the percentage of fat in the females' milk and the fasting ability of their pups. These traits covary among species, are probably not subject to much interannual variation, and may represent evolutionary constraints at the family level (Stearns, 1983).

Short-term options are flexible within or between seasons and probably relate to a specific, perhaps even ephemeral, set of conditions. These options are under behavioral control and may vary within a season as needed to rear a single young to weaning. Examples of such options are the varied combinations of attendance and diving behavior, which probably reflect the abundance, quality, and distribution of prey.

Some options may be flexible in one maternal strategy and fixed in another. In unpredictable environments the time to weaning is a flexible trait. In tropical species weaning can occur over a broad range of ages from less than 18 to 36 months, commensurate with yearly food supply. In increasingly predictable environments, the time to weaning becomes less and less flexible until at high latitudes it is so determined by environmental constraints that it becomes inflexible. The female's best strategy here is to unfailingly invest all resources in the young of the year. That is, the flexible portions of the maternal strategies are inseparable from the physiological, ecological, and behavioral factors that comprise the inflexible portions.

The maternal strategies in our work form an apparent gradient from the subpolar to the tropical species that is best characterized by its end points. Many variables other than time to weaning (Bester, 1981) differ along this gradient.

In the subpolar strategy, females face a highly predictable but seasonally changeable environment in which food resources, although not uniform across years, are not subject to massive failure. Given predictable food resources, females maximize their lifetime reproductive output by investing in pups to meet the same conditions each year. They produce and wean a pup in the brief season defined by inclement weather through a series of long-duration foraging trips involving many dives and dive bouts. They obtain large amounts of energy on each trip to sea and convert it to high-fat-content milk that the pup receives on infrequent but long visits to shore by the mother. The young are quickly brought to weaning weight and are weaned without parent-offspring conflict. Pups are weaned having excess fat on which they subsist until independent feeding begins. Preweaning mortality is low. The risk in this strategy is that pups may not survive the transition to independent feeding because they have acquired no foraging skills by then. Females invest in fat reserves for their young and risk the pup's survival on the availability of food. Even though postweaning mortality is high, large populations result from this strategy because in this predictable environment resource levels are high, and entire cohorts of young are never lost.

In the tropical strategy, females face a seasonally constant environment that is unpredictable over a series of years because food supplies are subject to massive, periodic failures. Under these conditions the best reproductive strategy is to retain flexibility in rearing young. The weaning period is not precisely defined and can vary depending on food supply. In good years females wean the offspring by 2 years of age and undertake rearing a new young. In poor years they continue to invest in the young of the previous year and allow the newborn offspring to die. In extremely poor years they allow all young to die in order to remain alive themselves. During suckling, which is prolonged, females make frequent, brief trips to sea from which they return with milk of low fat content. As the pup slowly approaches weaning weight, parent-offspring conflict develops which jeopardizes the survival of the next young. Pups are weaned with no excess fat, but stand a good chance of survival due to the feeding experience they have acquired. The low success of rearing newborns is thus offset by the flexibility that females retain in the face of uncertain food supply. Because entire cohorts and some adults may die from starvation during massive, unpredictable food failures, the populations grow at very slow rates.

Our data suggest that another strategy develops in the more temperate fur seals, or at least that these seals are intermediate in many aspects of attendance behavior. They tend to follow a yearly cycle of weaning, but with some variation. We cannot conclude from present evidence that their maternal strategies are closer to the tropical than to the subpolar seals, but we suggest that they are. More extensive data are needed on the New Zealand, subantarctic, and South American fur seals.

Our goal at the beginning of this project was to make a few simple comparisons among the seals we had studied. We discovered that the similarities and differences formed large patterns involving factors that we had not measured. As a result we have not completely characterized the maternal strategies we describe, nor have we identified all the possible maternal strategies that exist in fur seals. We have identified some questions for future research that, when answered, will complete the outline of broad patterns of adaptation in the eared seal family that we have begun in this work.

Literature Cited

Aguayo, A. L. 1978. The present status of the Antarctic fur seal *Arcto-cephalus gazella* at South Shetland Islands. *Polar Rec.* 19: 167–176.

Ainley, D. G., H. R. Huber, and K. M. Bailey. 1982. Population fluctuations of California sea lions and the Pacific whiting fishery off Central California. *U.S. Natl. Mar. Fish. Serv. Fish. Bull.* 80: 253–258.

Altmann, J. 1974. Observational study of behavior: Sampling methods. *Behaviour* 49: 227–267.

Anonymous. 1973. Coordinated Pribilof Islands-Bering Sea research proposal *Fed. Regist.* 38(147): 20599–20601.

Antonelis, G. A., and R. L. DeLong. 1985. Population and behavioral studies, San Miguel Island (Adams Cove and Castle Rock). In P. Kosloff, editor, *Fur Seal Investigations, 1983*. U.S. Dept. of Commerce, NOAA Tech. Memo. NMFS F/NWC-78. Northwest and Alaska Fisheries Center, Seattle, Wash.

Antonelis, G. A., C. H. Fiscus, and R. L. DeLong. 1984. Spring and summer prey of California sea lions, *Zalophus californianus*, at San Miguel Island, California, 1978–1979. *U.S. Natl. Mar. Fish. Serv., Fish. Bull.* 82: 67–76.

Ashworth, U. S., G. D. Ramaiah, and M. C. Keyes. 1966. Species differences in composition of milk with special reference to the northern fur seal. *J. Dairy Sci.* 49: 1206–1211.

Bailey, K. M., and D. G. Ainley. 1981/1982. The dynamics of California sea lion predation on Pacific hake. *Fish. Res.* (Amst.) 1: 163–176.

Barber, R. T., and F. P. Chavez. 1983. Biological consequences of El Niño. *Science* 222: 1203–1210.

Bartholomew, G. A. 1970. A model for the evolution of pinniped polygyny. *Evolution* 24: 546–559.

Bartholomew, G. A., and P. G. Hoel. 1953. Reproductive behavior of the Alaska fur seal, *Callorhinus ursinus. J. Mammal.* 34: 417–436.

Best, P. B. 1973. Seals and sealing in South and South West Africa. *S. Afr. Shipp. News Fish. Ind. Rev.* 28: 49–57.

Best, P. B., and P. D. Shaughnessy. 1975. Nursing in the Cape fur seal *Arctocephalus pusillus pusillus*. Unpublished report. Sea Fisheries Res. Inst., Cape Town.

———. 1979. An independent account of Captain Benjamin Morrell's sealing voyage to the south-west coast of Africa in the *Antarctic*, 1828/29. *Fish. Bull. S. Afr.* 12: 1–19.

Bester, M. N. 1977. Habitat selection, seasonal population changes, and behavior of the Amsterdam Island fur seal *Arctocephalus tropicalis* on Gough Island. D.Sc. thesis, Univ. Pretoria, Pretoria.

———. 1981. Seasonal changes in the population composition of the fur seal *Arctocephalus tropicalis* at Gough Island. *S. Afr. J. Wildl. Res.* 11: 49–55.

Boersma, P. D. 1978. Breeding patterns of Galapagos penguins as an indicator of oceanographic conditions. *Science* 200: 1481–1483.

Bonner, W. N. 1968. The fur seal of South Georgia. *Br. Antarct. Surv. Sci. Rep.* 56: 1–81.

———. 1981. Southern fur seals *Arctocephalus* (Geoffroy Saint-Hilaire and Cuvier, 1826). In S. H. Ridgway and R. J. Harrison, editors, *Handbook of Marine Mammals*, vol. 1, pp. 161–208. New York: Academic Press.

Brody, S. 1945. *Bioenergetics and Growth.* New York: Hafner Press.

Budd, G. M. 1972. Breeding of the fur seal at McDonald Islands, and further population growth at Heard Island. *Mammalia* 36: 423–427.

Burger, A. E., and J. Cooper. 1984. The effects of fisheries on sea birds in South Africa and Namibia. In D. N. Nettleship, J. Sanger, and P. F. Springer, editors, *Marine Birds: Their Feeding Ecology and Commercial Fisheries Relationships*, pp. 150–161. Can. Wildl. Serv., Spec. Publ.

Butterworth, D. S. 1983. Assessment and management of pelagic stocks in the southern Benguela region. In G. D. Sharp and J. Csirke, editors, *Proceedings of the expert consultation to examine changes in abundance and species composition of neritic fish resources, San Jose, Costa Rica, April 1983.* Food Agric. Organ. U.N., Rome. *FAO Fish Rep.* 291(2): 329–405.

Butterworth, D. S., J.H.M. David, L. H. Rickett, and S. Xulu. In press. Modelling the population dynamics of the Cape fur seal (*Arctocephalus pusillus pusillus*). In J. P. Croxall and R. L. Gentry, editors, *The Status, Biology, and Ecology of Fur Seals.* U.S. Dept. of Commerce, NOAA Tech. Rep., NMFS.

Cane, M. A. 1983. Oceanographic events during El Niño. *Science* 222:1189–1195.

Chapman, D. G. 1961. Population dynamics of the Alaska fur seal herd. *Trans. N. Am. Wildl. Nat. Resource Conf.* 26: 356–369.

Charnov, E. L. 1976a. Optimal foraging: The marginal value theorem. *Theor. Popul. Biol.* 9: 129–136.

———. 1976b. Optimal foraging: Attack strategy of a mantid. *Am. Nat.* 110: 141–151.

Cioffi, L. A., W.P.T. James, and T. B. Van Itallie, editors. 1981. *Body Weight Regulatory System: Normal and Disturbed Mechanisms.* New York: Raven Press.

Clark, T. W. 1979. Galapagos fur seal. In *Mammals in the Seas*, vol. 2, *Pinniped Species Summaries and Reports on Sirenians*, pp. 31–33. Food Agric. Organ. U.N., Rome. FAO Fish. Ser. 5.

Clarke, A. C., and P. A. Prince. 1980. Chemical composition and calorific value of food fed to mollymawk chicks *Diomedea melanophris* and *D. chrysostoma* at Bird Island, South Georgia. *Ibis* 122: 488–494.

Clarke, M. R., and F. Trillmich. 1980. Cephalopods in the diet of fur seals of the Galapagos islands. *J. Zool.* (Lond.) 190: 211–215.

Clutton-Brock, T. H., F. E. Guinness, and S. D. Albon. 1982. *Red Deer: Behavioral ecology of two sexes.* Chicago: Univ. of Chicago Press.

Colwell, R. K. 1974. Predictability, constancy, and contingency of periodic phenomena. *Ecology* 55: 1148–1153.

Condy, P. R. 1978. Distribution, abundance, and annual cycle of fur seals (*Arctocephalus* spp.) on the Prince Edward Islands. *S. Afr. J. Wildl. Res.* 8: 159–168.

Costa, D. P. 1978. Ecological energetics, water and electrolyte balance of the California sea otter, *Enhydra lutris*. Ph.D. thesis, Univ. of California, Santa Cruz.

Costa, D. P., S. D. Feldkamp, and R. L. Gentry. 1982. Bioenergetics of lactation in the northern fur seal. (Abstr.) *The Physiologist* 25: 279.

Costa, D. P., and G. L. Kooyman. 1984. Contribution of specific dynamic action to heat balance and thermoregulation in the sea otter *Enhydra lutris*. *Physiol. Zool.* 57: 199–203.

Costa, D. P., B. J. LeBoeuf, C. L. Ortiz, and A. C. Huntley. In press. The energetics of lactation in the northern elephant seal. *J. Zool.* (Lond.)

Crawley, M. C. 1975. Growth of New Zealand fur seal pups. *N.Z. J. Mar. Freshwater Res.* 9: 539–545.

Croxall, J. P., and P. A. Prince. 1979. Antarctic seabird and seal monitoring studies. *Polar Rec.* 19: 573–595.

Croxall, J. P., and M. N. Pilcher. 1984. Characteristics of krill, *Euphausia superba*, eaten by Antarctic fur seals, *Arctocephalus gazella*, at South Georgia. *Br. Antarct. Surv. Bull.* 63: 117–125.

Croxall, J. P., I. Everson, G. L. Kooyman, C. Ricketts, and R. W. Davis. 1985. Fur seal diving behavior in relation to vertical distribution of krill. *J. Anim. Ecol.* 54: 1-8.

David, J.H.M. In press. South African fur seal, *Arctocephalus pusillus pusillus*. In J. P. Croxall and R. L. Gentry, editors, *The Status, Biology, and Ecology of Fur Seals*. U.S. Dept. of Commerce, NOAA Tech. Rep.

Doidge, D. W., and J. P. Croxall. 1985. Diet and energy budget of the Antarctic fur seal *Arctocephalus gazella* at South Georgia. In W. R. Siegfried, R. M. Laws, and P. R. Condy, editors, *Antarctic Nutrient Cycles and Food Webs*, pp. 543–550. The Proceedings of the 4th SCAR Symposium on Antarctic Biology. Berlin: Springer-Verlag.

Doidge, D. W., J. P. Croxall, and J. R. Baker. 1984a. Density-dependent pup mortality in the Antarctic fur seal *Arctocephalus gazella* at South Georgia. *J. Zool.* (Lond.) 202: 449–460.

Doidge, D. W., J. P. Croxall, and C. Ricketts. 1984b. Growth rates of Antarctic fur seal *Arctocephalus gazella* pups at South Georgia. *J. Zool.* (Lond.) 203: 87–93.

Dunstone, N., and R. J. O'Connor. 1979a. Optimal foraging in an amphibious mammal. I: The aqualung effect. *Anim. Behav.* 27: 1182–1194.

———. 1979b. Optimal foraging in an amphibious mammal. II: A study using principal component analysis. *Anim. Behav.* 27: 1195–1201.

Edwards, M. J., and R. J. Martin. 1966. Mixing technique for the oxygen-hemoglobin equilibrium and Bohr effect. *J. Appl. Physiol.* 21: 1898–1902.

Eibl-Eibesfeldt, I. 1955. Ethologische Studien am Galapagos-Seelöwen. *Z. Tierpsychol.* 12: 286–303.

Erickson, A. W., and R. J. Hofman. 1974. Antarctic seals. Am. Georg. Soc., Antarct. map folio, ser. 18, *Antarctic Mammals*, pp. 4–13.

Evans, W. E. 1971. Orientation behavior of delphinids: Radio telemetric studies. *Ann. N.Y. Acad. Sci.* 188: 142–160.

Fagen, R. M., and D. Y. Young. 1979. Temporal patterns of behavior: Durations, intervals, latencies, and sequences. In P. W. Colgan, editor, *Quantitative Ethology*, pp. 79–114. New York: John Wiley and Sons.

Fedak, M. A., and S. S. Anderson. 1982. The energetics of lactation: Accurate measurements from a large wild mammal, the grey seal (*Halichoerus grypus*). *J. Zool.* (Lond.) 198: 473–479.

Fiscus, C. H., and G. A. Baines. 1966. Food and feeding behavior of Steller and California sea lions. *J. Mammal.* 47: 195–200.

Fisher, R. A. 1930. *The Genetical Theory of Natural Selection.* Oxford: Oxford Univ. Press.

Fonseca, T. R. 1983. El Niño, fenomeno digno de estudio. *Creces* 83,4(5): 24–29.

Foxton, P. 1956. The distribution of the standing crop of zooplankton in the Southern Ocean. *Discovery Rep.* 28: 191–235.

Foy, J. M., and H. Schneiden. 1960. Estimation of total body water in the rat, cat, rabbit, guinea pig, and man, and the biological half-life of tritium in man. *J. Physiol.* 154: 169–176.

Gentry, R. L. 1970. Social behavior of the Steller sea lion. Ph.D. thesis, Univ. of California, Santa Cruz.

————. 1975. Comparative social behavior of eared seals. In K. Ronald and R. W. Mansfield, editors, *Biology of the Seal. Rapp. P.-v. Réun. Cons. Int. Explor. Mer* 169: 189–194.

Gentry, R. L., and J. R. Holt. 1982. Equipment and techniques for handling northern fur seals. U.S. Dept. of Commerce, NOAA Tech. Rep., NMFS SSRF-758.

Gentry, R. L., M. E. Goebel, J. Calambokidis, and R. L. DeLong. In prep. Comparative growth rates of northern fur seal neonates. Unpubl. ms. National Marine Mammal Laboratory, Seattle, Wash.

Gonfiantini, R. 1978. Standards for stable isotope measurements in natural compounds. *Nature* 271: 534–536.

Green, B., and K. Newgrain. 1979. Estimation of the milk intake of sucklings by means of 22-Na. *J. Mammal.* 60: 556–559.

Grubb, T. C., Jr., and L. Greenwald. 1982. Sparrows and a bushpile: Foraging responses to different combinations of predation risk and energy cost. *Anim. Behav.* 30: 637–640.

Hanwell, A., and M. Peaker. 1977. Physiological effects of lactation on the mother. *Symp. Zool. Soc. Lond.* 41: 297–312.

Hisard, P. 1980. Observation de réponses de type "El Niño" dans l'Atlantique tropical oriental Golfe de Guinee. *Oceanol. Acta* 3: 69–78.

Hobson, E. S. 1966. Visual orientation and feeding in seals and sea lions. *Nature* 210: 326–327.

Hobson, E. S., W. N. McFarland, and J. R. Chess. 1981. Crepuscular and nocturnal activities of California nearshore fishes, with consideration of their scotopic visual pigments and the photic environment. *U.S. Natl. Mar. Fish. Serv. Fish. Bull.* 79: 1–30.

Holdgate, M. W., and P. E. Baker. 1979. The South Sandwich Islands: I. General description. *Br. Antarct. Surv. Sci. Rep.* 91: 1–76.

Holleman, D. F., R. G. White, and J. R. Luick. 1975. New methods for estimating milk intake and yield. *J. Dairy Sci.* 58: 1814–1821.

Houvenaghel, G. T. 1978. Oceanographic conditions in the Galapagos archipelago and their relationships with life on the islands. In R. Boje and M. Tomszak, editors, *Upwelling Ecosystems*, pp. 181–200. Berlin: Springer-Verlag.

Ichihara, T., and K. Yoshida. 1972. Diving depth of northern fur seals in the feeding time. *Sci. Rep. Whales Res. Inst.* (Tokyo) 24: 145–148.

Idyll, C. P. 1973. The anchovy crisis. *Sci. Am.* 228: 22–29.

Irving, L., L. J. Peyton, C. H. Bahn, and R. S. Peterson. 1962. Regulation of temperature in fur seals. *Physiol. Zool.* 35: 275–284.

Iwasa, Y. 1982. Vertical migration of zooplankton: A game between predator and prey. *Am. Nat.* 120: 171–180.

Johanesson, K., and R. Vilchez. 1980. Note on hydroacoustic observations of changes in distribution and abundance of some common pelagic fish species in the coastal waters of Peru, with special emphasis on the Anchoveta. Intergovernmental Oceanographic Commission, Workshop Report 28, pp. 287–323. Lima, Peru.

Jouventin, P., J. C. Stahl, and H. Weimerskirch. 1982. La recolonisation des Iles Crozet par les otaries. *Mammalia* 46: 505–514.

Kajimura, H. 1983. Opportunistic feeding of the northern fur seal, *Callorhinus ursinus*, in the eastern North Pacific Ocean and eastern Bering Sea. U.S. Dept. of Commerce, NOAA Tech. Rep., NMFS SSRF-779.

Kenyon, K. W., and F. Wilke. 1953. Migration of the northern fur seal, *Callorhinus ursinus*. *J. Mammal.* 34: 87–98.

Kerley, G.I.H. 1983. Comparison of seasonal haul-out patterns of fur seals *Arctocephalus tropicalis* and *A. gazella* on subantarctic Marion Island. *S. Afr. J. Wildl. Res.* 13: 71–77.

———. 1984. Relative population sizes, trends and hybridization of *Arctocephalus tropicalis* and *A. gazella* at Prince Edward Islands, Southern Ocean. *S. Afr. J. Zool.* 18: 388–392.

Kerr, R. A. 1983. Fading El Niño broadening scientists' view. *Science* 221: 940–941.

Keyes, M. C. 1965. Pathology of the northern fur seal. *J. Am. Vet. Med. Assoc.* 147: 1090–1095.

King, J. E. 1954. The otariid seals of the Pacific coast of America. *Bull. Br. Mus. (Nat. Hist.) Zool.* 2: 311-337.

———. 1964. *Seals of the World*. London: British Museum of Natural History.

Kleiber, M. 1975. *The Fire of Life*. New York: Robert Krieger.

Kooyman, G. L. 1963. Milk analysis of the kangaroo rat *Dipodomys merriami*. *Science* 142: 1467–1468.

———. 1965. Techniques used in measuring diving capacities of Weddell seals. *Polar Rec.* 12: 391–394.

———. 1968. An analysis of some behavioral and physiological character- istics related to diving in the Weddell seal. *Antarct. Res. Ser.* 11: 227–261.

———. 1973. Respiratory adaptations in marine mammals. *Am. Zool.* 13: 457–468.

———. 1975. A comparison between day and night diving in the Weddell seal. *J. Mammal.* 56: 563–574.

———. 1981. *Weddell Seal: Consummate Diver*. Cambridge, Eng.: Cambridge Univ. Press.

Kooyman, G. L., and C. M. Drabek. 1968. Observations on milk, blood and urine constituents of the Weddell seal. *Physiol. Zool.* 41: 187–193.

Kooyman, G. L., and E. E. Sinnett. 1982. Pulmonary shunts in harbor seals during simulated dives to depth. *Physiol. Zool.* 55: 105–111.

Kooyman, G. L., R. L. Gentry, and D. L. Urquhart. 1976. Northern fur seal diving behavior: A new approach to its study. *Science* 193:411–412.

Kooyman, G. L., E. A. Wahrenbrock, M. A. Castellini, R. W. Davis, and E. E. Sinnett. 1980. Aerobic and anaerobic metabolism during voluntary diving in Weddell seals: Evidence of preferred pathways from blood chemistry and behavior. *J. Comp. Physiol.* 138B: 335–346.

Kooyman, G. L., R. W. Davis, J. P. Croxall, and D. P. Costa. 1982. Diving depths and energy requirements of king penguins. *Science* 217: 726–727.

Kooyman, G. L., J. O. Billups, and W. D. Farwell. 1983a. Two recently de- veloped recorders for monitoring diving activity of marine birds and mammals. In A. G. Macdonald and I. G. Priede, editors, *Experimental Bi- ology at Sea*, pp. 197–214. New York: Academic Press.

Kooyman, G. L., M. A. Castellini, R. W. Davis, and R. A. Maue. 1983b. Aerobic dive limits in immature Weddell seals. *J. Comp. Physiol.* 151: 171– 174.

Lander, R. H. 1979. Alaskan or northern fur seal. In *Mammals in the Seas*, vol. 2, *Pinniped Species Summaries and Reports on Sirenians*, pp. 19–23. Food Agric. Organ. U.N., Rome, FAO Fish. Ser. 5.

———. 1981/82. A life table and biomass estimate for Alaskan fur seals. *Fish. Res.* (Amst.) 1: 55–70.

Lander, R. H., and H. Kajimura. 1982. Status of northern fur seals. In *Mammals in the Seas*, vol. 4, *Small Cetaceans, Seals, Sirenians, and Otters*, pp. 319–345. Food Agric. Organ. U.N., Rome. FAO Fish. Ser. 5.

Lavigne D. M., R.E.A. Stewart, and F. Fletcher. 1982. Changes in compo- sition and energy content of harp seal milk during lactation. *Physiol. Zool.* 55: 1–9.

Lenfant, C., R. Elsner, G. L. Kooyman, and C. M. Drabek. 1969. Respira- tory function of blood of the adult and fetus Weddell seal, *Leptonychotes weddelli*. *Am. J. Physiol.* 216: 1595–1597.

Lenfant, C., K. Johansen, and J. D. Torrance. 1970. Gas transport and oxygen storage capacity in some pinnipeds and the sea otters. *Respir. Physiol.* 9: 277–286.

Lieth, H. 1975. The measurement of caloric values. In H. Lieth and R. Whittaker, editors, *Primary Productivity of the Biosphere*, pp. 119–129. New York: Springer-Verlag.

Lifson, N., and R. McClintock. 1966. Theory and use of the turnover rates of body water for measuring energy and material balance. *J. Theor. Biol.* 12: 46–74.

Limberger, D., F. Trillmich, G. L. Kooyman, and P. Majluf. 1983. Reproductive failure of fur seals in Galapagos and Peru in 1982–83. *Trop. Ocean-Atmos. Newsl.*, Oct. 1983, pp. 16–17.

Lockyer, C. 1977. Observations on diving behavior of the sperm whale, *Physeter catodon*. In M. Angel, editor, *A Voyage of Discovery*, pp. 591–609. New York: Pergamon Press.

Longhurst, A. R. 1976. Vertical migration. In D. H. Cushing and J. J. Walsh, editors, *Ecology of the Seas*, pp. 116–140. Philadelphia: W. B. Saunders.

Lucks, D., A.I.L. Payne, and S. Maree. 1973. The trawl fishery of South West Africa. *S. Afr. Shipp. News Fish. Ind. Rev.* 28(9): 65–71.

Lynde, C. M. 1984. Juvenile and adult walleye pollock of the eastern Bering Sea: Literature review and results of ecosystems workshop. In D. H. Ito, editor, *Proceedings of the workshop on walleye pollock and its ecosystem in the eastern Bering Sea*, pp. 43–108. U.S. Dept. Commerce, NOAA Tech. Memo. F/NWC-62.

McCann, T. S. 1980. Territoriality and breeding behavior of adult male Antarctic fur seal, *Arctocephalus gazella*. *J. Zool.* (Lond.) 192: 295–310.

McEwan, E., and P. Whitehead. 1971. Measurement of milk intake of reindeer and caribou calves using tritiated water. *Can. J. Zool.* 49: 443–447.

McFarland, W. N., and F. W. Munz. 1975. The evolution of photopic visual pigments in fishes. *Vision Res.* 15: 1071–1080.

Macfarlane, W. V., B. Howard, and D. B. Siebert. 1969. Tritiated water in the measurement of milk intake and tissue growth of ruminants in the field. *Nature* 221: 578–579.

Macy, S. K. 1982. Mother-pup interactions in the northern fur seal. Ph.D. thesis, Univ. of Washington, Seattle.

Mattlin, R. H. 1978. Pup mortality of the New Zealand fur seal *Arctocephalus forsteri* (Lesson). *N.Z. J. Ecol.* 1: 138–144.

———. 1981. Pup growth of the New Zealand fur seal *Arctocephalus forsteri* on the Open Bay Islands, New Zealand. *J. Zool.* (Lond.) 193: 305–314.

———. In press. The New Zealand fur seal, *Arctocephalus forsteri*, within the New Zealand region. In J. P. Croxall and R. L. Gentry, editors, *The Status, Biology, and Ecology of Fur Seals*. U.S. Dept. of Commerce, NOAA Tech. Rep., NMFS.

Maxwell, D. C. 1974. Marine primary productivity of the Galapagos archipelago. Ph.D. thesis, Ohio State Univ., Columbus.

Merle, J. 1980. Variabilité thermique annuelle et interannuelle de l'ocean Atlantique equatorial Est: Hypothèse d'un "El Niño" Atlantique. *Oceanol. Acta* 3: 209–220.

Meyers, G. 1979. Annual variation in the slope of the 14°C isotherm along the equator in the Pacific Ocean. *J. Phys. Oceanogr.* 9: 885–891.

Milinski, M., and R. Heller. 1978. Influence of a predator on optimal foraging behavior of sticklebacks (*Gasterosteus aculeatus* L.). *Nature* 275: 642–655.

Millar, J. S. 1977. Adaptive features of mammalian reproduction. *Evolution* 31: 370–386.

Miller, E. H. 1975. Annual cycle of fur seals, *Arctocephalus forsteri* (Lesson) on the Open Bay Islands, New Zealand. *Pac. Sci.* 29: 139–152.

Miller, L. K. 1978. Energetics of the northern fur seal in relation to climate and food resources of the Bering Sea. U.S. Mar. Mammal Comm., Wash., D.C., Rep. MMC-75/08. (Available from U.S. Dept. Commerce, Natl. Tech. Info. Serv., Springfield, Va., as PB275 296.)

Mitchell, E., and R. H. Tedford. 1973. The Enaliarctinae, a new group of extinct aquatic carnivora and a consideration of the origin of the otariidae. *Bull. Am. Mus. Nat. Hist.* 151: 203–284.

Morejohn, G. V., J. T. Harvey, and L. T. Krasnow. 1978. The importance of *Loligo opalescens* in the food web of marine vertebrates in Monterey Bay, California. Calif. Dept. Fish and Game, *Fish Bull.* 169: 67–97.

Mrosovsky, N., and D. F. Sherry. 1980. *Animal Anorexias. Science* 207: 837–842.

Muntz, W.R.A. 1983. Bioluminescence and vision. In A. G. Macdonald and I.G. Priede, editors, *Experimental Biology at Sea*, pp. 217–238. New York: Academic Press.

Munz, F. W., and W. N. McFarland. 1973. The significance of spectral position in the rhodopsins of tropical marine fishes. *Vision Res.* 13: 1829–1874.

Murphy, R. C. 1936. *Oceanic Birds of South America.* New York: American Museum of Natural History.

Nagy, K. 1975. Water and energy budgets of free-living animals: Measurement using isotopically labeled water. In N. Hadley, editor, *Environmental Physiology of Desert Organisms*, pp. 227–245. Stroudsburg, Penn.: Dowsen, Huchinson, and Ross.

———. 1980. CO_2 production in animals: Analysis of potential errors in the doubly labeled water method. *Am. J. Physiol.* 238: R466–473.

Nagy, K., and D. P. Costa. 1980. Water flux in animals: Analysis of potential errors in the tritiated water technique. *Am. J. Physiol.* 238: R454-465.

Nagy, K. N., and K. Milton, 1979. Energy metabolism and food consumption by wild howler monkeys (*Alouatta palliata*). *Ecology* 60: 475–480.

Nagy, K. N., R. S. Seymour, A. K. Lee, and R. Braithwaite. 1978. Energy and water budgets in free-living *Antechnius stuartii. J. Mammal.* 59: 60–68.

Nagy, K. A., A. B. Huey, and A. F. Bennett. 1984. Field energetics and foraging mode of Kalahari lacertid lizards. *Ecology* 65: 588–596.

Niebauer, H. J. 1981a. Recent short-period wintertime climatic fluctuations and their effect on sea-surface temperatures in the eastern Bering sea. In D. W. Hood and J. A. Calder, editors, *The Eastern Bering Sea Shelf: Oceanography and Resources*, vol. 1, pp. 23–30. Wash., D.C.: U.S. Govt. Printing Office.

———. 1981b. Recent fluctuations in sea ice distribution in the eastern Bering Sea. In D. W. Hood and J. A. Calder, editors, *The Eastern Bering Sea Shelf: Oceanography and Resources*, vol. 1, pp. 133–140. Wash., D.C.: U.S. Govt. Printing Office.

North, A. W., J. P. Croxall, and D. W. Doidge. 1983. Fish prey of the Antarctic fur seal *Arctocephalus gazella* at South Georgia. *Br. Antarct. Surv. Bull.* 61: 27–37.

North Pacific Fur Seal Commission. 1982. Workshop on population trends of northern fur seals, appendix E. In *Proceedings 25th Annual Meeting* (April 13-16, 1982, Ottawa), pp. 36–42. (Available from headquarters of the Commission, Wash., D.C.)

Orians, G. H. 1969. The number of bird species in some tropical forests. *Ecology* 50: 783–801.

Orians, G. H., and N. E. Pearson, 1979. On the theory of central place foraging. In D. J. Horn, R. D. Mitchell, and R. G. Stairs, editors, *Analysis of Ecological Systems*, pp. 155–177. Columbus: Ohio State Univ. Press.

Orr, R. T. 1967. The Galapagos sea lion. *J. Mammal.* 48: 62–69.

Ortiz, C. L., D. P. Costa, and B. J. LeBoeuf. 1978. Water and energy flux in elephant seal pups fasting under natural conditions. *Physiol. Zool.* 238: 166–178.

Ortiz, C. L., B. J. LeBoeuf, and D. P. Costa. 1984. Milk intake of elephant seal pups: An index of parental investment. *Am. Nat.* 124: 416–422.

Paulik, G. J. 1971. Anchovies, birds and fishermen in the Peru current. In W. N. Murdock, editor, *Environment, Resources, Pollution, and Society*, pp. 156–185. Stanford, Calif.: Sinauer Press.

Payne, M. R. 1977. Growth of a fur seal population. *Philos. Trans. R. Soc. Lond. (B). Biol. Sci.* 279: 67–79.

———. 1979a. Fur seals *Arctocephalus tropicalis* and *A. gazella* crossing the Antarctic Convergence at South Georgia. *Mammalia* 43: 93–98.

———. 1979b. Growth in the Antarctic fur seal *Arctocephalus gazella. J. Zool.* (Lond.) 187: 1–20.

Peterson, R. S. 1968. Social behavior in pinnipeds with particular reference to the northern fur seal. In R. J. Harrison, R. C. Hubbard, R. S. Peterson, C. E. Rice, and R. J. Schusterman, editors, *The Behavior and Physiology of Pinnipeds*, pp. 3–53. New York: Appleton-Century-Crofts.

Peterson, R. S., and G. A. Bartholomew. 1967. The natural history and behavior of the California sea lion. *Am. Soc. Mammal.*, Spec. Publ. 1.

Pilson, M.E.Q., and A. L. Kelly. 1962. Composition of milk from *Zalophus californianus*, the California sea lion. *Science* 135: 104.

Poulter, T. C., T. C. Pinney, R. Jennings, and R. C. Hubbard. 1965. The rearing of Steller sea lions. In *Proceedings of the 2nd Annual Conference on Diving Mammals*, pp. 49-62. Menlo Park, Calif.

Prince, P. A. 1980. The food and feeding ecology of grey-headed albatross

Diomedea chrysostoma and the black-browed albatross *D. melanophris. Ibis* 122: 476–488.

Pruter, A. T. 1973. Development and present status of bottomfish resources in the Bering Sea. *J. Fish. Res. Board Can.* 30: 2373–2385.

Pyke, G. H., H. R. Pulliam, and E. L. Charnov. 1977. Optimal foraging: A selective review of theory and tests. *Quart. Rev. Biol.* 52: 137–154.

Rand, R. W. 1950a. Branding in field work on seals. *J. Wildl. Manag.* 14: 128–132.

———. 1950b. On the milk dentition of the Cape fur seal. *Off. J. Dent. Assoc. S. Afr.* 5: 462–471.

———. 1955. Reproduction in the female Cape fur seal, *Arctocephalus pusillus* (Schreber). *Proc. Zool. Soc. Lond.* 124: 717–740.

———. 1956. The Cape fur seal *Arctocephalus pusillus* (Schreber): Its general characteristics and moult. S. Afr. Div. Fish., *Invest. Rep.* 21: 1–52.

———. 1959. The Cape fur seal (*Arctocephalus pusillus*). Distribution, abundance, and feeding habits off the south western coast of the Cape Province. S. Afr. Div. Fish., *Invest. Rep.* 34: 1–75.

———. 1967. The Cape fur seal (*Arctocephalus pusillus*). 3. General behaviour on land and at sea. S. Afr. Div. Fish., *Invest. Rep.* 60: 1–39.

———. 1972. The Cape fur seal *Arctocephalus pusillus*. 4. Estimates of population size. S. Afr. Div. Fish., *Invest. Rep.* 89: 1–28.

Randolph, P. A., J. C. Randolph, K. Mattingley, and M. M. Foster. 1977. Energy cost of reproduction in the cotton rat, *Sigmodon hispidus. Ecology* 54: 1166–1187.

Reiter, J., N. L. Stinson, and B. J. LeBoeuf. 1978. Northern elephant seal development: The transition from weaning to nutritional independence. *Behav. Ecol. Sociobiol.* 3: 337–367.

Repenning, C. A. 1976. Adaptive evolution of sea lions and walruses. *Syst. Zool.* 25: 375–390.

Repenning, C. A., and R. H. Tedford. 1977. Otarioid seals of the Neogene. U.S. Geol. Surv., Prof. Pap. 992.

Repenning, C. A., R. S. Peterson, and C. L. Hubbs. 1971. Contributions to the systematics of the southern fur seals, with particular reference to the Juan Fernandez and Guadalupe species. *Antarct. Res. Ser.* 18: 1–34.

Repenning, C. A., C. E. Ray, and D. Grigorescu. 1979. Pinniped biogeography. In J. Gray and A. J. Boucot, editors, *Historical Biogeography, Plate Tectonics, and the Changing Environment*, pp. 357–369. Corvallis: Oregon State Univ. Press.

Ridgway, S.H. 1972. Homeostasis in the aquatic environment. In S. H. Ridgway, editor, *Mammals of the Sea: Biology and Medicine*, pp. 590–747. Springfield, Ill.: C. C. Thomas.

Riedman, M., and C. L. Ortiz. 1979. Milk composition during lactation in the northern elephant seal. *Physiol. Zool.* 52: 240–249.

Rimmer, D. W., and B. F. Phillips. 1979. Diurnal migration and vertical distribution of phyllosoma larvae of the western rock lobster *Panulirus cygnus. Mar. Biol.* (Berl.) 54: 109–124.

Rothwell, N. S., and M. S. Stock. 1981. Regulation of energy balance. *Ann. Rev. Nutr.* 1: 235–256.

Roux, J.-P., and A. D. Hes. 1984. The seasonal haul-out cycle of the fur seal *Arctocephalus tropicalis* (Gray, 1872) on Amsterdam Island. *Mammalia* 48: 377–389.

Schaeffer, M. B. 1970. Men, birds, and anchovies in the Peru current: Dynamic interactions. *Trans. Am. Fish. Soc.* 99: 461–467.

Scheffer, V. B. 1958. Seals, sea lions, and walruses, a review of the Pinnipedia. Stanford, Calif.: Stanford Univ. Press.

Scheffer, V. B., and B. S. Kraus. 1964. Dentition of the northern fur seal. U.S. Fish Wildl. Serv., *Fish. Bull.* 63: 293–342.

Scheid, P., and M. Meyer. 1978. Mixing technique for study of oxygen-hemoglobin equilibrium: A critical evaluation. *J. Appl. Physiol. Respir. Environ. Exercise Physiol.* 45: R818–R822.

Schmidt-Nielsen, K., and B. Schmidt-Nielsen. 1952. Water metabolism of desert mammals. *Physiol. Rev.* 32: 135–160.

Schoeller, D. A., and E. van Santen. 1982. Measurement of energy expenditure in humans by doubly labeled water method. *J. Appl. Physiol.* 53: 955–959.

Scholander, P. F. 1940. Experimental investigations on the respiratory function in diving mammals and birds. *Hvalradets Skr.* 22: 1–131.

Schreiber, R. W., and E. A. Schreiber. 1983. Reproductive failure of marine birds on Christmas Island, fall 1983. *Trop. Ocean-Atmos. Newsl.* 16: 10–12.

Schusterman, R. J. 1981. Behavioral capabilities of seals and sea lions: A review of their hearing, visual, learning, and diving skills. *Psychol. Rec.* 31: 125–143.

Schusterman, R. J., and R. F. Balliet. 1971. Aerial and underwater visual acuity in the California sea lion (*Zalophus californianus*) as a function of luminance. *Ann. N.Y. Acad. Sci.* 188: 37–46.

Shanon, L. V. 1983. Preliminary report of the Southern Benguela warm event, 1982–83. *Trop. Ocean-Atmos. Newsl.* 22: 8–9.

Shaughnessy, P. D. 1979. Cape (South African) fur seals. In *Mammals in the Seas*, vol. 2, *Pinniped Species Summaries and Reports on Sirenians*, pp. 37–40. Food Agric. Organ. U.N., Rome. FAO Fish. Ser. 5.

———. 1982. The status of seals in South Africa and Namibia. In *Mammals in the Seas*, vol. 4, *Small Cetaceans, Seals, Sirenians, and Otters*, pp. 383–410. Food Agric. Organ. U.N., Rome. FAO Fish. Ser. 5.

Shaughnessy, P. D., and D. S. Butterworth. 1981. Historical trends in the population size of the Cape fur seal (*Arctocephalus pusillus*). In J. A. Chapman and D. Pursley, editors, *Worldwide Furbearer Conference Proceedings*, vol. 2 (August 3–11, 1980, Frostburg, Maryland).

Shaughnessy, P. D., A. Semmelink, J. Cooper, and P.G.H. Frost. 1981. Attempts to develop acoustic methods of keeping cape fur seals, *Arctocephalus pusillus*, from fishing nets. *Biol. Cons.* 21: 141–158.

Shoemaker, V. H., K. A. Nagy, and W. R. Costa. 1976. Energy utilization and temperature regulation of jack rabbits in the Mojave Desert. *Physiol. Zool.* 49: 364–375.

Sivertsen, E. 1953. A new species of sea lion, *Zalophus wollebaeki*, from the Galapagos Islands. *Det Kongr. Nor. Videnesk. Sel. Forh.* 26: 1–3.

Smith, G. B. 1981. The biology of walleye pollock. In D. W. Hood and J. A. Calder, editors, *The Eastern Bering Sea Shelf: Oceanography and Resources*, vol. 1, pp. 527–551. Wash., D.C.: U.S. Govt. Printing Office.

Smith, R. L. 1976. Waters of the sea: The ocean's characteristics and circulation. In D. H. Cushing and J. J. Walsh, editors, *The Ecology of the Seas*, pp. 23–58. Philadelphia: Saunders and Co.

Stearns, S. C. 1976. Life-history tactics: A review of the ideas. *Q. Rev. Biol.* 51: 3–47.

———. 1977. The evolution of life history traits: A critique of the theory and a review of the data. *Ann. Rev. Ecol. Syst.* 8: 145–171.

———. 1983. The influence of size and phylogeny on patterns of covariation among life-history traits of mammals. *Oikos* 41: 173–187.

Stewart, R.E.A., and D. M. Lavigne. 1984. Energy transfer and female condition in nursing harp seals, *Phoca groenlandica. Holarct. Ecol.* 7: 182–194.

Stirling, I. 1971. Studies on the behavior of the South Australian fur seal, *Arctocephalus forsteri* (Lesson). II. Adult females and pups. *Aust. J. Zool.* 19: 267–273.

———. 1975. Factors affecting the evolution of social behavior in the Pinnipedia. In K. Ronald and A. W. Mansfield, editors, *The Biology of the Seal. Rapp. P.-v. Réun. Cons. Int. Explor. Mer* 169: 205–212.

———. 1983. The evolution of mating systems in pinnipeds. In J. Eisenberg and D. Kleinmann, editors, *Advances in the Study of Mammalian Behavior*, pp. 489–527. Am. Soc. Mammal., Spec. Publ. 7.

Strange, I. J. 1973. The silent ordeal of a south Atlantic archipelago. *Nat. Hist.* 82: 30–39.

Studier, E. H. 1979. Bioenergetics of growth, pregnancy and lactation in the laboratory mouse, *Mus musculus. Comp. Biochem. Physiol.* 64A: 473–481.

Toole, J. M. 1983. Preliminary observations of the equatorial Pacific, fall 1982. *Trop. Ocean.-Atmos. Newsl.* 16: 12–14.

Townsend, C. H. 1899. Pelagic sealing with notes on the fur seals of Guadalupe, the Galapagos, and Lobos Islands. In D. S. Jordan, editor, *The Fur Seals and Fur-Seal Islands of the North Pacific Ocean*, vol. 3, pp. 223–274. Wash., D.C.: U.S. Govt. Printing Office.

Trillmich, F. 1979. Galapagos sea lions and fur seals. *Not. Galapagos* 29: 8–14.

———. 1981. Mutual mother-pup recognition in Galapagos fur seals and sea lions: Cues used and functional significance. *Behaviour* 78: 21–42.

———. 1983. Ketamine xylazine combination for the immobilization of Galapagos sea lions and fur seals. *Vet. Rec.* 112: 279–280.

———. 1984. The natural history of the Galapagos fur seal, *Arctocephalus galapagoenis*, Heller, pp. 215–223. In R. Perry, editor, *Key Environments: Galapagos*. Oxford: Pergamon Press.

———. In press. The Galapagos fur seal, *Arctocephalus galapagoensis*. In J. P. Croxall and R. L. Gentry, editors, *The Status, Biology, and Ecology of Fur Seals*. U.S. Dept. of Commerce, NOAA Tech. Rep., NMFS.

Trillmich, F., and P. Majluf. 1981. First observations on colony structure, behavior and vocal repertoire of the South American fur seal (*Arctocephalus australis* Zimmermann 1783) in Peru. *Z. Säugetierkd.* 46: 310–322.

Trillmich, F., and W. Mohren. 1981. Effects of the lunar cycle on the Galapagos fur seal, *Arctocephalus galapagoensis*. *Oecologia* (Berl.) 48: 85–92.

Trillmich, F., and H. Wiesner. 1979. Immobilization of free-ranging Galapagos sea lions. *Vet. Rec.* 105: 465–466.

Trivers, R. 1974. Parent-offspring conflict. *Am. Zool.* 14: 249–264.

Vaz-Ferreira, R. 1982. *Arctocephalus australis* Zimmermann, South American fur seal. In *Mammals in the Sea*, vol. 4, *Small Cetaceans, Seals, Sirenians, and Otters*, pp. 497–508. Food Agric. Organ. U.N., Rome. FAO Fish. Ser. 5.

Vaz-Ferreira, R., and A. Ponce de Leon. In press. South American fur seal (*Arctocephalus australis*) in Uruguay. In J. P. Croxall and R. L. Gentry, editors, *The Status, Biology, and Ecology of Fur Seals*. U.S. Dept. of Commerce, *NOAA Tech. Rep., NMFS*.

Vladimirov, V. A. 1983. On reproductive biology of sea bear females on the Urilye rookery (Mednyi Island). *Byull. Mosk. O-va Ispyt. Prir. Otd. Biol.* 88(4): 52–61. (In Russ., Engl. summary.)

Warneke, R. 1979. Australian fur seal. In *Mammals in the Sea*, vol. 2, *Pinniped Species Summaries and Reports on Sirenians*, pp. 41–44. Food Agric. Organ. U.N., Rome. FAO Fish. Ser. 5.

Wells, R.M.G. 1978. Observations on the hematology and oxygen transport of the New Zealand fur seal, *Arctocephalus forsteri*. *N.Z. J. Zool.* 5: 421–424.

Wilbur, H. M., D. W. Tinkle, and J. P. Collins. 1974. Environmental certainty, trophic level, and resource availability in life history evolution. *Am. Nat.* 108: 805–817.

Williams, T. M., and G. L. Kooyman. 1985. Seal swimming performance and hydrodynamic characteristics. *Physiol. Zool.* 58(5): 576–589.

Yates, M. G., W. V. Macfarlane, and R. Ellis. 1971. The estimation of milk intake and growth of beef calves in the field using tritiated water. *Aust. J. Agric. Res.* 22: 291–306.

York, A. E. 1979. Analysis of pregnancy rates of female fur seals in the combined United States-Canadian pelagic collections, 1958–74. In H. Kajimura, editor, *Preliminary Analysis of Pelagic Fur Seal Data Collected by the United States and Canada during 1958–74*, pp. 50–122. Unpubl. ms. Natl. Mar. Mammal Lab., U.S. Natl. Mar. Fish. Serv., Seattle, Wash.

York, A. E., and J. R. Hartley. 1981. Pup production following harvest of female northern fur seals. *Can. J. Fish. Aquat. Sci.* 38: 84–90.

Zeusler, F. A. 1936. Report of the oceanographic cruise of the United States Coast Guard Cutter *Chelan*, Bering Sea and Bering Strait, 1934, and other related data. Unpublished report. Wash., D.C.: U.S. Coast Guard Headquarters.

Zuta, S., T. Rivera, and A. Bustamante. 1978. Hydrologic aspects of the marine upwelling areas off Peru. In R. Boje and M. Tomczak, editors, *Upwelling Ecosystems*, pp. 235–257. Berlin: Springer-Verlag.

Author Index

Aguayo, A. L., 102
Ainley, D. G., 216
Albon, S. D. *See* Clutton-Brock et al., 1982
Altmann, J., 28
Anderson, S. S., 80, 97, 98, 99
Anonymous, 41
Antonelis, G. A., 7, 216, 235
Ashworth, U. S., 81

Bahn, C. H. *See* Irving et al., 1962
Bailey, K. M., 216. *See also* Ainley et al., 1982
Baines, G. A., 216
Baker, P. E., 102
Baker, R. J. *See* Doidge et al., 1984a
Balliet, R. F., 251
Barber, R. T., 5, 153, 260
Bartholomew, G. A., 4, 43, 48, 53
Bennett, A. F. *See* Nagy et al., 1984
Best, P. B., 17, 128
Bester, M. N., 112, 223, 225, 263
Billups, J. O. *See* Kooyman et al., 1983a
Boersma, P. D., 153
Bonner, W. N., 16, 19, 95, 102
Braithwaite, R. *See* Nagy et al., 1978
Brody, S., 83
Budd, G. M., 102
Burger, A. E., 151
Bustamante, A. *See* Zuta et al., 1978
Butterworth, D. S., 17, 127, 151

Calambokidis, J. *See* Gentry et al., in prep.
Cane, M. A., 5, 153
Castellini, M. A. *See* Kooyman et al., 1980
Chapman, D. G., 41, 58
Charnov, E. L., 250
Chavez, F. P., 5, 153, 260
Chess, J. R. *See* Hobson et al., 1981
Cioffi, L. A., 245
Clark, T. W., 21
Clarke, A. C., 255
Clarke, M. R., 182, 193
Clutton-Brock, T. H., 96

Collins, J. P. *See* Wilbur et al., 1974
Colwell, R. K., 5, 235
Condy, P. R., 112, 223
Cooper, J., 151
Costa, D. P., 77, 80, 81, 83, 98, 242
Crawley, M. C., 223
Croxall, J. P., 16, 17, 102, 113, 114, 118, 121, 122, 124, 247, 250

David, J.H.M., 224. *See also* Butterworth et al., in press
DeLong, R. L., 7, 235. *See also* Antonelis et al., 1984
Doidge, D. W., 16, 17, 102, 113, 121, 223, 224
Drabek, C. M., 94, 95
Dunstone, N., 249, 253

Edwards, M. J., 155
Eibl-Eibesfeldt, I., 24
Ellis, R. *See* Yates et al., 1971
Elsner, R. *See* Lenfant et al., 1969
Erickson, A. W., 14
Evans, W. E., 10
Everson, I. *See* Croxall et al., 1985

Fagan, R. M., 28
Farwell, W. D. *See* Kooyman et al., 1983a
Fedak, M. A., 80, 97, 98, 99
Feldkamp, S. D. *See* Costa et al., 1982
Fiscus, C. H., 216. *See also* Antonelis et al., 1984
Fisher, R. A., 96
Fonseca, T. ., 153
Foster, M. M. *See* Randolph et al., 1977
Foxton, P., 109, 234
Foy, J. M., 81
Frost, P.G.H. *See* Shaughnessy et al., 1981

Gentry, R. L., 10, 32, 33, 57, 207, 223
Goebel, M. E. *See* Gentry et al., in prep.
Gonfiantini, R., 85
Green, B., 81

Greenwald, L., 183
Gregorescu, D. *See* Repenning et al., 1979
Grubb, T. C., Jr., 183
Guinness, R. E. *See* Clutton-Brock et al., 1982

Hanwell, A., 97
Hartley, J. R., 260
Harvey, J. T. *See* Morejohn et al., 1978
Heller, R., 183
Hes, A. D., 223
Hisard, P., 7
Hobson, E. S., 76, 151, 256
Hoel, P. G., 43, 48, 53
Hofman, R. J., 14
Holdgate, M. W., 102
Holleman, D. F., 81
Holt, J. R., 32, 33
Houvenaghel, G. T., 168
Howard, B. *See* MacFarlane et al., 1969
Hubbard, R. C. *See* Poulter et al., 1965
Hubbs, C. L. *See* Repenning et al., 1971
Huber, H. R. *See* Ainley et al., 1982
Huey, A. B. *See* Nagy et al., 1984
Huntley, A. C. *See* Costa et al., in press

Ichihara, T., 10
Idyll, C. P., 153
Irving, L., 112
Iwasa, Y., 182

James, W.P.T. *See* Cioffi et al., 1981
Jennings, R. *See* Poulter et al., 1965
Johanesson, K., 163
Johansen, K. *See* Lenfant et al., 1970
Jouventin, P., 102

Kajimura, H., 11, 28, 41, 76, 84, 246
Kelly, A. L., 95
Kenyon, K. W., 41
Kerley, G.I.H., 102, 223
Kerr, R. A., 153
Keyes, M. C., 80. *See also* Ashworth et al., 1966
King, J. E., 14, 17, 22

Kleiber, M., 81, 97, 236
Kooyman, G. L., 10, 22, 28, 29, 30, 31, 36, 61, 62, 77, 94, 95, 98, 194, 230, 233, 236, 237, 240, 242
Krasnow, L. T. *See* Morejohn et al., 1978
Kraus, B. S., 233

Lander, R. H., 11, 41, 233
Lavigne, D. M., 80, 94
LeBoeuf, B. J. *See* Costa et al., in press
Lee, A. K. *See* Nagy et al., 1978
Leith, H., 85
Lenfant, C., 155, 166, 236
Lifson, N., 83
Limberger, D., 5, 22, 24, 235, 247
Lockyer, C., 10
Longhurst, A. R., 249, 251
Lucks, D., 126
Luick, J. R. *See* Holleman et al., 1975
Lynde, C. M., 75

McCann, T. S., 105, 113
McClintock, R., 83
McEwan, E., 81
McFarland, W. N., 76
Macfarlane, W. V., 81
Macy, S. K., 47, 96
Majluf, P., 157. *See also* Limberger et al., 1983
Maree, S. *See* Lucks et al., 1973
Martin, R. J., 155
Mattingley, K. *See* Randolph et al., 1977
Mattlin, R. H., 223, 224
Maue, R. A. *See* Kooyman et al., 1983b
Maxwell, D. C., 168
Merle, J., 7
Meyer, M., 155
Meyers, G., 154
Milinski, M., 183
Millar, J. S., 80
Miller, E. H., 223
Miller, L. K., 84, 97, 98, 100, 255
Milton, K., 98
Mitchell, E., 10
Mohren, W., 171, 182, 200
Morejohn, G. V., 216
Mrosovsky, N., 245

Muntz, W.R.A., 251
Munz, F. W., 76
Murphy, R. C., 153

Nagy, K., 79, 81, 83, 98
Newgrain, K., 81
Niebauer, H. J., 6
North, A. W., 17
North Pacific Fur Seal Commission, 11

O'Connor, R. J., 249, 253
Orians, G. H., 5, 207, 234, 247
Orr, R. T., 24
Ortiz, C. L., 80, 81, 83, 85, 94, 97, 98

Paulik, G. J., 154
Payne, A.I.L. *See* Lucks et al., 1973
Payne, M. R., 14, 16, 102, 113, 223, 224
Peaker, M., 97
Pearson, N. E., 207, 247
Peterson, R. S., 43, 48
Peyton, L. J. *See* Irving et al., 1962
Phillips, B. F., 182
Pilcher, M. N., 17, 121
Pilson, M.E.Q., 95
Pinney, T. C. *See* Poulter et al., 1965
Ponce de Leon, A., 223
Poulter, T. C., 95
Prince, P. A., 102, 113, 114, 247, 255
Pruter, A. T., 41
Pulliam, H. R. *See* Pyke et al., 1977
Pyke, G. H., 249

Ramaiah, G. D. *See* Ashworth et al., 1966
Rand, R. W., 17, 95, 126, 127, 128, 133,
    139, 149, 150, 151, 223, 224, 225
Randolph, J. C. *See* Randolph et al., 1977
Randolph, P. A., 97
Ray, C. E. *See* Repenning et al., 1979
Reiter, J., 96
Repenning, C. A., 10, 17, 76
Rickett, L. H. *See* Butterworth et al., in
    press
Ricketts, C. *See* Croxall et al., 1985
Ridgway, S. H., 166

Riedman, M., 94
Rimmer, D. W., 182
Riviera, T. *See* Zuta et al., 1978
Rothwell, N. S., 245
Roux, J.-P., 223

Schaeffer, M. B., 154
Scheffer, V. B., 22, 233
Scheid, P., 155
Schmidt-Nielsen, B., 95
Schmidt-Nielsen, K., 95
Schneiden, H., 81
Schoeller, D. A., 99
Scholander, P. F., 240
Schreiber, E. A., 153
Schreiber, R. W., 153
Schusterman, R. J., 251
Semmelink, A. *See* Shaughnessy et al.,
    1981
Seymour, R. S. *See* Nagy et al., 1978
Sharon, L. V., 7
Shaughnessy, P. D., 17, 19, 128, 149, 151
Sherry, D. F., 245
Shoemaker, V. H., 83
Siebert, D. B. *See* MacFarlane et al., 1969
Sinnett, E. E., 236, 240
Sivertsen, E., 22
Smith, G. B., 58, 234
Smith, R. L., 252
Stahl, J. C. *See* Jouventin et al., 1982
Stearns, S. C., 7, 8, 9, 220, 261, 262, 263
Stewart, R.E.A., 80
Stinson, N. L. *See* Reiter et al., 1978
Stirling, I., 4, 57, 223
Stock, M. S., 245
Strange, I. J., 19
Studier, E. H., 97

Tedford, R. H., 10
Tinkle, D. W. *See* Wilbur et al., 1974
Toole, J. M., 154
Torrence, J. D. *See* Lenfant et al., 1970
Townsend, C. H., 41, 42
Trillmich, F., 22, 24, 157, 171, 182, 193,
    200, 203, 209, 224, 259
Trivers, R., 258

Urquhart, D. L. *See* Kooyman et al., 1976

Van Itallie, T. B. *See* Cioffi et al., 1981
van Santen, E., 99
Vaz-Ferreira, R., 19, 223
Vilchez, R., 163
Vladimirov, V. A., 247

Wahrenbrock, E. A. *See* Kooyman et al., 1980
Warneke, R., 17
Weimerskirch, H. *See* Jouventin et al., 1982
Wells, R.M.G., 166
White, R. G. *See* Holleman et al., 1975
Whitehead, P., 81

Wiesner, H., 209
Wilbur, H. M., 5, 9, 261
Wilke, F., 41
Williams, T. M., 36

Xulu, S. *See* Butterworth et al., in press

Yates, M. G., 81
York, A. E., 53, 260
Yoshida, K., 10
Young, D. Y., 28

Zeusler, F. A., 41, 42
Zuta, S., 153

Subject Index

Accommodation versus adaptation, 220
Activity budget, 155, 220
   comparative, subpolar/tropical, 231
   effects on metabolism of, 242
   environmental factors, 185
   measurement of, 32, 170
   pelagic, 63, 72, 73, 74, 77, 78, 119, 125,
      159, 167, 188, 189, 195, 213, 219,
      261; Antarctic fur seal, 118; Galapa-
      gos fur seal, 189; Galapagos sea lion,
      215; northern fur seal, 64; South
      American fur seal, 160
   terrestrial, 77, 130, 158, 170, 180
Adaptive responses, 7
Aerobic dive limit, 236, 237, 238, 252,
      254; and body size, 237; conse-
      quences of exceeding, 237
Afro-Australian fur seal, 26
Algoa Bay, 126
Alveoli, 240
Anchovy, 150
Annual cycle: Antarctic fur seal, 102;
      northern fur seal, 46; South African
      fur seal, 126
Antarctic convergence, 14, 102, 109
Antarctic fur seal, 4, 5, 19, 27, 32, 80, 182,
      191, 221, 223, 226, 234, 237, 244,
      246, 251, 255, 257
Antipredator functions, 113
Arrival, relative to parturition, 133
Arrival/departure rates, 45, 49, 59, 105,
      114, 200, 208; and age of offspring,
      175; hour of day, 131, 156, 177, 202;
      northern fur seal, 46; South African
      fur seal, 129
Atka mackerel, 76
Attendance behavior, 4, 7, 8, 9, 28, 198,
      263
   comparisons, 221, 222; historical, 53,
      59, 60; phocids versus otariids, 97;
      sea lions versus fur seals, 207
   as component of maternal strategies,
      220
   effects of: age of young, 183; lactation

on, 45, 53, 58, 60, 138, 139, 140, 141,
      157, 166, 184; pregnancy on, 45;
      Time-Depth-Recorder on, 216
   flexibility in, 57, 230
   indexes of: environmental change, 103;
      fish stocks, 59
   perinatal, 141
   postpartum, 141, 201
   prepartum, 130, 132, 141
   sources of variation, 221; environment,
      60, 113; food, 184; hour of day, 47,
      129, 130, 141, 156, 198, 205; island,
      206; lunar cycle, 172; population den-
      sity, 113; season, 103, 109, 128, 141,
      197; temperature, 129; yearly, 129,
      179
   by species: Antarctic fur seal, 102, 106,
      110, 114; California sea lion, 207;
      Galapagos fur seal, 176, 177, 185;
      Galapagos sea lion, 208; northern fur
      seal, 28, 41, 48, 59, 95; South African
      fur seal, 133, 137, 141; Steller sea
      lion, 207
   study methods, 103, 127, 154, 169, 196
Australia, 17

Barnacles, 179
Behavior, at capture, 143
Bering Sea, 5, 7, 11, 41, 59, 76, 234
Bioluminescence, 194
Bird Island, South Georgia, 16, 103, 105,
      109, 112, 115, 122, 124, 246
Blood chemistry, 163, 164, 167; effects on
      diving, 165; sample analysis, 155;
      sample collection, 155; South Ameri-
      can fur seal, 162
Blubber layer, 94, 233, 244, 245
Blue-footed Booby, 183
Body:
   condition, 159, 164
   size (mass), 4, 176, 186; drag to power
      output, 252; intraspecific variation,
      225; oxygen stores, 240; oxygen use,

Body: size (*cont.*)
    236; regulation of, 245; temperature, 241
Bogoslof Island, Alaska, 11
Breath-hold limit, 218, 237
Breeding:
    effects of feeding patterns on, 76
    habitat, 4
    range, otariid, 4
    season duration, 24, 128, 141, 157, 166, 169, 172, 185, 200
    sources of variation in: clinal variation, 223; compression, 234; island differences, 200, 208; prolongation, 234; yearly shifts, 200
    timing of biological events during: Antarctic fur seal, 104; South African fur seal, 134, 135

Cabo Hammond, Fernandina Island, 168, 185, 186, 194, 209, 218
California, 235
California sea lion, 22, 34, 200, 241
Calling activity, 200
Caloric density, 84
Capelin, 91
Capture methods, 28
    drugs, 33, 155
    effects of temperature on, 142
    nets, 32
    noose, 32
    by species: Antarctic fur seal, 32, 117; Galapagos fur seal, 32, 186; Galapagos sea lion, 33; northern fur seal, 32, 62; South African fur seal, 32; South American fur seal, 33, 155
Carbon dioxide production, 83, 91
Census methods, 172, 198, 205
Central American seaway, 10
Central Place Foraging Theory, 207, 247
Cephalopods, 91, 140
Colonization, 11
Commander Islands, USSR, 11, 41, 247
Commercial fishing:
    effects of El Niño on, 154
    effects on fur seals, 41; northern fur seal, 41; South African fur seal, 19, 126, 149, 151
Comparisons, general interspecific, 9
Competition, sibling, 9, 201

Continental shelf edge, 41, 61, 64, 234, 246
Copulation, 175
Critical temperature, 241, 242
Crozet Island, South Atlantic, 102
Current systems, 234; Agulhas current, 126; Benguela current, 126, 140, 142; California countercurrent, 7; Cromwell countercurrent, 168; Gulf stream, 10; Humboldt current, 168; Peru countercurrent, 7, 168

Data analysis, 28
Data collection, 43
Deciduous teeth, comparative, 233
Deep scattering layer, 76, 217, 251
Defecation, 180
Departures to sea, 166; by hour of day, 185; effects of lunar cycle on, 185
Development to weaning, 233
Diet:
    comparisons, 26
    feeding generalists versus specialists, 11, 17, 26, 59, 115, 247
    hypothetical, 91
    by species: California sea lion, 216; Galapagos fur seal, 21, 192; Galapagos sea lion, 24, 216; northern fur seal, 41, 76, 101; South African fur seal, 17, 150; South American fur seal, 19
Dilution rate, 81
Disease, 24
Dispersal, Antarctic fur seal, 102
Distance to forage areas, 231, 246
Distribution, 12; Antarctic fur seal, 14, 16, 102; Galapagos fur seal, 20, 24; Galapagos sea lion, 24; northern fur seal, 11, 14, 41; South African fur seal, 16, 17, 126; South American fur seal, 19, 22
Disturbance, at capture, 186
Dive:
    ascent/descent: angle, 239; rate, 150, 195, 239, 241, 254; rate and prey capture, 255-256
    behavior, 28, 263; as component of maternal strategy, 220; individual variation in, 64, 74, 149, 230; interspecies comparisons in, 209, 225, 227; measurement of, 117; by species: Antarctic

fur seal, 103, 115, 117, 124; Galapagos fur seal, 188, 194; Galapagos sea lion, 211, 218; northern fur seal, 61, 63, 77; South African fur seal, 144, 151; South American fur seal, 153, 159-160, 166

Dive bout:

characteristics for: Antarctic fur seal, 123; Galapagos fur seal, 190; Galapagos sea lion, 215; northern fur seal, 67; South African fur seal, 147; South American fur seal, 159-160

criterion, 62, 64, 67, 78, 119, 145, 151, 160, 167, 189, 194, 213, 219, 230; methods of computation, 38, 39

depth, 3, 67, 147; changes with time, 78, 118, 124; comparisons, 217; contours within, 67; limit, theoretical, 164, 239, 241; maximum, 78, 118, 125, 145, 152, 160, 167, 188, 195, 211, 219; mean, 3, 64, 78, 118, 125, 145, 152, 159-160, 167, 186, 188, 190, 195, 211, 219; most frequently attained, 78, 119, 120, 146, 148, 152, 160, 162, 167, 192, 195, 213, 219, 226, 228, 231; relative to: arterial oxygen tensions, 240, dive durations, 70, 78, 145, 146, 152, 225, lung shunt, 240, prey, 122, 124, 256; time spent at maximum, 3, 146, 152

duration of, 67, 78, 124, 152, 160, 167, 186, 189, 213, 219; maximum, 114, 118, 125, 159-160, 167, 188, 195, 211, 219, 226; mean, 3, 8, 78, 118, 125, 145, 152, 159-160, 167, 188, 194, 211, 219, 226; subpolar/tropical fur seal comparison, 257

effects of size on, 142

effort, 149

exploratory, 64, 77, 150, 215

number per trip, 8, 64, 78, 119, 124, 145, 152, 167, 190, 194, 219

pattern: deep divers, northern fur seal, 68, 73, 75, 76, 77, 79, 99; effects of age and experience on, 254; effects of local environment on, 231; exceptions to, 253; mixed divers, northern fur seal, 73, 75, 76, 252, 253, 256, 257; shallow divers, northern fur seal, 68, 73, 75, 76, 77, 79, 99, 230, 252, 257

proportion of time spent submerged, 124, 145

rates: comparative, 202, 218; per hour within dive bouts, 5, 8, 67, 69, 119, 124, 145, 152, 167, 186, 189, 195, 213, 218, 230, 219; per trip to sea, 64, 77, 119, 124, 167, 194, 212, 219; profiles, 64, 146, 147, 167, 219

recovery times, 69

time, depth, frequency relationships, 3, 8, 67, 68, 69, 71, 72, 73, 76, 77, 119, 120, 121, 124, 148, 149, 151, 160, 161, 163, 167, 181, 186, 190, 192, 193, 194, 212, 213, 214, 216, 219, 226, 229, 230, 232, 249, 253

Diving: absence of, 251; effects of TDR on, 28, 36, 77, 91; metabolic cost of, 182; in other marine mammals, 10; physiological limits to, 3, 230, 236; seasonal changes in, 75

Doubly labeled water, 27, 83, 84, 98, 245

Drag: effects of TDR on, 36; measurement of, 34, 37

East Reef Rookery, St. George Island, 43, 59, 61, 77, 101

Ecological roles, 4

El Niño, 5, 7, 21, 24, 59, 153, 154, 155, 162, 164, 166, 221, 235, 244, 247, 260, 261, 262

Elsehul, South Georgia, 103, 113, 115, 124

Emaciation syndrome, 80

Enaliarctidae, 10

Energetic: cost of carrying TDR, 94; requirements of pup, 79, 133, 256, 257; summary for northern fur seal, 93

Energy:

acquisition, 231

budget, 79; comparative, 243; components of, 80, 101: foraging costs, 79, 91, 98, 101, foraging strategy, 99, lactation costs, 79, 80, 82, 83, 90, 97, 99, 101, measurement of, 80, parturition costs, 83, 90; effect of pup mass on, 99; effect of pup sex on, 99; summary for northern fur seal, 100, 101; transfer, daily rate, 27, 79, 97, 225, 242, 243

Environment, comparative, 26; factors in environmental uncertainty, 4, 5, 7, 8,

Environment (*cont.*)
　　9, 99, 225, 234, 261, 263; factors in
　　seasonality, 5, 7, 9, 109, 234
Equator, 7, 168, 260
Española Island, 201, 202, 203, 206
Estrus: feeding relative to, 49, 141, 175;
　　timing of, 49, 59, 105, 114, 133, 141,
　　175, 185, 201, 208
Evolutionary history, 10
Experimental methods, 46

Falkland Islands, 19
False Cape Frio, South Africa, 126
Fasting: adaptations for, 243; adult males,
　　252; metabolism, 82; phocid seals, 4,
　　95; pups (otariid), 80, 81, 243, 263;
　　role in intraspecific competition, 252
Fat: as energy store, 95; oxidation, 95; -to-
　　lean ratio, 245
Feeding:
　　area, distance to, 119, 126, 165, 191,
　　　215, 261
　　bouts, termination of, 244
　　competition, 113, 217
　　cycle: proportion of time spent on land,
　　　59, 105, 114, 166, 203, and effects of
　　　age of mother's offspring, 176, hour
　　　of day, 175, 202, lunar cycle, 179, sea-
　　　son, 108, 200, year, 176; proportion
　　　of time spent at sea, 105, 107, 113,
　　　and effects of hour of day, 175, 202,
　　　and effects of season, 107, 139
　　ecology, 3, 250
　　frequency, 150
　　success, 123
　　suckling alternation, 259, 262
　　surface, unrecorded, 119, 191
　　trips to sea: comparison among sites, 53,
　　　231; duration of, 8, 49, 105, 107, 113,
　　　114, 137, 138, 141, 157, 164, 166,
　　　178, 186, 194, 203, 204, 208, 218,
　　　261; effects of: age of offspring on, 9,
　　　capture on, 211, drugs on, 214, 218,
　　　environment on, 111, 179, 185, indi-
　　　vidual variation on, 53, 183, late par-
　　　turition on, 52, prey location on, 230,
　　　reproductive status on, 54, 55, re-
　　　source level on, 247, season on, 49,
　　　51, 58, 59, 106, 112, 114, 137, 140,
　　　175, 178, 204, 207, 208, TDR on, 34,

63, 118, 124, 151, 167, 188, 194, 218;
　　as index of food resources, 247; num-
　　ber of, birth to weaning, 8, 105, 139,
　　179, 184, 185, 207; prepartum, 138,
　　174, 185; relative to estrus, 105, 185,
　　208; by species: Antarctic fur seal,
　　105, 106, 112, Galapagos fur seal,
　　177, northern fur seal, 50, South Af-
　　rican fur seal, 137, South American
　　fur seal, 156; transit costs relative to
　　feeding, 163; transit costs between
　　shore and feeding areas, 8, 77, 119,
　　124, 151, 159, 167, 186, 189, 194,
　　213, 215, 218, 261: comparative, 62,
　　64, 231, 247, 259, as determinant of
　　trip duration, 248, 249
　　by unweaned juveniles, 181, 201
Female: aggression, 201; comparative
　　sizes, 26; loss of recruits, 260
Fernandina Island, 20, 201
Flight response, 117, 143, 154, 186
Food: availability, 113; consumption, 83,
　　84; depletion of, 51, 58, 76, 102, 140,
　　247; motivation, 250; requirements of
　　mothers, 112, 193; requirements of
　　pups, 112, 245
Foraging:
　　constraints: economic, 249, 253; oxy-
　　　gen, 249, 253
　　costs, interspecies comparisons, 98
　　effects of TDR on, 36, 165
　　efficiency, yearly comparisons, 98
　　effort, 245
　　experience, comparative, 233
　　ranges, 113, 119, 140, 239, 246
　　strategies, 79, 165, 193, 209, 249; subpo-
　　　lar/tropical fur seal comparison, 253
　　success, 165, 166
　　time of, 150, 217, 218
Functional depth limit, calculation of, 239
Fur seals/sea lions, general differences,
　　221

Galapagos archipelago, 20, 235, 242, 246,
　　260
Galapagos fur seal, 5, 19, 23, 26, 27, 34,
　　80, 112, 158, 163, 196, 205, 207, 209,
　　217, 221, 223, 226, 231, 233, 242,
　　243, 246, 247, 257
Galapagos sea lion, 5, 22, 25, 76, 191, 196,

209, 221, 226, 231, 243, 246, 249, 252, 253, 257
Garua (drizzle) season, 168, 186
Gas exchange, 240
Gray seal, 80, 97
Gregariousness, 4
Grooming, 180, 233
Growth rate:
  absolute, 223
  effect of TDR, 188
  efficiency by sex, 95, 96
  pups, 8, 112, 128, 140, 203, 208, 220, 223, 230; comparative, 224; relative, 223, 225, 226, 242
Gut clearance time, 76, 251

Habitat choice, 196, 208; description of, 209
Handling: of Antarctic fur seal, 40; of Galapagos fur seal, 40; of Galapagos sea lion, 40; of northern fur seal, 40; of South African fur seal, 40; of South American fur seal, 40; tractability of species, 28, 40
Harp seal, 80
Heard Island, 102
Hunting: tactics, 253; theoretical rules for, 253-256
Hypothermia, 242

Identification marks, 43
Immobilization, drug-induced, 209
Independent feeding, onset of, 128, 233
Instrument recovery, 29
Interactions: female-female, 181; male-female, 181
Interdive interval, 3, 69, 70, 78
Interspecies comparisons, 26
Isabella Island, 20
Isotopic tracers, 101

Juan Fernandez fur seal, 26
Juveniles, unweaned, 173

Ketamine, 33, 209
King penguins, 194
Kitovi Rookery, 43, 59

Kleensee, 142, 143, 151
Krill, 102, 115, 124, 234, 247; availability of, 113; commercial harvest of, 103, 113, 115
Kuril Islands, 11

Lactation: in excess of pup need, 206; periods, 109, 112
Lactic acid, 237
Lag effects, population trends, 260
Leopard seal, 113
Life history, 4
  otariid, 4, 5
  phocid, 4
  strategy, 261
  theory, 9, 261; bet hedging, 9, 262; components of, 261; *r* vs. *K* selection, 9, 261, 262
Light levels, 251
Lung: collapse, 240; function, in seals, 240; shunt, 240; volume, 240
Lunar cycle effects, 171, 173, 180, 184, 186, 205, 217

Maasbankers, 150
McDonald Island, 102
Maintenance metabolism: effects of lactation on, 92; females, 80, 83, 99, 101; pups, 80, 82, 95
Management, seal, 41
Mass (body): gain in females, 91, 176; gain in pups, 92, 206; loss in females, 92, 174; loss in pups, 203; of pups, 113; at weaning, 8, 112
Marking methods, 103, 154, 197
Maternal:
  behavior, 7
  investment, 80, 95, 163
  strategies, 8, 9, 79, 196, 220, 253; and bet-hedging, 262; comparative, 26, 28, 231, 234; definition, 262; land, 8; latitude changes, 220, 263; pelagic, 231; and population dynamics, 261; subpolar otariids, 9, 263; temperate otariid, 264; tropical otariid, 9, 264
Mating systems, 4
Metabolic acidosis, 237
  efficiency, 84

Metabolic acidosis (*cont.*)
  rate: effects of TDR on, 36, 84, 91, 245;
    errors of measuring, 83; in water, 242
  water, 81, 83
Metabolizable energy, 84
Migration, 141, 225, 245, 259, 260
  absence of, 234
  comparative, 26, 106
  effects of food supply, 140
  by species: Antarctic fur seal, 14, 114;
    Galapagos fur seal, 20, 168, 171, 185,
    186; Galapagos sea lion, 24, 199, 208;
    northern fur seal, 41, 42, 59; South
    African fur seal, 17, 126; South
    American fur seal, 19, 163, 166
Milk:
  caloric content, 81, 85
  changes over time, 85, 86, 87, 94, 245;
    effects on age at weaning, 225; fat
    content, 80, 85, 86, 94, 95, 100, 101,
    243, 263; protein content, 43, 85, 94,
    101; water content, 80, 85, 101
  collecting methods, 34, 56, 82
  composition: ash content, 80, 85; in
    northern elephant seal, 225; in north-
    ern fur seal, 86, 225
  ingestion: effects of pup age on, 89, 95,
    101; effects of pup mass on, 89, 90,
    95, 101; effects of pup sex on, 88, 90,
    95, 101; in perinatal period, 88; rate,
    80, 81, 86, 89, 96, 101; validation tests
    for, 82
  production, upper limit, 96
Molt, 201, 233
Morphology, 4
Mortality:
  causes of, 3, 80; siblings as, 259
  rate: adult and juvenile, 262; pup, 7,
    113, 159, 164, 167
Mother-young bond, 259
Movements, effects of temperature on,
  142

Namibia, 17
Natural selection, 9
New Zealand fur seal, 26, 57, 223, 264
Neonate dependency, 4, 46; in Galapagos
  sea lion, 24; in Northern fur seal, 51
Niche separation, 208
Northern elephant seal, 80, 96, 97

Northern fur seal, 4, 7, 11, 13, 34, 80, 109,
  112, 126, 140, 145, 149, 193, 221,
  223, 226, 231, 234, 241, 243, 244,
  245, 246, 247, 249, 251, 259

Observation effort, northern fur seal, 43
Optimal foraging theory, 249, 250
Otaria, South American sea lion, 22
Otariids, 3, 262
Oxygen tension, arterial and venous, 240
Oxytocin, 80

Pacific Ocean, 41; whiting, 216
Parent-offspring conflict, 258, 259, 263
Pelagic behavior, 3, 8, 9
Perinatal attendance, 81, 108, 109
Peru, 5, 19, 153, 221, 235
Pilchards, 150
Plankton, 109
Polygyny, 4
Population:
  density, 103, 114
  dynamics, 260
  growth rate, 114, 151
  size, 141; comparisons, 26; controls on,
    260; daily trends, 157, 199, 200; envi-
    ronmental uncertainty and, 260; of
    Galapagos sea lion, 24; hourly trends,
    205; insolarization effects, 172; lunar
    effects, 171, 200; seasonal trends,
    171, 199; of South American fur seal,
    19; windspeed effects, 172
  trend, 103; with Antarctic fur seal, 14,
    16, 102, 115; with Galapagos fur seal,
    21; with northern fur seal, 11; with
    South African fur seal, 17, 142; with
    South American fur seal, 19
Predation, 260
Predator avoidance, 3
Pregnancy rate, 260
Presence/absence, distribution differences,
  203
Pressure/depth relationship, 3
Prey:
  abundance, 114, 183, 233, 243
  assimilation efficiency, 256
  bioluminescent, 252
  capture rates, 123, 151, 193, 194, 218,
    251, 256, 257
  consumption, estimated, 98

content: caloric, 83, 84, 91, 98, 99, 243, 256; water, 84, 98
depth relative to diving, 250, 253
density, 249, 251
mass, 193, 217
pursuit of, 194
requirements, 218, 256, 258
silhouetting of, 151, 251, 256, 257
vertical movement of, 76, 115, 118, 121, 124, 145, 150, 165, 182, 193, 249, 250, 251, 252
visibility of, 251
Pribilof Islands, 11, 41, 235, 242, 260
Prince Edward Islands, 102
Productivity, 5
Punta Baquerizo, Santiago Island, 196, 208
Punta San Juan, Peru, 154, 166
Punta Suarez, Española Island, 196
Pup-rearing strategies, 221, 223

Radio telemetry, 28, 32, 211
Reproductive: contribution by sex, 4; efforts, 261; life span, 5; success, 259
Research goals, 115
Resource depletion, 248; partitioning, 209. *See also* Food, depletion of
Rest, pelagic, periods: duration of, 8, 64, 73, 78, 241; effect of SDA on, 242; limited to thermoregulation, 241; measurement of, 31, 63; timing of, 73, 74
Rest, terrestrial, 179
Restraint methods, 28, 33, 62
Reunion, mother-pup, 55, 113, 245
Robben Island, 11

Santiago Island, 200, 201, 212
San Miguel Island, 11, 216
Sardinops, 183
Schlieper Bay, 103, 109, 247
Scomber, 183
Scripps Institution of Oceanography, 36
Sealing, 10
interspecies comparisons, 26
pelagic, 11, 41
by species: Antarctic fur seal, 14, 102; Galapagos fur seal, 21; Galapagos sea lion, 22; northern fur seal, 11, 41; South African fur seal, 17, 19, 127,

142; South American fur seal, 19
Sea of Okhotsk, 11
Sea surface temperature, 5, 6, 102, 153, 235
Sea water ingestion, 84, 91, 98
Sebastes, 216
Sex ratio, 4. *See also* Polygyny
Sexual dimorphism, 4
comparisons, 26
and food competition, 252
in pups, 90
Phocidae, 4
by species: Antarctic fur seal, 14, 16; Galapagos fur seal, 19, 23; Galapagos sea lion, 22, 25; northern fur seal, 11, 13; South African fur seal, 17, 18; South American fur seal, 19, 20
Sexual selection, theory of, 96
Shark attack, 182
Shivering, 242
Shore visits:
durations, 4, 47, 106, 109, 114, 138, 156, 157, 178, 204; comparison over years, 49; effects of: age of offspring, 185, prereunion interval, 55, pup demand, 56, 57, reproductive status, 53, 54; of last visit to shore, 51; of perinatal visit, 49, 51, 104, 108, 174, 201, 208; of postpartum visits, 105, 110, 166, 185, 202, 203, 208
nightly, 208
at nonsuckling sites, 179, 189
number of, birth to weaning, 7, 59, 114, 141
seasonal change in, 51, 113, 138, 175
termination of, 244
Sinclair Island, 126, 141
Social: behavior, 4; groupings, 4; interactions, 181
South Africa, 17
South African fur seal, 17, 18, 31, 223, 238, 255
South American fur seal, 5, 19, 20, 32, 76, 221, 244, 248, 264
South Atlantic Ocean, 7
Southern Ocean, 14
South Georgia Island, 14, 19, 102, 103, 104, 115, 122, 124, 242
South Shetland Islands, 14
Space, amount available, 260

Specific Dynamic Actions (SDA), 77, 242
Standard Metabolic Rate (SMR), 97, 98,
        101, 241
Starvation, 157, 245, 259; in adults and
        young, 5; in pups, 221; and sibling
        competition, 172
Steller sea lion, 57
St. George Island, 41, 43, 44, 58, 59, 61,
        77, 101, 246
St. Paul Island, 41, 43, 44, 58, 59, 246
Study sites, characteristics of, 43, 127, 143,
        168, 169
Subantarctic fur seal, 26, 112, 264
Subpolar areas, 7
Subpolar fur seal group, 4, 221, 242; char-
        acteristics of, 112; comparative dives,
        226; homogeneity of, 221
Suckling:
    effect on shore visit, 158
    frequency of, 8, 96; and age of young,
        158, 181, 182, 185; changes over
        time, 181; per visit, 158, 205, 206; to
        weaning, 184, 185
    of multiple young, 174, 185, 208
    posture, 181
    sites, movement between, 51, 103, 105,
        143, 171, 199
Surface: activity, 3; feeding, unrecorded,
        118, 124, 188
Survival, postweaning, 233, 260
Swim speed, 117, 119, 149, 191, 207, 215,
        238, 246, 252, 253, 255; effects of
        TDR on, 34
Sympatry, 209

Tasmania, 17
Temperate fur seal group, 4, 7, 26
Thermal budget, 242
Thermocline, 153
Thermoneutral environment, 242
Thermoregulation, 129, 141, 158, 196,
        208, 242; and fat layer, 244; at sea, 77
Tierra del Fuego, 19
Time budget, proportion spent: at sea,
        109, 111, 113, 157; on land, 157;
        suckling, 158, 166
Time-Depth-Recorder, 3, 8, 27, 30, 84,
        142, 144, 155, 170, 176, 182, 209, 248

analysis of records, 38
baseline "chatter," 30, 31, 63, 186
calibration of, 38
description of, 29
design requirements, 28
development of, 29
harness for, 34, 35, 61
hysteresis, 29, 31
light-emitting diodes, 31
photographic film, 31
pressure-sensitive paper, 29, 31
pressure transducer, 29, 142, 144
recapture, 34
resolution: depth, 188, 251; time, 31,
        144, 145, 188, 211
timing circuit, 31, 144
Tooth rings, 103
Transition to feeding independence, 244
Tritiated water, 27, 81, 82, 83, 84
Tropical areas, 7
Tropical fur seal group, 5, 7, 26, 221, 226,
        242
True seals (Phocidae), 94
Twilight hypothesis, 76
Time budget, proportion spent: on land,
        157; at sea, 109, 113, 157; suckling,
        158, 166

Unimak Pass, Alaska, 246
Unweaned juveniles, 128, 141, 157, 166,
        172, 184, 201
Upwelling, 4, 5, 19, 20, 24, 142, 153, 168,
        234, 260
Uruguay, 19

Van Reenen Bay, 127, 129, 141
Visual discrimination, 251

Walleye pollock, 5, 41, 58, 59, 75, 247
Water:
    flux, 81, 82, 91, 95, 99, 101; as index of
        prey fluctuation, 99, 101; measure-
        ment of, 81, 83, 85; rate of, 81, 82;
        validation tests, 84, 91, 198
    metabolic, 81, 83
    preformed, 81

reserves, phocids vs. otariids, 94

Weaning, 4, 9; abruptness of, 46, 128, 166, 185, 234, 268; age at, 9, 20, 43, 59, 105, 109, 114, 128, 138, 141, 157, 166, 172, 185, 208, 263; coincident with migration, 259; comparative, 225, 233; determinants of, 225, 234; effect of birth date on, 109, 114; mother's role in, 141, 185, 259; mother-young conflict during, 173, 201; in otariids, 4; pup's role in, 47, 113, 114, 258; sibling conflict in, 259

Weddell seal, 10, 29, 31, 142, 237

Weighing methods, 169, 170, 196

Xylosine, 33, 209

Zapadni Rookery, St. George Island, 43, 59

LIBRARY OF CONGRESS CATALOGING-IN-PUBLICATION DATA

Main entry under title:
Fur seals : maternal strategies on land and at sea.

Bibliography: p.
Includes indexes.
1. Eared seals—Behavior. 2. Parental behavior in animals. I. Gentry, Roger L.
II. Kooyman, Gerald L.
QL737.P63F87 1986   599.74'6   85-43282

ISBN 0-691-08399-1 (alk. paper)   ISBN 0-691-08400-9 (pbk. : alk. paper)

54,579

© THE BAKER & TAYLOR CO.